CATHOLIC EMANCIPATIONS

Irish Studies

James MacKillop, *Series Editor*

Charles Russell (1852–1910). *The O'Connell Centenary Celebrations,*
1875, oil on canvas, 104 × 163 cm. National Gallery of Ireland.

CATHOLIC EMANCIPATIONS

Irish Fiction from Thomas Moore to James Joyce

Emer Nolan

 Syracuse University Press

LEABHARLANN
UIMHIR
RANG
Dhun na nGall

Copyright © 2007 by Syracuse University Press
Syracuse, New York 13244-5160
All Rights Reserved

First Edition 2007
07 08 09 10 11 12   6 5 4 3 2

The paper used in this publication meets the minimum requirements of
American National Standard for Information Sciences—Permanence of
Paper for Printed Library Materials, ANSI Z39.48-1984.∞™

For a listing of books published and distributed by Syracuse University Press,
visit our Web site at SyracuseUniversityPress.syr.edu.

ISBN-13: 978-0-8156-3120-0 (cloth)
ISBN-10: 0-8156-3120-0 (cloth)

ISBN-13: 978-0-8156-3175-0 (pbk.)
ISBN-10: 0-8156-3175-8 (pbk.)

Library of Congress Cataloging-in-Publication Data
Nolan, Emer, 1966–
    Catholic emancipations : Irish fiction from Thomas Moore to James Joyce / Emer
Nolan. — 1st ed.
        p. cm. — (Irish studies)
    Includes bibliographical references and index.
    ISBN 978-0-8156-3120-0 (alk. paper) — ISBN 978-0-8156-3175-0 (pbk. : alk. paper)
    1. English fiction—Irish authors—History and criticism. 2. English fiction—19th
century—History and criticism. 3. English fiction—Catholic authors—History and
criticism. 4. Moore, Thomas, 1779–1852—Criticism and interpretation. 5. Joyce, James,
1882–1941—Criticism and interpretation. 6. English fiction—20th century—History
and criticism. 7. Literature and society—Ireland—History—19th century. 8. Literature
and society—Ireland—History—20th century. I. Title.
PR8801.N65 2007
823.009'9222—dc22   2007012381

Manufactured in the United States of America

In memory of

Rachel MacRory

(1967–2002)

Emer Nolan lectures in English at the National University of Ireland, Maynooth. She is the author of *Joyce and Nationalism* (1995) and editor of *Thomas Moore: Memoirs of Captain Rock* (2007).

Contents

Preface

This is a study of the Irish Catholic novel from its origins in the era of Catholic political resurgence in the 1820s to its culmination and transformation in the work of James Joyce. The latter's modernist epic, *Ulysses* (1922), is by no means an unexpected endpoint for any account of Irish fiction before the twentieth century, but I will approach this destination by a relatively unfamiliar route. The aim is not to offer a comprehensive history of Irish fiction in the nineteenth century; instead, I concentrate on key moments in the evolution of the peculiarly significant subgenre of the Irish "national" novel.

The novels considered here cast a revealing light on the story of the emergence of the native Catholic middle class from its penal bondage, and even more so on its quest for a concept of Irish national identity that would be at once faithful to a revamped notion of the traditional and appropriate to a modern civil polity. The effort to create new forms of expression that were specific to the Catholic community and that yet would be effective within established conventions was most famously successful in the organization of mass politics within the Catholic Association and the new kind of leadership offered by Daniel O'Connell in the campaign for Catholic Emancipation. But accompanying that exemplary version of a new modernity, there was a recasting of native cultural materials for the creation of an Anglophone Irish culture, one that embraced new modes of musical performance as well as an innovative printed literature in poetry and prose. Much recent discussion in Irish cultural studies has been animated by an effort to decry these various forms of cultural nationalist enterprise. This hostile critique is founded in the claim that the bourgeois nationalism of the nineteenth century quickly surrendered its emancipatory ambitions to become the conservative orthodoxy of the independent Irish state between 1922 and the late 1960s. In particular, in literature, the attempt to adapt metropolitan or realist novelistic modes to the depiction of Irish Catholic society—often understood as an effort to make the archaic and the advanced congruent with one another—has generally been regarded as an especially fraught and misguided project.

Thus commentators have proposed that twentieth-century Irish modernism, in fiction as in poetry and drama, was obliged to sweep away its "embarrassing antecedents"[1] in nineteenth-century Irish writing. They have characterized fiction written by nineteenth-century Catholic authors as governed by a didactic commitment to narrowly conceived political aims and thereby condemned to aesthetic failure. In Thomas Flanagan's account, these novels often lapsed into melodrama, sensationalism, or sentimentality as they struggled to represent Irish life within conventions that were uncongenial to it.[2] One underlying assumption is that Catholic nationalist authors were adherents of a religion and supporters of a political ideology that were both profoundly at odds with the Protestantism and the liberalism that had fostered the English realist novel. Realism was evidently better suited to a society that sought to modernize itself by the approved processes of secularization and industrialization. In its most sophisticated form, criticism of Irish realism, while characterizing it as inadequate, has nevertheless acknowledged the power of its revelation of the country's troubled social conditions and remarked on its prefiguration of a later, more assured modernism.[3] But partly as a result of such an analysis, the best Irish Catholic novelists (besides Joyce) are usually presumed to be the twentieth-century naturalists, defined as a daring, challenging group by virtue of their critique of the Catholic-dominated independent Irish state. These are also the very writers taken to emphasize most emphatically the damaging cultural and economic effects of Catholic hegemony in Ireland. In this view of things, it was not emancipation for but emancipation from Catholicism that would mark the beginnings of modernity in Ireland. Thus, the first Irish Catholic author to gain the status of a nineteenth-century original, one in whose work the terms of that crucial transition began to be realized, was William Carleton, who converted to Protestantism at an early age. He saw religious conversion as the key to modern advancement. Protestantism was the religion of the state; that way lay modernity. Unlike other national novelists of Catholic provenance, he did not search for any other form of modern rationality.

I will trace an alternative line in the development of Irish Catholic fiction, beginning not with Carleton but with Thomas Moore, the first Irish Catholic writer in the English language to attain both a national and an international reputation. A central emphasis here will be on the efforts of early Irish novelists, such as John and Michael Banim, Gerald Griffin, and Charles Kickham, to conform or find alternatives to the protocols of English realism in their fiction, accepting that realism (the supposed Irish penchant for the fantastic or surreal aside) is the main form of Irish Catholic literary endeavor in the field of the novel. This represents a departure from a more familiar critical stress on Anglo-Irish fiction in the nineteenth century and especially on the Gothic modes that were increasingly adopted by Irish Protestant writers after the granting of Catholic Emancipation in 1829. Anglo-Irish Gothic has hitherto been held to represent a more continuous and fertile tradition than "native" realism as well as offering more compelling insights into the national political unconscious, at least from the point of view of the minority population. In particular, the image of the Ascendancy "Big House," threatened by the advance of the uncultured natives, has enjoyed a long tenure in Anglo-Irish fiction. Catholic novelists generally take a different view of the surge toward power of the Irish masses over the nineteenth and early-twentieth centuries. They too are anxious about the religious and cultural practices of the majority, but they attempt to describe how these practices might be reformed and yet preserved in a modern, democratic dispensation. The occasional quandaries of the Irish national novelists reveal the stress of their search for some new, undiscovered passage from tradition to modernity. But their variations on national themes are not dismissible as signs of nostalgia or incoherence; rather, they are a response to the antinomies of modern capitalism, which promises to bring individual freedom while also delivering mass conformity.

There is still considerable disagreement about the significance of classical or English realism in any critical evaluation of the nineteenth-century Irish novel.[4] Certainly some of the authors considered here imitated metropolitan genres, from the historical fiction of Walter Scott to the domestic sentimentalism and social critique of Charles Dickens. They self-consciously set out to produce Irish Catholic versions of exemplary British novels and were frequently distressed by a suspicion that they had failed to achieve anything on the same scale. Yet this "minor" literature sought to perform a "major" cultural function.[5] One way we can begin to describe this function is by stressing some of the formally innovative and politically progressive features of the texts. Two novels, Griffin's *The Collegians* (1829) and Kickham's *Knocknagow* (1873), are of particular importance in this regard simply because of their enormous popularity. For example, Daniel Corkery declared that these two works were part of the submerged popular literature of Ireland that "lives by Irish suffrage." He observed that *Knocknagow* was "one of the few books which have furnished living figures to the Irish consciousness, as the *Pickwick Papers* has to the English or *Père Goriot* to the French."[6] Although judging these works to be utterly unsophisticated, Corkery nonetheless suggests that if a school of genuine Anglo-Irish literature were ever to emerge, it would grow from this tradition rather than from its "Ascendancy-minded" relation "above in the drawing room."[7] Even though Corkery would wish for Griffin and Kickham to be even more committed to representing what Corkery considered the defining forces in Irish national life, he acknowledges the massive cultural influence of the nineteenth-century Irish popular novelists—even by comparison with their Anglo-Irish contemporaries and Revivalist or modernist twentieth-century successors. (Indeed, it was probably only in the 1970s that the Irish readership of *Ulysses* exceeded that of *Knocknagow*.)[8]

Throughout this work, I will use the term *Catholic* in primarily a sociological and political sense rather than a denominational one. In any case, Ireland provides few examples of the Catholic novel as it is generally understood in a wider European context.[9] The difficulties nineteenth-century Irish Catholic writers had with realist form seem to owe as much to their concern with depicting a largely oral or premodern culture as to any clash between Catholic belief and the supposedly Protestant or secular premises of realism.[10] Even in the late nineteenth or the twentieth century, Irish Catholic writers did not explore in any sustained way how the secular assumptions of realism could be challenged while retaining some of its protocols—in contrast to their French or English Catholic counterparts such as Mauriac, Bernanos, Julien Green, or Graham Greene.[11] This is surely an indication of largely uncritical commitment on the part of many Irish writers to realism as the sovereign form of the novel. Nevertheless, there is an underacknowledged Catholic tradition in nineteenth-century Irish letters—one that sporadically recognizes the limitations of realism, even though it remains in thrall to its prestige and popularity. The works in this tradition offer an account of Catholic Ireland that is considerably more complicated than the standard image of a Victorianized Irish Catholicism may suggest.

The book begins with Thomas Moore, who is not in any ordinary sense a novelist at all. Yet as the most successful Irish writer of his age, celebrated as a poet of liberty throughout postrevolutionary Europe, his influence on his native coreligionists is incalculable. Moore has often been accused of having transformed the radical Enlightenment heritage of the 1798 Rebellion (he was a student in Dublin at the time of the rebellion as well as a friend of the revolutionary leader Robert Emmet) into the sentimental Romantic nationalism of the nineteenth century, so congenial to the socially aspirant Catholic middle class. I meet this charge (which is currently under revision anyway) in order to estimate, from a new angle, what this alleged transformation involves.

The sentimentalism of Moore's astonishingly popular *Irish Melodies* (1808–34) enjoyed a long afterlife in nineteenth-century Irish fiction, especially in the work of Griffin initially and of Kickham in the post-Famine period. But the narrative innovations and the fierce political satire of Moore's contentious prose work, *Memoirs of Captain Rock* (1824), also had a huge impact, formally and politically, on Irish fiction; indeed, as I demonstrate, it became a seminal work for Irish Catholic novelists, especially the Banims. It has regularly been observed that agrarian insurgence, so prominent a feature of Irish society between the 1820s and the Land War of the 1880s, was difficult to represent within the narrative conventions that prevailed in the nineteenth century. Moore's *Captain Rock* as well as many of the novels of the Banims are remarkable for the prominence they give to this issue. In contrast, Kickham seems to avoid it altogether by depicting an idealized Ireland from which such violence has been expunged. Yet Kickham's pastoralism is carefully constructed to create this inverse, counterfactual condition as a defense against the cultural trauma and despair with which he is actually preoccupied. In his other life as a Fenian leader and propagandist, Kickham had pleaded with the Catholic Church to drop its opposition to this separatist, underground organization; in his fiction, too, we see evidence of the some of the tensions between nationalist and Catholic versions of how the Irish masses were to be recuperated, culturally and politically.

During the 1820s, Catholic leaders had campaigned for political inclusion in the British state on equal terms with members of the Established Church. They denied that Catholics were inherently disloyal or violent, or that their religion was inimical to self-discipline and economic improvement. The national novelists too set out to challenge such bigotries. Yet for Gerald Griffin, whose work *The Collegians* proved to be the paradigmatic national novel of the era, the real anxiety lay in the nature of modernization itself. He presents the process of becoming "modern" in a generally negative light—as the imposition of a sterile discipline, or as the ethically ambiguous release of the individual from the restraints imposed by a subsistence economy and communal values. He does not see these developments as occurring in any particular temporal sequence, although we might relate them to the successive phases of industrial and consumer capitalism. It may seem astonishing that Griffin considered that the overcoming of economic scarcity would be a possibility, never mind a problem, for the fast-growing, impoverished Irish masses. Nevertheless, doubts about the moral benefits of a modernizing nationalism created an ideological crisis for Griffin, who eventually gave up writing fiction altogether in order to pursue a religious vocation. But key questions first raised by Griffin preoccupied Irish Catholic writers over the course of the nineteenth and early-twentieth centuries. For him (as later for others), a degree of economic improvement that met basic needs was an ideal threatened by overproduction and luxury. According to him, frugality was a basis for virtue. Capitalist development was desirable to a certain degree and no further. Beyond that, the integrity of "traditional" life was imperiled, just as it was by the underdevelopment that afflicted Ireland. This remained an ideal by no means peculiar to Ireland, but peculiarly important to its developing nationalist ideology.

In his famous St. Patrick's Day radio broadcast of 1943, Eamon de Valera declared:

> The Ireland that we dreamed of would be the home of a people who valued material wealth only as the basis for right living, of a people who were satisfied with frugal comfort and devoted their leisure to the things of the spirit—a land whose countryside would be bright with cosy homesteads, whose fields and villages would be joyous with the sounds of industry, with the romping of sturdy children, the contests of athletic youths and the laughter of comely maidens, whose firesides would be forums for the wisdom of serene old age. It would, in a word, be the home of people living the life that God desires that man should live.[12]

Griffin and more especially Kickham are often taken to be the sources of this pastoral vision and its accompanying rhetoric that survived into the middle years of the twentieth century, providing the economic and cultural core of the autarkic policies of the independent Irish state up to the 1960s. Many would argue that this vision of Ireland was never more than a mirage—an idyllic Catholic pastoral landscape over which the cloud shadows of emigration and emptiness had always loomed. Nevertheless, an idealized image of Irish rural life retained its influence for a long time. It is now almost doctrinal to say that this central element in the Irish national imaginary was finally abandoned only when it was deemed incompatible with the imperatives of economic modernization in the late 1960s. Although a version of it had clearly facilitated survival and modernization in the aftermath of the Famine, the myth of a pastoral Ireland ultimately came to be regarded as endangering development in the new era. But it did not simply become defunct; it remained alive as the counterimage of contemporary Ireland, necessary for the late twentieth century's own sense of legitimacy and radical newness. For example, the critical awareness of Irish novelists over the past fifty years has been confined almost exclusively to pointing up the squalid realities hidden within the pastoralized and pasteurized ideology of the immediately preceding generations.

The Irish national novelists had not given their wholehearted approval to the outcome of the agrarian and political struggles of the nineteenth century. Even in the 1820s, Griffin evidently feared that the strict discipline favored by an increasingly centralized and authoritarian Catholic Church would destroy the communal ethos that had enabled the Irish people to endure oppression. Especially after the Famine, the Church clearly sought to overcome the demoralization of its flock; it also wanted to protect the people from what it saw as the corruptions of modern liberalism and consumerist luxury. When the final demise of landlordism came, in the wake of the Land League campaign of the 1880s, it was succeeded not by a national, collective repossession of the soil, but by a society of small landholders. No radical, communal solution was achieved. The new establishment had the support of the Church. For many, the settlement was a grave disappointment, heralding a social order dominated by farmers in alliance with the Catholic priests and the exploitative *gombeen* capitalists of the towns. Despite the fact that *Knocknagow* has been so insistently read as the national epic of the Irish middle class, Kickham was repelled by the narrowly materialistic nature of this setup, even at the moment of its emergence. Rather than celebrating the achievement of peasant ownership of the land as the final resolution of the agrarian question—which had dominated fictional narratives as well as political discussion for much of the nineteenth century—Irish novelists in general sounded a note of disenchantment and regret.

Several notable Catholic writers sponsored a more spiritual and collective idea of advancement than that of individual material success. The popular novelist Canon Sheehan, while active in assisting his parishioners in County Cork to buy their farms under the terms of the Land Purchase Acts, advocated much broader conceptions of Catholic spirituality and of clerical social engagement than those that had been current at the Catholic seminary he had attended in Maynooth. The ex-priest Gerald O'Donovan criticized the Church in his novels for having insufficient respect for the inherited cultural resources of the people, especially the Irish language, and for its opposition to cooperative movements for agricultural and industrial development. Although the ideal of "cooperation" was regarded suspiciously by some of the clergy as dangerously socialist in tendency, supporters (including the radical James Connolly) believed it to be rooted in traditional Irish attitudes toward material possessions, particularly toward the land. However, after *Knocknagow*, there is no important novel devoted either to the ratification or to the systematic critique of the evolving politics of the national project around the turn of the twentieth century. Thus, a variety of responses to social developments manifested, however briefly, in Catholic-authored novels of the period have been overshadowed by the emergence of the critique of twentieth-century Ireland that was pioneered in fiction by George Moore, a disciple of the French naturalist novelist Émile Zola.

Moore introduced a new literary model for Irish novelists—one that was in many ways to prove less troublesome than English realism. Naturalist fiction in general, and especially in the last decades of the nineteenth century, flaunted a pessimistic determinism, announcing the inescapable dominance of heredity and environment on the individual. The alarm occasioned by Henrik Ibsen's dramas, or Thomas Hardy's and George Gissing's novels, gave to naturalism a radical edge that it has never been able to emulate since the 1890s. In Ireland, however, its prestige was preserved long after that. Thanks to Moore's French borrowings and then, later, to the notoriety of Joyce's *Dubliners* (1914), naturalism won for itself the reputation of being subversive and cosmopolitan, the "noir" genre of its day and since.[13] The grimness of Moore and the young Joyce was rendered seductive by the linguistic virtuosity and technical control by which it was realized. This helps to explain why later Irish writers were so addicted to the naturalistic representation of the banal and ugly "realities" of Irish life, primarily as a way to critique the crowd mentality that formal religion, especially in its Roman Catholic version, supposedly nourished. The older realist ambition to depict individual characters as "typical"—in the sense that their lives would be representative of a larger collective fate, or that their actions could help the reader make sense of historical conflict and change—no longer compelled the admiration and imitation it once had.

It can certainly be argued that Moore and his followers are more stylistically accomplished than some of the nineteenth-century Irish authors considered here. But they tend to dismiss any creative idea of collective or political agency, focusing instead on minutely detailed recreations of the sordid environments in which the demoralized victims of social and historical circumstance are forced to live. Hence they are less attentive to the traumatic history of the Irish than to the repressed, depoliticized throng that was its consequence. While characters in naturalist fiction rarely achieve any escape from their bleak conditions, they may demonstrate an admirable capacity to survive or even to arrive at some understanding of their incarceration. Abandoning the realist faith in a general social progress, the naturalists concentrate on the heroicization of individual consciousness as the only important site of resistance to mass culture—despite their putatively scientific dismissal of autonomous individuality. Emily Lawless, an author who is in many ways entirely at odds with the mainstream Irish realist tradition that I have been discussing here, anticipates Moore's seizure of that moment of transition between predominantly communal protest at injustice and the claim of the individual to precedence over social and political solidarities. Thus, in Lawless's work, we witness both the end of the novel of agrarian violence and the birth of the modern Irish novel of individualistic protest, particularly on behalf of women. Joyce shares with both Lawless and Moore a preoccupation with subjectivity and especially with sexuality. His *Dubliners* is the most significant and influential achievement of Irish naturalism. But in *Ulysses*, the individual, who had seemed so threatened by dissolution in Joyce's early work, has begun to become merely dissolute—a consumer. Joyce expresses his skepticism about the economic system that produces both conformity and the individualist resistance to it. In this regard, he is not merely the outstanding figure among a group of fin de siècle dissidents in whose hands the novel of native Irish life finally comes of age. He is also heir to the older project of the national novel. Joyce's works experiment with new ways of representing mass consciousness in Ireland over the course of the country's historical evolution from colony to partitioned states. In *Finnegans Wake* (1939), "character" is reabsorbed by the "type," creating a startling new mode of national allegory. In this way, the *Wake* can be regarded as the last phase of an experiment that began in Ireland with Thomas Moore's *Captain Rock*, where, in his satiric vein, the captain tells us that Irish history is the selfsame story of subordination and insubordination repeated over and over again.

We know that Joyce asked for editions of works by Kickham, Griffin, Carleton, and the Banims to be sent to him in Paris, but it seems that they never arrived; still, they remain a presence in his work, called for, in a sense undelivered. Yet his predecessors in Irish fiction do illuminate his work. His most obvious direct "influence" is Joseph Sheridan Le Fanu's *The House by the Churchyard* (1863), from which he borrowed many details in *Finnegans Wake*, although, equally directly, he venerated Moore's *Melodies*, and alluded to every one of them in the *Wake*.[14] His slightly older contemporary George Moore certainly provoked in Joyce a sense that he had something to emulate. His hostile reaction to, for example, *The Lake* (1905) may in fact signal his appreciation that with this work Moore had given to the Irish Literary Revival "its first and only novel of distinction."[15] This novel had features that would remain dominant in Irish fiction after both the revival and modernism had ebbed. As we shall see, Joyce's rejection of Moore signals his distaste for some of the most important tropes of Irish naturalism. And yet, Griffin's hero, Lowry Looby, speculating about why anyone in the world would want to eat anything other than potatoes, or Kickham's Mat the Thrasher, gazing with amazement through the window of a ladies' dress shop in Dublin's Sackville Street, may appear to inhabit a universe of representation that could only appear in Joyce as parody. Joyce's skill in exposing the hidden dimensions of the "real" world, his exploration of sexual fantasy and the unconscious, his interest in urban culture and the technologies of print, cinema, and even—in *Finnegans Wake*—of radio and television are all inescapable features of his mature work, as well as the fact that he managed to command the attention of a global audience to works that were so centrally concerned with depicting Catholic Ireland. But there was a history of Catholic novel-writing in Ireland before Joyce, even if he remakes its concerns in ways that are completely different to the earlier writers. One of the chief interests they share is the refashioning of Irish history and culture in new literary forms, especially those that include music and song. Like Joyce, the national novelists frequently depict scenes of musical performance and experiment with the connections between musical and narrative form. Joyce understood that recycling the past often resulted in fake "revivals." While he may have scorned such kitsch, Joyce never underestimated its emotional potency, for he himself certainly seems to have been affected by it. So he pays his homage to Thomas Moore, who first turned Ireland into a commodity and then became one himself.

In *Ulysses*, Joyce dwells on the seductive appeal of mass culture under capitalism, specifically on its utopian promise to overcome the nightmares of history. His proleptic representation of Ireland as a consumer society is profoundly linked to his apprehension of the upheavals, deprivations, and transformations of nineteenth-century Ireland—the Ireland Joyce was born into and grew up in. His precocious treatments of commodification, consumption, advertising, and technology also make Joyce's work relevant to the contemporary globalized condition of independent Ireland in the wake of the economic boom of the 1990s. Joyce explores the "dreamworld"[16] of modernity with an intensity and ambivalence that connects him back to the earliest novelists in the Irish Catholic lineage. For them, the project of the national novel had repeatedly raised questions of representation to which perhaps only Joyce found appropriately radical responses. Nevertheless, by revisiting their work, we can supply a vital missing chapter in the prehistory of Joyce's distinctively Irish modernism.

Acknowledgments

I wish to thank the Irish Research Council for the Humanities and Social Sciences for their award of a Government of Ireland Research Fellowship, which enabled me to complete this book. I am indebted to many people for their kind support for this project. Particular thanks are due to Brian Cosgrove, former Head of the Department of English at the National University of Ireland, Maynooth, and to my departmental colleagues, for creating such a stimulating and friendly environment for academic research. I am grateful for the advice and assistance of Glenn Wright, Acquisitions Editor, and James MacKillop, Series Editor, at Syracuse University Press.

Numerous colleagues in the area of nineteenth-century Irish studies, at Maynooth and elsewhere, have shared their knowledge and in many cases their forthcoming work with me. I would especially like to thank Jacqueline Belanger, Claire Connolly, Margaret Kelleher, Ronan Kelly, Siobhán Kilfeather, Jason King, Heather Laird, Breandán MacSuibhne, Chris Morash, Willa Murphy, and Tadgh O'Sullivan. I am grateful for the insightful responses of Marjorie Howes and Declan Kiberd to an initial outline of this work. Kevin Whelan read an early version of the opening chapter of this book and made several extremely useful suggestions. Special thanks also to Luke Gibbons for support and inspiration. I am fortunate to have benefitted so much from the generosity and critical acumen of Joe Cleary over many years, as both a scrupulous reader and a much valued interlocutor.

The Red Stripe Seminar sustained lively intellectual debate in Dublin and Maynooth for more than a decade; in particular, I would like to thank Kevin Honan, Sinéad Kennedy, Siobhán Long, and Conor McCarthy for their unfailing comradeship. Richard Bourke, Rachel Potter, Denise Meagher, and Ingrid Scheibler provided long-distance counsel and friendship. I would also like to acknowledge the kindness of John Cahill, the

MacRory family, and the whole "army," especially Sheila Morris and Aisling O'Donoghue.

I was often amused, when reading some of the early Irish novels I discuss in this book, to come across words and phrases that I had only ever heard before from my mother Eileen or my late father Patrick Nolan. I am glad to have heard those echoes of another Ireland, and I am also thankful to my father for having conveyed such a strong sense of the importance and excitement of the printed word to all his children. I owe another huge debt to Rachel MacRory for the wonderful gift of her friendship over her whole short, extraordinary life.

My research for this book was facilitated at every stage by the critical engagement and practical help of Seamus Deane.

It has to be said that Iseult Deane did very little to advance this work. However, her incredulity at my slow progress and her impatience to commandeer my computer for her own—no doubt more important—purposes, may eventually have helped it toward a speedier conclusion.

Earlier versions of some of the material in this book have been published in *The Irish Novel in the Nineteenth Century*, ed. Jacqueline Belanger (Dublin: Four Courts Press, 2005) and *The Field Day Review*, vol. 2 (2006). I am grateful to the editors and publishers for allowing revised material to be reprinted here.

CATHOLIC EMANCIPATIONS

1

Thomas Moore

Irish Melodies and Discordant Politics

Irish History in the *Irish Melodies*

The Irish nineteenth century, as a distinct cultural entity, may be said to have begun in 1808 with the publication of the first volume of Moore's *Irish Melodies*. Thomas Moore (1779–1852) was the son of a Dublin grocer and a socially ambitious mother. Unusually for a Catholic of his day, he was a graduate of Trinity College, Dublin, and his literary career in London had been advanced by the patronage of prominent Whig aristocrats. Moore was a political satirist of note and also wrote several innovative biographies and a wildly successful "Orientalist" romance, *Lalla Rookh* (1817). But it was the phenomenon of the *Melodies*, published in ten volumes between 1808 and 1834, that made of their author a celebrity. Moore's performances of the songs, all of which were based on traditional Irish airs, created a sensation in the drawing rooms of English Regency society. In Ireland, the *Melodies* were rapidly incorporated into a whole new repertoire of music and story that became as important for an emergent Irish nationalism as opera was for its later counterpart in Italy. Moore's enduring popularity exceeded even that of the poets of *The Nation*, the newspaper of the Young Ireland movement in the 1840s, and of the now much more highly regarded writers of the Irish Literary Revival.

Many of the airs adapted by Moore had first been written down by Edward Bunting at the Belfast Harp Festival of 1792, from the playing of ten elderly harpists. These musicians had represented for their audience a frail surviving link with the culture of the ancient Irish bards. But for Bunting, as for his United Irish associates who organized the festival, this tradition could still be rescued and revived. And so controversy over the

Melodies began with Bunting's own objections to the "drawling, doleful and die-away manner" in which Moore performed some of the airs that Bunting had collected in his *A General Collection of the Ancient Irish Music* (1796): "The world have [sic] been too apt to suppose our music of a highly plaintive and melancholy character, and that it partook of our National feeling at the state of our country in a political view, and that three parts out of four of our tunes were of this complaining nature. Now there never was anything more erroneous than this idea."[1]

Moore has been accused not just of betraying the generally animated and joyful spirit of traditional Irish culture but also the political optimism of the United Irish movement that had helped to save this music from oblivion.[2] For the airs had not just been modified by Moore's predominantly nostalgic and melancholic verses; they had been, so the accusation went, transmogrified.

Much had changed in Ireland's political fortunes between the 1790s and the first appearance of the *Melodies*. The United Irishmen's Rebellion in 1798, which had been preceded by extreme provocation, was followed by extreme repression. Irish parliamentary autonomy, such as it had been, was finally extinguished by the Act of Union in 1800. The disenfranchised Catholics had been promised concessions after the Union, but during the first decade of the new century the prospect of Catholic Emancipation seemed as remote as ever. Moore has been characterized as a grieving commemorator of the lost revolutionary moment of 1798 (and of Robert Emmet's rebellion of 1803). The elegies for Lord Edward Fitzgerald and Robert Emmet in *Melodies*, and Moore's laudatory biography of Fitzgerald in 1831, would appear to confirm this view. Yet debate still continues over Moore's attitude toward the 1798 Rebellion. This issue remains important because of its relation to the larger question of how we should understand the largely Catholic nationalism that eventually emerged in Ireland with O'Connell's mass political campaign for emancipation in the 1820s.

O'Connell created the Catholic masses as a political force. He helped to break the confessional nature of the British state, winning for the Irish cause the support of liberal opinion in Europe and beyond. He presented the Irish as essentially docile, loyal, and civil, quite unlike the ferocious mobs or radicalized *peuple* of the French Revolution. His Catholic

Association sought to wean the disaffected away from both local agrarian secret societies and campaigns of retaliatory violence. Moore's *Melodies* provided a powerful reinforcement to O'Connell's project. They drew their inspiration from the "folk," but they were arranged for the pianofortes of "the rich and the educated" by Moore and his collaborator John Stevenson.[3] In the *Melodies*, it has been argued, Moore in effect consigns both the heroism of ancient Ireland and the United Irishmen's brand of revolutionary activism to the past. In their place, he offers an inauthentic translation of oral culture into "civilized" forms. Hence Moore, who was admired by Byron, Shelley, Goethe, and Stendhal, and who was particularly renowned in France and Poland as a passionate literary advocate of political liberty, has also been described as no more than "the public relations man of the movement whose political leader was O'Connell."[4] (This is despite Moore's own occasional disdain for O'Connell's personality and politics.) The very popularity of the *Melodies*, from this point of view, testifies to the blandly modular nature of bourgeois nationalism, which steals elements from traditional culture in order to serve its modernizing, homogenizing program.[5] The paradox is that Moore, who did more than any other single figure in the nineteenth century to create an Irish nationalist sensibility, and who used the success of the *Melodies* to open up a new public sphere in letters for previously excluded Irish Catholics, nonetheless stands accused of operating in the classic mode of "imperial sentimentality," which merely "cathects that which it is in the process of destroying."[6]

Daniel Maclise's illustrations for the 1846 edition of the *Melodies* highlight some important aspects of Moore's understanding of Irish history in the songs. Except in the case of a small number of the *Melodies* with an unmistakably contemporary setting, Maclise's drawings are executed in a highly ornamented medievalist style, complete with warriors in full armor, ladies in flowing gowns, and sad-faced lovers in flower-bedecked bowers. "Gaelic" Ireland is signified only by the many depictions of harps and harpists and in some of the framing borders entwined with shamrocks. But in a few of the pictures, these knights and damsels give way to modern young gentleman in frock coats (some in mortarboards), half asleep over their wine.[7] It is indeed hard to imagine these drinkers as anything other than remote and degenerate descendants of their heroic forbears.

In the *Melodies*, Moore resorts to what he elsewhere candidly admits may merely be "flattering fictions" about the ancient Gaels. This permits him, in his own words, to escape "the sad degrading truths" of later times.[8] But it also could be argued that Moore's construction of the past makes present-day realities appear to be the inevitable outcome of a process of historical evolution. And while he obviously cultivates nostalgia for the primal, heroic condition, there is also a satisfaction here with the civil present. Moore draws an opposition between an idealized and simplified bardic past, as opposed to the sensual pleasures of a corrupt modernity about which he professes much guilt. Although he frequently exhorts his audience to armed resistance on behalf of freedom and Irish independence, this rhetoric is less than convincing. The poems about war dwell as much on bloodshed and self-sacrifice as they do on heroic victories ("After the Battle"). He may long for "The Swords of former time," but he also wishes for "the men who bore them"—as it indeed seems most unlikely that men like himself will ever be ready to wield them. The era of kings, warriors, and all their pomp is gone, yet often the joys of good company, wine, song, and a possibly self-deceiving historical memory seem compensation enough ("This life is all chequer'd with pleasures and woes," "They may rail at this life"). Historical change is envisioned as analogous to the sad mutability of individual human experience in its various phases. The many lyrics about young love, loss, and mortality emphasize an obsession with personal development or degeneration ("Love's young dream," "I saw thy form in youthful prime," "In the morning of life"). The youth of the nation is imagined in heroic, martial terms, yet the occasional calls to recreate this past have a bogus political quality and are as futile as the wish to be young again.[9]

The juxtaposition of antiquity and modernity in the lyrics is stark because it is not mediated by much specific reference to an actually (or even *recently*) existing Irish culture. The "we" who weep together in these lyrics, or who pass around the bowl to cheer themselves up, are apparently united by a shared emotional relationship to Ireland's semihistorical, semilegendary past, but it is not a past that proves usable in any clear way. Instead, we uncover a narrative of ever-increasing isolation and individualism and a corresponding retreat to the realm of private comfort and solace. In several songs, the relationship between two lovers is explicitly offered as a more dependable substitute for other forms of community—even the vestigial community signified by the solidarity of drinking-mates. (See "Tho' the last glimpse of Erin with sorrow I see," in which the exiled woman comforts herself with the thought that her lover's body is "Erin to me," and "Oh! Had we some bright little isle of our own," "I'd mourn the hopes.")

Moore's real achievement in the *Melodies* is to convert the military and political disaffection of the past into an appealing form of lamentation for the world that such disaffection had failed to recover. The history of Irish resistance is thereby converted into *cultural* opposition, and the music itself pleads Ireland's case for recognition and justice: "Thy masters themselves, as they rivet thy chains,/Shall pause at the song of their captive, and weep" ("Oh! Blame not the Bard"). We can understand why William Hazlitt complains that "There are no tones here to waken Liberty, to console Humanity."[10] Such apparently political allegories as "Silent O Moyle," and laments like "'Tis gone, and for ever," transform an activist project of mass politicization, such as that attempted by the United Irish movement, into a merely passive longing for the indefinitely deferred dawn of freedom in Ireland. The emotional appeal of some of the *Melodies* obscures the political impasse they depict. We might say that in these song-cycles the fight for liberty and for Ireland *must* go on, but *can't* go on—partly because of the ways in which "fighting" itself is conceptualized and aestheticized.

But against this, we could equally stress Moore's contribution to the cultivation of what we might call colonial memory. At least, Moore never entirely surrenders to a catastrophic history, even when he laments his inability to influence or change it; as Luke Gibbons puts it, contrasting Moore's attitude to Gaelic culture with Walter Scott's more purely nostalgic regard for an antiquated Scottish Highland culture, "1798 is no Culloden where Ireland is concerned."[11] It is surely arguable that the songs register collective traumas too painful to be spoken of with clarity, and that have not been absorbed into any coherent or easily communicable historical narrative. But my purpose here is not so much to adjudicate the question of the ultimate political significance of the *Melodies*, as to examine how their emphasis on the heroism of the past, contrasted with the sentimental sensibility of the present, makes it extremely difficult to fit 1798 into the dualistic time scheme so vividly illustrated by Maclise's drawings. (The best-known songs about Fitzgerald and Emmet, "Oh! Breathe not his name," "She is far from the land," and "When he, who adores thee," are not illustrated in the 1846 edition.)[12] Ireland had no Culloden, and not only in the sense that the gleams of Gaelic culture can never be extinguished ("And thus Erin, my country tho' broken thou art,/There's a lustre within thee, that ne'er will decay"),[13] but also because 1798 did not involve any equivalent military engagement in which the brave warriors of an old, doomed civilization confronted the more powerful forces of England and "modern" civilization. Indeed, despite his regard for the deeply romantic figures of Emmet and Fitzgerald, Moore betrays contradictory feelings both about the United Irishmen and about the many thousands of common Irish people whom they recruited to their cause. Hence his lament, in the appendix to "Corruption and Intolerance," that neither the history of oppression, nor that of resistance, reflect much glory on the Irish:

> It is true that this island has given birth to heroes who, under more favorable circumstances, might have left in the heart of their fellow countrymen recollections as dear as those of a Bruce or a Wallace; but success was wanting to consecrate resistance, their cause was branded with the disheartening name of treason, and their oppressed country was such a blank among nations, that . . . the fame of their actions was lost in the obscurity of the place where they achieved them. . . . Hence it is that the annals of Ireland, through a lapse of six hundred years, exhibit not one of those shining names, not one of those themes of national pride, from which poetry borrows her noblest aspiration; and that history, which ought to be the richest garden of the Muse, yields no growth to her in this hapless island but cypress and weeds.[14]

One way in which Moore commemorates the dead is by displacing recent history into a distant, heroic past. Thus, "the wounded companions" tied to stakes on the battlefield in order than they can fight on ("Remember the glories of Brien the brave"), or "the few and faint, but fearless still"

("After the Battle"), represent the men of 1798.[15] At times, this serves to confer on the figure of Fitzgerald, for example, a kind of archaic, ultramasculine glamour that his biographer so self-consciously lacks. As he notes in his journal, Moore received a "sort of *boudoir* education" as the precocious only son of a doting mother, who ran something of a minor *salon* from their house in Aungier Street. He states, "The only thing that conduced to brace and invigorate my mind was the strong political feelings that were stirring around me when I was a boy, and in which I took a deep and most ardent interest."[16] Hence his daring friends were a healthy, manly influence, and he himself showed considerable moral courage at various moments in his university career.[17] Yet he was never inducted into the underground world of United Irish organization and conspiracy. Both his mother and Emmet himself dissuaded Moore from more active involvement; as he later discovers, his friends had kept their real secrets from him. They had "implicated themselves far more deeply in the popular league against power than I could ever have suspected."[18]

He followed (or so he tells us in 1831) the United Irishmen for every step of their journey toward rebellion, "but the last."[19] They became martyrs; after the forced exile of his friend Edward Hudson and Emmet's public execution in 1803, Moore was left with the airs from Bunting's songbooks, which Hudson and Emmet had performed together, out of which Moore created the *Melodies*. At one level, then, the United Irishmen are warriors like Brian Boru and other champions of Gaeldom. But at another level, Moore would *wish* them to be no more extreme than John Philpot Curran and Henry Grattan and the reforming, patriotic Irish Whigs. He asserts that the government, in effect, turned the United Irishmen into revolutionaries by prohibiting their meetings: "The whole body, thus debarred from the right of speaking out, as citizens, passed naturally to the next step, of plotting as conspirators."[20] But he cannot entirely deny that the United Irishmen also had a radical ideological agenda of their own. They took advantage of the vacuum that had been created by the failure of the Whigs to stand up for the Irish people as a whole because, blinded by their hatred of popery, the people's "legitimate guardians . . . took no account of the great mass of living materials, out of which alone the pile of national liberty can be constructed"—that is, the Catholic masses of Ireland. Hence, the people lost faith in what Moore seems to have regarded as their natural leaders and instead looked "to that ominous light now kindled in the north as their sole and sure beacon of invitation and hope."[21] The radicals thus invited the masses into their movement, but the latter took it over and destroyed it. Moore argues that, because of his incarceration and death, Fitzgerald had no influence on the military conduct of the rebellion, and therefore bore no responsibility for those "outrages and crimes" that were perpetrated under the name of the United Irishmen in those areas where the uprising had "degenerated into Defenderism"—by which Moore denotes the excessive violence of the poor.[22] But the rebellion cost the lives of such men as Fitzgerald and Emmet, whose "gifts would have made them the ornaments and supports of a well-regulated community."[23] That Fitzgerald, the author of the many personal letters that Moore quotes in the biography—letters telling of his family life, his firstborn baby, his love of gardening, these "simple and,—to an almost feminine degree,—fond letters"— should so shortly afterwards plunge into "a sea of conspiracy and revolt" is in itself an indictment of the government: "The government that could drive such a man into such resistance—and there were hundreds equal to him in goodness, if not in heroism, so driven,—is convicted by this very result alone, without any further enquiry into its history."[24]

Moore recalls the only occasion, in 1797, on which he saw Lord Edward in the flesh, walking down Dublin's Grafton Street, and states that "I ran anxiously after him, desirous of another look at one whose name had, from my school-days, been associated in my mind with all that was noble, patriotic and chivalrous. Though I saw him but once, his peculiar dress, the elastic lightness of his step, his fresh, healthful complexion, and the soft expression given to his eyes by their long dark eyelashes, are as present and familiar to my memory as if I had intimately known him."[25]

This passage is consonant with Moore's emphasis, throughout the text, on Fitzgerald's personal charm and attractiveness as much as on his skill as a military strategist. In the biography, an impassioned defense of the right to resist unjust government and a coherent analysis of various tactical mistakes made by the leaders are countered by Moore's plea to the reader to ignore Lord Edward's deeds, and to concentrate on his personal virtues alone. In a concluding passage, Moore quotes from the life of Fitzgerald's contemporary, Curran, written by his son, who remembered that "his [Lord Edward's] private excellencies were so conspicuous that the officer of the Crown, who moved for leave to bring in the Bill of Attainder, could not refrain from bearing ample testimony to them: 'His political offences he could not mention without grief; and were it consistent with the principles of public justice, he would wish that the recording angel should let fall a tear and wash them out for ever.'"[26]

For Moore, too, what actually happened in 1798 should be washed out by tears, for it is not to the credit of either the people or their leaders. The memory of these sweet-natured, self-sacrificing gentlemen is foremost among what must be salvaged from the catastrophes of 1798 and 1803. Yet their names are not to be breathed in the songs that commemorate them; what it means is to be "too faithful" to Ireland ("When he, who adores thee") or to die for your country ("She is far from the land") is decorously veiled. Violence in the distant past can be celebrated in poetry, but not the violence of the recent past. Revolutionaries and angry peasants represent too great an aesthetic (as well as a political) problem for the author of the *Melodies*. But native Catholic leadership under O'Connell is also regarded by Moore with suspicion. In one of the late *Melodies*, "The dream of those days when first I sung thee is o'er," generally presumed to be addressed to the Great Liberator, Moore asserts that O'Connell's conduct since emancipation has revealed him still to be wearing "the dark brand" of slavery in his heart: "And Freedom's sweet fruit, for which thy spirit long burn'd,/Now, reaching at last thy lip, to ashes hath turn'd?" It is difficult to judge, from this lyric, whether Moore is expressing a principled objection to the cult of personality and the supposed Catholic sectarianism of O'Connell's movement, or whether he is merely voicing a snobbish distaste for Irish democracy.[27] In either case, this Irish hero does not even begin to rival Emmet or Fitzgerald in Moore's Irish pantheon.

Moore's rather truncated version of Irish history then compels him to treat the country's Golden Age—early Christian to medieval in most of its incarnations in the *Melodies*—with great reverence. However, it has often been noted that the tone of Moore's works—poems, prose, and satires in several modes—varies considerably, and that he expresses mixed and maybe even contradictory opinions about English and Irish politics.[28] Some have claimed that a consistent but veiled politics lies behind these disparate texts: Moore's own views, so the argument goes, remained essentially as they were when he was an undergraduate at Trinity, but he was obliged to adopt various disguises or masks in changed political times, especially because of his dependence on the London literary marketplace. However, his *Memoirs of Captain Rock* (1824), a history of English rule in Ireland narrated by a fictional Irish rebel, seems to represent a break with the indirection and the pessimism of the *Melodies*, and a return to the United Irish Moore. (The name "Captain Rock," affixed to countless threatening notices and letters over a period of particularly intense unrest in the south of Ireland during the previous five years, had become synonymous with Irish agrarian terrorism.) This alteration in Moore's mode of political avowal has been ascribed to various historical factors, or theorized in terms of the determining power of genre.[29]

The issue of Moore's political consistency is less important here than the question of the contrasting ways in which the *Melodies* and *Captain Rock* render polite literary versions of the traditional, the barbarous, or the wild. The contrast is not produced by a "development" in Moore's work from a sentimental to a satiric treatment of Irish political issues. Indeed, these two modes alternate quite regularly in his writing. But in *Captain Rock* we do have something unique—a work in which he finds something to do with Irish history other than merely to bewail it. For example, the account of 1798 in *Captain Rock* is in many ways similar to that in the biography of Fitzgerald. Moore emphasizes the government's culpability in fomenting the rising, and how the "lowest of the population" were lashed into "a fury as blind as that of the Cyclops in his cave, but only the more ferocious for being unenlightened"; in this way, "the cause of the people in Ireland" was disgraced.[30] But in *Captain Rock*, there is no paean of praise for Emmet or Fitzgerald and no allusion whatever to O'Connell or to the changed complexion of Irish political opposition after the rebellion and the Act of Union. (Rock describes the union as "that last grand *bouquet* of the *feux d'artifice* of Corruption" [*Captain Rock*, 216].) Nor, as Moore assumes the voice of Captain Rock, does he fear to speak of even the worst aspects of '98:

With respect to the atrocities committed by some members of my Family, during the paroxysm of that re-action which the measures of the Government had provoked, it is far from my intention to enter into any defence of them. I will merely say, that they who, after having read the preceding pages, can still wonder at such events as even the massacre of Scullabogue, have yet to learn that simple theory of the connexion of events with their causes, which is the sovereign cure for wonder on all such occasions. (361–62)[31]

For in the fictional biography of Captain Rock, that "lover of discord" (21), Moore writes about native leadership and popular agency in startlingly new ways. He turns to an imagined version of the secret history of the Irish masses (and even to what he characterizes in the biography of Fitzgerald as "Defenderism") in order to write about historical catastrophe without euphemism or mystification. In so doing, he demonstrates how an atrocious history contains the seeds not just of tragedy, but of comedy as well.

Ventriloquizing Captain Rock

The contemporary reception of *Captain Rock* tells us a good deal about the political impact of the work on the conventional pieties of the readership of the day in all that concerned the representation of Ireland. One of the first reviews complained that "It is scarcely possible that any reader should not, from the title of this book, be led to anticipate some account of the late insurrections in Ireland. Of this, however, there is not one word."[32]

This misreading is not at all surprising given its provenance in the Tory *Blackwood's Edinburgh Magazine*. There are at least a few words about "the late insurrections" in *Captain Rock*, but clearly they were not taken seriously by the *Blackwood's* reviewer. We can only imagine that he may have preferred something more expressive of the thrilling horror of agrarian violence, as it appeared from the point of view of the gentry: "When we read Captain Rock's Memoirs, and remembered the scenes of blood which for three years have desolated the fairest provinces of Ireland—while, with fear and trembling, we at this hour think of the insecurity of our friends there, the first feeling excited by the book, was sorrow that any one could be found to jest with such a subject."[33]

The notice in the *Westminster Review*, although obviously written by an admirer of Moore and from a more liberal political viewpoint, is also critical. (*Captain Rock* was published anonymously, although Moore's authorship was an open secret from the outset.) This reviewer, too, is surprised by the lack of "reality" in *Captain Rock* and is disappointed that Captain Rock is not "a real potatoe and milk, or gun-powder and whisky, Irishman, but a sort of abstraction of Irish riot."[34] He remarks:

> When we heard that Mr. Moore was editing the captain's life, we hoped to see such a picture as might be given by a man of imagination and knowledge, by a man acquainted with his own country and the human heart, of the manner in which a Captain Rock and his followers are made, of the manner in which individual Irishmen are worked up into that state of excitement and ferocity of which we see the daily fruits in almost every part of Ireland. We hoped for such a Captain Rock as the author of Old Mortality might make, if he chose, instead of strengthening absurd prejudices which exist, or directing his strength against the caricatures of follies which have passed away, to acquire some claim to the gratitude of the age.[35]

Moore would have written a more responsible and important book, the writer argues, if he had created a fictional representative of this colorful but violent culture in the manner of a Walter Scott, "the author of Old Mortality."

But the meaning of Moore's literary experiment was not at all more obvious to Irish readers. One of the most extraordinary responses to *Captain Rock* came from Roger O'Connor, who is mentioned by Moore in the text. As Captain Rock informs us, the origins of his family name is disputed, but "an idea exists in certain quarters that the letters of which it is composed are merely initials, and contain a prophetic announcement of the high destiny that awaits, at sometime or other, that celebrated gentleman, Mr. Roger O'Connor, being, as they fill up the initials, the following awful words,—Roger O Connor King!" (6).

This Roger O'Connor—a brother of the United Irish leader Arthur O'Connor—was a radical and, in the words of Joep Leerssen, "a living reminder of 1798," chiefly notorious for his *Chronicles of Eri* (1822)—"translations" of nonexistent Irish source texts that traced the origins of the Irish race back to the Mediterranean, in the style of the Phoenician model of Charles Vallancey.[36] In his *Letters to His Majesty, King George the Fourth, by Captain Rock,* O'Connor reappropriates the Rock name, but also makes a number of important criticisms of Moore's text.

O'Connor notes the difference between the English taste for Scottish and for Irish subject matter. He charges Moore with the attempt to make Ireland charming and amusing in the "Caledonian" mode, but he also suggests that such a treatment will not hold English interest for very long and, more significantly, that Moore's own self-conscious stylism in *Captain Rock* falsifies the misery and suffering of the Irish poor:

> How could you handle so lightly matter so weighty, that lies so heavily on millions of our flesh and blood, drawing off attention, which should be undivided, from the most tragic scenes to your wit and sportiveness?. . . . the blasted heaths; the craggy cliffs; poesy made tame; history run wild; the goblins and hobgoblins, hags, witches and tartan of Caledonia,—dressed up in Pictish phrase,— have had the power to attract the notice, and fix the attention of England during some seasons: these are charming playthings, fit for the chimney-corner or parlour-window; but I much doubt whether the interest you have roused by your version of my memoirs will survive next winter.[37]

Moore indeed admits in his journal that he had never seen the true degradation of Irish rural poor until his 1823 tour in the company of Lord Lansdowne: "Saw at Collan for the first time in my life, some real specimens of Irish misery and filth; three or four cottages together exhibiting such a naked swarm of wretchedness as never met my eyes before."[38]

During that trip he conversed with Daniel O'Connell, John O'Driscol, and others, and took the tourist trail around the lakes of Killarney. Although the journal records his many inquiries as to the religious consciousness of the people, the state of their education, and the motivation of the secret Whiteboy societies, the origins of *Memoirs of Captain Rock*, as O'Connor correctly suggests, do not lie in the experience of the peasantry. Despite Moore's "questioning of the existing colonial stereotypes of agrarian insurgency"[39] in the journal, we must also admit that he is excessively concerned with exonerating his friend Lansdowne from the charge of being a bad landlord, as well as with his own enormous fame in Ireland, which pleased him greatly. Moore's actual distance from the peasant culture that he invoked was also mocked by another of the respondents to the book, Mortimer O'Sullivan, author of the anonymously published *Captain Rock Detected*. As the title of his own book suggests, O'Sullivan, a convert to the Church of Ireland, was concerned with detecting what he regarded as the true identity of the rural insurgents. In an aside, he scoffed at the spectacle of "a peer and a poet" (Lansdowne and Moore) who "made a rather hasty exit from Killarney last year." Lansdowne's conduct was contrasted by O'Sullivan with that of another landlord, Stanley, who was, at the time of Moore's visit, "visiting in person and alone the cabins of the tenantry; seeing with his own eyes their condition."[40]

Perhaps the most telling contrast to Moore is provided by the Limerick novelist Gerald Griffin (1803–40), generally regarded as being close to the common people and concerned to capture their language and their spirit. In works such as *The Collegians* and *Tracy's Ambition* (both published in 1829), he produced remarkable accounts of upper-class guilt and self-division, but these are dramatized by the *projection* of various forms of violence onto the poor. Rather than offering an analogous exploration of the brutalized or criminal Irish peasant mind, *Captain Rock* is a contribution to the little-understood "role of humour, albeit bitter humour, in the psychodynamics of oppression,"[41] its "wit and sportiveness"[42] as offensive to a Roger O'Connor as to a Mortimer O'Sullivan (and the latter announces proudly that his own work will be unadorned by "the graces of wit or eloquence").[43] In this sense, some of those who excoriated *Captain Rock* (this "pernicious missal,"[44] "the most exceptionable publication, in all its bearings as to Ireland, that I have yet seen")[45] appear to have read it more sensitively than those who welcomed it. His biographer made the impossible claim that Daniel O'Connell described the book as being to the struggle for Catholic

Emancipation what *Uncle Tom's Cabin* was to the abolition of slavery.[46] This interestingly misrepresents the text, however, for indeed it would be hard to imagine anything further removed from Harriet Beecher Stowe's sentimental fiction than Moore's *Captain Rock.*

Moderate Catholic admiration for Moore's book stems from his belief that it would attract support for the cause of Catholic Emancipation. Tadhg O'Sullivan agrees that Moore reorients "the 'Rock' signifier away from the nom-de-guerre of threatening letters and toward the new strident voice of Catholic middle-class politics in the mid 1820s."[47]

According to this reading, *Captain Rock* civilized or sanitized the most fearful features of Irish popular culture. It was therefore integral to the O'Connellite project of weaning the peasantry away from violent, local agrarian movements and leading them into nonviolent, national politics. O'Sullivan argues that the "'merry reign of Captain Rock and his family' is fundamentally as damaging and threatening to the class that Moore is championing"[48] as it is to the Ascendancy class in Ireland. This is consistent with readings of the *Melodies*, which would claim that something wild was tamed and domesticated in them. To be sure, Moore cannot entirely be absolved from the charge of appropriating popular insurgency for his own political ends, especially in his stress on tithes and religious grievances rather than on rent and land. For example, Michael Davitt wrote in *The Fall of Feudalism in Ireland* (1904) that O'Connell and other Catholic leaders entered into "a tacit, if unacknowledged, co-operation" with "the spirit of Whiteboyism" during the tithe war—only to resume their usual denunciations of secret societies after the Tithe Commutation Act of 1838, which effectively settled the question of tithes.[49] But I will contend that we are dealing with something much more far-reaching and unsettling in this text than the middle-class adoption of the Rock name for specifically constitutional nationalist purposes.

Roger O'Connor asserts that the book ignored the necessity for radical change: "And now, at the end of all these many days of many years, the account of all the spoliations, massacres, degradations, and insults heaped on the Irish people is proposed to be balanced by the one *pitiful* item— *Catholic Emancipation.*"[50] But his summary of the text's concluding polemic is somewhat misleading. Rock's direct appeal for emancipation (that point in the text where the political concerns of the 1820s are most explicitly addressed) comes at the end of the penultimate chapter, before the account of 1798 and of Decimus Rock's capture and transportation. The book does not *end* with a plea for emancipation, in the apparently conciliatory style of, for example, John Banim's novel *The Boyne Water* (1826).

It was despite rather than because of Moore's lack of intimacy with Irish rural life that *Memoirs of Captain Rock* was produced. The text betrays none of the familiar anxiety so prevalent when an elite observer attempts to make sense of the aberrant behavior of the lower orders—although traces of it are indeed present in the much more conventional form of Moore's journal of his fact-finding mission in Ireland. Ultimately, *Captain Rock* fails to provide the kind of knowledge that will serve the interests of the landowners themselves—the real reason for seeing with one's "own eyes," as Mortimer O'Sullivan puts it. In some senses, *because* of Moore's decision to ignore the moral panic about agrarian violence, he created in *Captain Rock* a persona, a historical narrative, and a representation of Irish turbulence, all of which may indeed be closer than any novel or official report to the spirit of Irish "outrage," which historians have only recently attempted to decipher in terms of its complex articulation with folk culture, ritual, and festival.[51]

Moore offers, in the voice of the book's eponymous hero, a unique account of Irish popular disaffection in the 1820s. But this act of ventriloquism—so significant and so notorious in its own time—has effectively been lost to Irish literary history.[52] This may be in part a result of the fact that Moore's text appears simply to ignore the difficulties that early-nineteenth-century Ireland evidently presented to writers of all kinds—difficulties particularly associated with Irish peasant culture and its supposedly endemic violence. And while agrarian violence had been a significant feature of the Irish rural scene since about 1760, the events of 1798 (especially in Armagh and Wexford) helped to intensify fears concerning widespread unrest that might otherwise have been regarded as merely local, spontaneous, or pre-political.

Many authors at this time—producers of Irish sketches, travelogues, tales, and novels—comment repeatedly on the strangeness of the Irish peasant.[53] Whether these works dwell on the charm of the hospitable, sentimental Irish, or express terror at the spectacle of a brutal, degraded Irish folk culture, they clearly reflect the strains of translating rural Ireland into terms comprehensible to metropolitan English readers—or even to Ascendancy or middle-class Irish readers. Many of these texts, particularly those by Irish Catholic writers, bear obvious and important resemblances to the modernizing program pursued in the political realm by O'Connell and other nationalist leaders. The aesthetic and political projects are equally committed to the reform of the Irish national character, displayed in its purest form by the peasantry. Cultural change, it seemed, is necessary to redeem the Irish in English public opinion, and ultimately in order to create a modern Irish political state.

But Moore then fails to depict Captain Rock as a "typical" Irishman. The captain is, in fact, described only briefly in the text, in the framing narrative that introduces and concludes the *Memoirs*. There he encounters the narrator, an English Protestant missionary who has come to Ireland to convert "the poor benighted Irish" (*Captain Rock*, iv). (This was at the height of the proselytizing crusade of the so-called "Second Reformation.")[54] The missionary is treated ironically from the outset; he never develops into the kind of guide to the peculiarities of Irish life which the early-nineteenth-century reader might have expected to encounter, either in fiction or in nonfictional texts. Instead, authority in the text is effectively handed over to the native himself. Most of the text is written by Captain Rock in the form of a scholarly manuscript, complete with classical quotations and references to authorities on Irish history. Captain Rock presents this manuscript to the missionary, who contributes only a few remarks to the footnotes. Moore then bypasses the moral and political problem (as the *Westminister Review* understands it) of how a representative of a marginal culture should be exhibited to the metropolitan culture, fully and properly historicized and psychologized. He also bypasses the question of how to represent Irish speech, or how to translate an oral culture into literature, which so preoccupied Moore's Irish contemporaries. Captain Rock may speak with a brogue (viii), but he writes in standard English, of a particularly satiric kind. The text does engage with the question of Irish oral culture and the threat it evidently presented to modern civility—but, again, in very different terms to those of other writers of the time.[55] For in departing from novelistic modes, particularly those associated with Scott, Moore departs too from the conception of character appropriate to realist fiction, and especially the versions of historical consciousness and racial character that had become central to the historical novel.

It has, of course, always been difficult in any period of modern Irish history to characterize accurately the relationship between insurrection and constitutional politics, and especially so soon after 1798. For instance, O'Connell could outrightly condemn the Whiteboys and yet willingly represent them in the law courts, and as late as 1881, Irish Parliamentary Party leader Charles Stewart Parnell threatened the government: "[I]f I am arrested, Captain Moonlight will take my place."[56] This ambivalence is also central to Moore's text. Hence, we must address Moore not merely as the domesticator of wildness, but also as an analyst of the subtle as well as of the obvious relationships between political violence and political civility that obtained in Ireland.

Mortimer O'Sullivan (arguing for the irrelevance of Catholic Emancipation) denies that the "outrages in the south of Ireland, are only, as it were, a keeping time to the music of this commanding body [the Catholic Association]. 'So Orpheus fiddled, and so danced the brutes.'"[57] But by giving the speaking part, in this text, to the brutes themselves (and so, according to his critics, "words and wit to vulgar errors lending"),[58] Moore presents us with a new conception of Irish rural unrest. He depicts an ongoing tradition of insurgence that heroically defies both "misery and Malthus" (Captain Rock, 256)—although this is perhaps a vision of Irish resistance that could not have survived the devastation that was to come with the Great Famine of the 1840s.

In recent decades, a number of powerful critical commentaries have addressed these central preoccupations of nineteenth-century Irish writing, including—among other issues—questions about national character and violence, oral culture, translation, and civility.[59] As we have already seen, Moore's Melodies, the best-known work of the most popular Irish writer of his time, can be understood as song-cycles in which a lost Gaelic civilization and the necessity for cultural renovation are explored. Yet, in Captain Rock, we have also a text that borrows for its very title the most notorious signifier of rural unrest and outrage, and which, unlike so many of the prose narratives and especially the fictional narratives of the day, appears to be flagrantly uninterested in thick description of peasant life, in verisimilitude, and in the critique (or in the anxious defense) of Irish national character. Nor do we find here any attempt at the formal "resolution" of historical and political problems, which is so marked a feature of stories and novels by both Protestant and Catholic writers at this time.

The Campaign of Captain Rock

Gerald Griffin claimed that the campaign of agrarian violence pursued by the followers of Captain Rock created a new appetite among the English public for narratives about Ireland. Certainly, various commentators agree that the Rockite campaign in Munster marked a watershed in the history of disturbances in the Irish countryside, although Whiteboy secret, oath-bound societies had been sporadically active throughout large parts of rural Ireland for decades.[60] Griffin writes that it was the "subtle and murderous insurrection of 1821, 1822, so wonderful in its unity of purpose, so fearful and mysterious in its mode of operation [that] first excited in England an alarmed interest and a strong curiosity respecting the habits of the [Irish] people."[61] He implies that it is hard for outsiders to comprehend how any population could produce and sustain such "a system of terrorism."[62] It is a widely shared belief, found in much of the official as well as the literary writing of the time, that the enigma of the Irish people can only be resolved if the causes and nature of agrarian violence are understood. Equally, we can appreciate that the explanation of the phenomenon of Captain Rock offered by Moore's text (and, perhaps, the style and the form in which it was presented, so utterly different from, for example, Griffin's own fiction) baffled the expectations of both the English and Irish readerships that Moore had already created for his works. And it could be argued that an entirely new subgenre of Irish fiction, concerned with peasant violence, was born out of the reaction to *Captain Rock*. Various shades of political opinion were represented in that reaction; many regarded the book as scandalous, but even some of those who considered it to be a great boon for the cause of Irish Catholics misrepresented or sanitized the book in their own work. The radical novelty of *Captain Rock* can be illustrated by comparison with some of the peasant fiction of Catholic contemporaries, such as Gerald Griffin and John and Michael Banim who, although profoundly influenced by *Memoirs of Captain Rock,* were unable fully to embrace its unprecedented representation of peasant or subaltern agency. No one, it seems, was entirely comfortable with its particular blend of history, literature, and politics.

Questions about the leadership and aims of the agrarian secret societies were debated with particular urgency in official and gentry circles during the Rockite campaign of 1819–23. The immediate causes of this outbreak of violence lay in the Irish agricultural crisis following the Napoleonic wars, and in the famine and typhus epidemic of 1817. But this ferocious campaign by the followers of Captain Rock had certain distinctive and, to the eyes of the authorities, terrifying features.[63]

The week-long peasant jacquerie of January 1822 raised the specter of "scattered protest giving place to the mobilization of peasant armies in a full-scale insurrection."[64] In addition, the Rockites were responsible for some particularly notorious attacks, such as the rape of the wives of men of the 1st Rifle Brigade in February 1822,[65] and the murder of three members of the Franks family of rack-renting middlemen. The latter incident seems to have been particularly ritualistic in nature, thus contributing to commentators' horror at the "barbarism" of the perpetrators. The twenty or so men who carried out the killings were dressed in women's clothing, sang and danced at the scene, and symbolically washed their hands in bowls of water.[66] Most significantly, this phase of peasant unrest involved an important millenarian element that made it more difficult to believe that the insurgents were merely engaged in a spontaneous protest against local conditions, or that they were not essentially hostile to the Established Church or the government. The dissemination of the so-called "Pastorini prophecies" in Munster appears to correlate with areas of intensive Rockite activity, just as some of Captain Rock's letters appear to allude to Pastorini's foretelling of the imminent destruction of Protestantism.[67] For example, Donnelly cites one threatening notice sent to a Catholic tithe-collector in Kanturk in October 1822: "You are not to join these bloody Protestants, for you know there [sic] time is expired. I will slatar [sic] them like dogs."[68] These are the kind of associations invoked by Moore when

Captain Rock tells us that Pastorini was the theological textbook at his hedge-school (*Captain Rock*, 187).

Captain Rock's mysterious signature appeared on hundreds of threatening notices and letters that were secretly delivered by peasant protestors to their chosen victims—landlords, agents, tithe-collectors, and neighbors in their own community who had broken the insurgents' code.[69] This code was regarded as older and more legitimate than the official laws. Kevin Whelan cites a statement from Donegal, made in 1831: "We are bound to obey the law of the land; but we find that in practice, especially among unlettered people, there is a law which is paramount to it; it is the law of nature, which the very worm when trodden upon acknowledges and which disposes men to resent suffering when it exceeds the power of endurance."[70]

Captain Rock is then, first of all, one among a number of Whiteboy captains or leaders (others would include Fear No, Starlight, Terry Alt, Steel Ribes) whose imaginary authority was invoked by the people during periods of particularly intense hardship and turmoil. The term *captain* itself "derived as much from rural practice as military usage. One of the first Whiteboys ever caught admitted 'I have acted one night among them as Captain, such as the Mayboys have.'"[71]

Hence, such figures are the embodiments of a collective identity. Behind the brutality, the grim humor, and the parodies of official discourse that we find so often in the anonymous letters lay powerless and vulnerable individuals. For example, one notice posted in Clonakilty in May 1823 announced: "This is to let the Protestants know there is a scourge over them from the almighty God. I am the man . . . that will give it. Jack Rock." The authorities were "mildly relieved to discover that the writer of this notice was only an adolescent journeyman weaver . . . who had 'not long left school.'"[72] But the mask of collective identity "signifies the dissolution of the individual personality and the assumption of the communal, the timeless, the impersonal. . . . the power of judgement, and of exemplary intimidation";[73] removing this mask to expose a single guilty individual was rarely a straightforward procedure.

Because the secret societies appear to have been organized by committees rather than by individuals, and because they enjoyed widespread support among their own communities and were generally not betrayed to the authorities, Whiteboy ringleaders were rarely identified or punished. During the panic over Pastorini, official fears concerning a coherent, widespread, underground conspiracy intensified. The influence of the prophecies on the Rockites suggested that the peasants were being manipulated by external agitators disseminating inflammatory texts. (O'Connell, however, claimed that Pastorini was spread "very much by persons inimical to the Catholic claims" to damage the Catholic Association and the campaign for reform.)[74] The motif of the mysterious upper-class agitator is central to the fictional texts inspired by *Captain Rock*.[75] Some of these stories and novels were produced in outraged reaction to Moore's handling of the issues of peasant consciousness and leadership. So, in "The Ruin," a novelistic fragment that Mortimer O'Sullivan incorporates into his *Captain Rock detected*, we encounter a gentleman General Rock, who addresses his troops by moonlight in a ruined abbey—men whom he secretly regards as clods and mere instruments who will serve to "make the privileged orders feel their insignificance, and wither in our sight." This shadowy character later takes his place at a respectable dinner table, recognized only by the narrator who had stumbled on his nighttime meeting.[76] Charlotte Elizabeth's *The Rockite: An Irish Story* also presents us with a captain of genteel physiognomy and superior education, who is ultimately revealed as a mere agent of Ireland's real enemy, the Roman Catholic Church. Charlotte Elizabeth concludes:

> In surveying the successive links of this formidable chain, now fast encircling the devoted island, it was impossible to fail of the conclusion that some unseen directing power, incomparably mightier than what either personal or political influence could put forth, stood paramount, to form, to fix, and to direct, the ponderous and destructive machinery. . . . This was, and is, the master-spring of those terrific movements which incessantly convulse the turbulent mass, in Ireland.[77]

Of course, the theme of the opacity and illegibility of peasant movements (and the attempt to decipher their secrets) is by no means limited to Irish historiography or literature, but occurs in any place where the actions

of illiterate people, generally embedded in an oral culture whose mytho-
logical or religious points of reference may be entirely alien to the upper
classes, are read by their social superiors—and generally read in ways that
elide popular autonomy or agency. But such movements also represent a
significant challenge for radical historians, or for historians of anticolonial
nationalism, who seek to reconstruct the history of *rebellious* traditional cultures.[78] For many of these intellectuals are themselves heirs to intellectual
traditions that regard modernization and indeed urbanization as inherently
progressive, transforming peasants from what Marx describes as so many
"potatoes in a sack" into potentially politicized citizens.[79] They are not then
well placed to understand peasant movements that may appear hostile to
the logic of modernization and at odds with modern political culture—"not,
or as in some views, 'not yet'" nationalist or revolutionary.[80]

According to Ranajit Guha, it is this way of thinking that allowed for
the complete omission of peasant consciousness from all kinds of histories
of the rural masses in India:

> The omission is indeed dyed into most narratives by assimilating
> peasant revolts to natural phenomena: they break out like thunder
> storms, heave like earthquakes, spread like wildfires, infect like epi-
> demics. In other words, when the clod of earth turns, this is a matter
> to be explained in terms of natural history. Even when this histori-
> ography is pushed to the point of producing an explanation in rather
> more human terms it will do so by assuming an identity of nature
> and culture, a hall-mark, presumably, of a very low state of civili-
> zation and exemplified in "those periodical outbursts of crime and
> lawlessness to which all wild tribes are subject," as the first historian
> of the Chuar rebellion put it. Alternatively, an explanation will be
> sought in the enumeration of causes—of, say, factors of economic
> and political deprivation which do not relate at all to the peasant's
> consciousness or do so negatively—triggering off rebellion as a
> sort of reflex action, that is, as an instinctive and almost mindless
> response of physical suffering of one kind or another (e.g., hunger,
> torture, forced labour, etc.) or as a passive reaction to some initiative
> of his superordinate enemy.[81]

But understanding peasant agency also remains a problem for later commentators, even those who are sympathetic to the insurgents but who may simply assimilate the subaltern masses into some other, more recognizable, historical agent or agency, such as the nation-in-emergence or the working class. And, indeed, Guha's remarks have an obvious bearing on the historiography of Irish peasant movements.[82]

E. P. Thompson and E. J. Hobsbawm, both associated with the English "history from below" school of social history, apparently regard their attempt to recover plebeian consciousness as of great historical and ethical interest, but not of urgent political significance. Hobsbawm's "primitive rebels," for example, are described as inhabitants of "the sort of peasant society which, it is safe to guess, is as remote from most readers as ancient Egypt, and which is as surely doomed by history as the Stone Age."[83] But Guha and others of the Indian "Subaltern Studies" school evidently view peasant resistance not as archaic at all, but as registering a form of opposition to the modern state, which is still active and important, especially in postcolonial societies.[84] Yet the uncovering of silenced subaltern voices has been fraught with conceptual and political difficulties.[85] Even in Guha's seminal essay, we must balance his opening declaration that insurgency was "a motivated and conscious undertaking on the part of the rural masses" with his concluding remarks about the importance of subaltern religious mentalities (often dismissed by secular radicals) as, on occasion, making the rebels "look upon their own project as predicated on a will other than their own."[86]

In his journal for the Irish trip of 1823, Moore reports on John O'Driscol's claim that the Rockites constitute a well-organized, politically motivated conspiracy, but comments that he finds this view "exaggerated and incredible." Moore is instead inclined to agree with John Scully, his brother-in-law, who "says it is merely a war of the poor against the rich."[87] In this, Moore articulates the familiar liberal Catholic view that there is nothing inherently wrong with poor Irish Catholics that predisposes them to unruly behavior, and that they are not simply the dupes of foreign conspirators or revolutionaries. Nevertheless, on that basis it would appear absurd to look to Moore for an authentic subaltern view of the conflict. But by providing a particular historical context and cultural meaning for peasant revolt in *Captain Rock*, Moore elevates its importance as part of a longer struggle against what he understands as British tyranny in Ireland—yet the meaning of Captain Rock is articulated in this text *by* a Captain Rock (however fantastical a figure Moore's narrator might be). And I will argue that, partly by doing precisely what Guha says that the upper-class commentator will always tend to do, in "assimilating peasant revolts into natural phenomena" and "assuming an identity between culture and nature," Moore in fact goes far beyond the limitations of elite historiography. In the light of this text, Irish peasants can be imagined as bringing much more than just "their despair and their numbers" (*Captain Rock*, 334) into progressive or radical movements.

"In spite of misery and Malthus":
The Comedy of Insurgence

In his portrayal of Captain Rock, Moore borrows elements from both the Anglo-Irish national tale and the Irish folk tradition of the heroic bandit. This character also represents Moore's response to controversial questions about the nature of agrarian insurgence, combining, as Rock does, aspects of the external commentator and the native insider, and of both individual and collective agency. And indeed, I suggest, Moore ultimately makes of his hero a kind of "Lord of Misrule"—a figure who presides over a Bakhtinian inversion of civilized values, although within an ostensibly civil discourse.

It has been has observed that in Anglo-Irish fiction of this period, "bringing a sophisticated and bored stranger into a romantic Irish setting and then permitting a love affair with a native to develop" is a formula.[88] Leerssen comments on the importance of these cosmopolitan strangers in persuading the hostile or reluctant English reader to be more sympathetic toward Ireland: The seduction of the narrator in the story is supposedly paralleled by seduction of the metropolitan reader. Moreover, the intensity of other characters' native exoticism in such narratives is usually mediated through a buffer, a relatively "de-Irishized" character, who may act as an interpreter of the "authentic, unmitigated Irish outlook." In the classic case of Lady Morgan's *The Wild Irish Girl*, we can regard Mortimer as the cosmopolitan focalizer, the Prince of Inismore as the archaic, real Irish character, and the wild Irish girl, Glorvina herself, as the mediating character. For although Glorvina, the sweet-voiced, beautiful, Romantic Irish harpist, is "exceptional in her heightened nationality,"[89] she also makes vital concessions to Mortimer's cultural and political perspectives. She announces her preference for Macpherson's Ossian poems over "the wild effusions" of the Irish bards on which she believes they are based, and she is also remarkably willing to distance herself from the superstition of Irish Catholics. All of this conveniently sets the scene for the eroticization of national difference in the Mortimer/Glorvina relationship, and for what Robert Tracy has described as the "Glorvina solution" to the violence generated by colonialism—the joining of cultural legitimacy with legal right in the national marriage that concludes the text.[90]

But turning from Morgan to Moore's *Captain Rock*, we can see how the latter reshuffles this cast of characters, familiar from earlier Anglo-Irish fiction, in the course of the framing narrative. If we regard the missionary editor as occupying the position of the typical English newcomer and Captain Rock as the mediating Irish figure, we can see how Moore transforms Morgan's national allegory—not least by altering the gender relations. In addition, Captain Rock's Irish-speaking father is an example of an "authentic, unmitigated" native. Rock the elder, once a member of the Gaelic elite, has been reduced to poverty by the Penal Laws and bears an array of distinguishing Irish national characteristics (234–51). Yet his role and significance in the text is very different to that of Morgan's Prince of Inismore, whose fate at the end of *The Wild Irish Girl*, when he is in his death agony and unable to speak, is to learn that his daughter is apparently going to marry into the family of his great enemy. The prince's view of this solution to colonial conflict is not really relevant at the end of the story. His time has gone—or so Morgan hopes.

Moore's editor is a very frail representative indeed of his native culture. While in *The Wild Irish Girl*, Mortimer's cultural prejudices against Ireland begin to collapse with suspicious rapidity almost as soon as he sets foot in Dublin, they are replaced by a curiosity about Irish culture and a hunger for new romantic adventures in the far-flung regions of the West. The Rock editor, once he reads the captain's manuscript, simply aborts his Irish mission and leaves without even trying to see the papist natives for himself. The missionary is foolish rather than cosmopolitan, and, significantly, somewhat emasculated by his association with the earnest and naive women of the missionary society in his small home town in the West of England. He is afraid of traveling to Ireland but more afraid of what these pious ladies might think of him if he refuses to go (v). The comedy of this introduction depends on the extent to which the English missionary and his friends underestimate the incommensurability of English and Irish culture, as they send over "a whole edition" of a religious work by "Miss _____ of our Town, to the effect of which upon the Whiteboys we all looked forward very sanguinely" (vi). But these well-meaning evangelists, who are anxious that the County of Worcester has, for want of Christian preachers, become "a waste and a howling wilderness," cannot begin to imagine what "the mountains of Macgillicuddy" must be like (iv). And, in complex ways, Rock both confirms and confounds the missionary's expectations of Irish barbarism.

The authority of the English narrator evaporates after his discovery of Rock. The missionary first encounters the garrulous, expansive captain, "an extraordinary personage," outlandishly disguised in "green spectacles and a flaxen wig" (vii), on the Limerick coach. Rock has therefore already strayed beyond the usual habitats of "real Irish" characters in Anglo-Irish fiction, which tends to marginalize and quarantine its native exotics in remote glens or crumbling ruins.[91] This ringleader of Irish outrage is first glimpsed in daylight, in ordinary space and time, rather than in any isolated, archaic Romantic enclave; he is eccentric, almost dandy-like, but also mobile, sophisticated, communicative, and "civilized." In the course of their journey, although it becomes obvious that this Irishman prefers "monologue to dialogue" with the missionary (vii), he also seems at least as well able to read the missionary as the missionary is able to read him. Rock merely smiles "rather significantly" when he is told of the visitor's object in traveling to the south of Ireland; later, he gently dissuades him from wasting his time (x, xiii). Only some days later does the missionary recognize Rock's true identity, as the leader of the band of "some hundreds of awful-looking persons—all arrayed in white shirts" (xi), which he stumbles across when exploring a ruined abbey by moonlight. And here it is (for once) the English visitor who tells us that he was too drunk to be able to give a very full account of his adventures. Nonetheless, he enjoys a private conversation with Rock about which he does not reveal any details, and having taken delivery of and read Rock's manuscript, concludes that the people of Ireland need neither instruction nor conversion, and that it is their rulers who require enlightenment (xiii). But we appreciate that his is not a message that the missionary can easily convey back to his lady friends. One of them succeeds in turning the story of Captain Rock into a romance, which the missionary expects will be "much more extensively read, than the Captain's own authentic Memoirs" (xiv). This satiric comment on Irish romance, as opposed to Rockite authenticity, is especially interesting from Moore, himself often criticized as feminizing or domesticating the traditional Irish culture on which he drew for his *Melodies*.[92]

The narrating missionary makes a final appearance at the conclusion of the text, when we hear that Captain Rock is to be transported to Botany Bay. The captain's true crimes have gone undetected, but he has been found guilty of being out by moonlight and (ironically enough, given the preceding manuscript) for "not being able to give an account of himself" in court (371). But here the missionary serves merely as the recorder of an eyewitness account of the bizarre figure of Rock as he embarks at Cobh, attired "in an old green coat—supposed to be the same, but without the yellow facings, which was made up for Napper Tandy, as an officer of the Irish National Guard—a pair of breeches, the colour of which the reporter unluckily could not ascertain, and stockings, of the staple manufacture of Mr. Dick Martin's Kingdom of Connemara" (372).[93]

The last words of the text all belong to Rock, quoted from his final letter to the missionary (who evidently is not tempted to betray him to the authorities). Rock is triumphant and undefeated in spirit, confident that his campaign against the unreformed English government will continue under the leadership of his son. He comments on the state of Ireland in 1824:

> A Lord Lieutenant, whose enlightened and liberal intentions alarm and offend the stronger party; while his limited powers and embarrassed position incapacitate him from gaining the confidence of the weaker—a Secretary, worthy of the good old Anti-popery times,

and to whose spirit I would ensure a safe passage over Mahomet's bridge into Paradise, if *narrowness* (as it is probable) be a qualification, for the performance of that hair-breadth promenade—the Orange Ascendancy flourishing under the very eyes of the Government, and imitating that Oligarchy mentioned by Aristotle, whose oath was "We will do the multitude all the evil in our power"—the Established Clergy still further enriched, and threatening to "push" the Landed Gentry "from their stools"—more than a million spent annually upon soldiers, to keep down the Catholics, and only a few thousands per annum given to educate them—with such actual results of the policy of our present rulers, and with Mr. Peel, Lord Eldon, and the Duke of Wellington in the Cabinet, to answer for the complexion of their future measures, I may safely, I think, reckon upon the continuance of the Rock Dynasty, through many a long year of distraction and tumult; and may lay my head on my pillow at Botany Bay, with the full assurance that all at home is going on as prosperously as ever. (374–75)[94]

This passage is typical of Moore's style of argument in this text. We can note the wealth of detailed political analysis, improbably put into the mouth of an Irish peasant leader, and juxtaposed with the novel concept of a transhistorical and transgenerational "Rock Dynasty," for which tumult is prosperity. Rock is a fictionalized individual, but he is both like and unlike Mr. Peel or the Duke of Wellington, for he also represents a collective, even a primal, force. His removal from Ireland and his individual fate are irrelevant because he believes that a tyrannized people will *always* resist. Human energies can be repressed, but the repression can never entirely succeed.

Novels such as *The Wild Irish Girl* (1806) and Scott's *Waverley* (1814) offer, as an image of historical progress, the marriage of the central English character to the child of a former leader of the old, defeated culture. Such stories seek to teach us that with the passage of time, the pain of historical loss will lessen, and conciliation will become possible. In figures such as Glorvina or Scott's Rose Bradwardine, Gaelic national character is also softened and feminized. Rock is, in some regards, less stereotypically

Irish than his father, but Moore does not attempt to persuade us that a new generation will automatically be less bitter than its predecessors. Indeed, the present-day Rock cites as an example of his own degeneracy his foolish excitement, in 1782, at seeing the "prospects of peace and freedom" opening up around him. He "was ready, in the boyish enthusiasm of the moment, to sacrifice all my own personal interest in all future riots and rebellions, to the one bright, seducing light of my country's liberty and repose" (*Captain Rock*, 234–35). But his father's superior wisdom and pessimism win the day, as the false hopes of the 1780s give way to the chaos of the 1790s. He assures his son that the Rocks have "a Power on our side that 'will not willingly let us die'; and, long after Grattan shall have disappeared from earth . . . the family of the ROCKS will continue to flourish in all their native glory" (238); he orders his heir to give up "the foolish romance" (240) of reform. But the father's politics, unfortunately for Ireland, are not simply antiquated or irrelevant—he correctly perceives that, in Ireland, progress is impossible. And while the fact that the missionary meets old Captain Rock's son, rather than his daughter, obviously precludes a marital resolution to the story (one which might foreshadow a harmonious union of the two countries), it is notable that Moore's male character also confounds national gender stereotypes. The missionary is certainly less courageous and manly than Rock, but neither is the latter simply the purely masculine barbarian that the Englishman might have expected to encounter at the civilizational level of the Irish peasant. Of the pair, the captain is both the more exotic *and* the more polished, the more romantic *and* the more rational.

It is surely not surprising that loyalist authors responded, explicitly or implicitly, to this scandalous narrativization of an English encounter with Irish violence. The editor's brief and almost casual description of the ruined abbey, the meeting place of hundreds of disguised Whiteboys, is rewritten by Mortimer O'Sullivan, who emphasizes that the ruin is a place of disorder and savagery. In O'Sullivan's account, the men form not a united community, but "a horde of wolves who have made their league of blood, but can hold no converse together."[95] We first encounter O'Sullivan's upper-class General Rock addressing his demonic crew by moonlight, and only later see him as an ordinary gentleman in a neighbor's house. Charlotte

Elizabeth's more extended fictional treatment of the Rockites postpones our glimpse of the insurgents' lair until late in the story. There, in a dungeon of a ruined castle, we witness what is at once a seditious political meeting, a riotous wake complete with a keening woman, and a blasphemous religious ceremony presided over by a Catholic priest.[96]

Gibbons has remarked on the similarity between this scene from *The Rockite* and Daniel Maclise's painting, *The Installation of Captain Rock* (1834). But while Maclise also depicts many of the stock figures of the Irish peasant rabble—keeners, drinkers, political priests, inflammatory schoolmasters—he also endows some of the figures present "with the dignity and bearing of classical heroes." It was this confusion of history painting and the burlesque, the hybridization of high and low genres, which so dismayed contemporary reviewers of the painting.[97] While Moore passes up the opportunity of offering a depiction of Captain Rock's men in the framing narrative, settling instead for the rather bland assumption of complete harmony between Captain Rock and his supporters, it is perhaps not far-fetched to see Moore's Rock himself as the personification of the motley crowd of heroic and terrible bandits that Maclise portrays in this canvas. Certainly, neither Maclise nor Moore betray the anxiety and defensiveness of, for example, Griffin, in a text such as *Tracy's Ambition*, who is so concerned to explain how oppression and despair transform decent men into agrarian terrorists. As the virtuous elderly peasant, Moran tells his landlord, whose wife has been murdered by Whiteboys: "A set o' poor boys are distressed an' sazed, an' driven out o' house an home, without either country or carakter, or religion, an' they grow desperate, an' go fairly astray, an' their doings are to be charged upon the poor country after!" (*Rivals; Tracy* 3:6). In this regard, too, Moore opts not to pathologize rural insurgency. As Captain Rock remarks of his late father:

> He could never, indeed, understand the horror that was expressed, at the occasional violences committed by him and his followers, in this desperate game between them and their masters. . . . Caesar is supposed to have sent a million men out of the world, and Caesar is therefore a hero—while, if Captain ROCK, in what the laws have taught him to consider as fair fighting as Caesar's, puts a merciless

driver *hors de combat,* or pushes a middleman's middleman off his step in the ascending scale of tyrants, he is a ferocious, brutal and irreclaimable savage. This my father could never understand; and if he was wrong, his betters are to blame, not he. (*Captain Rock,* 250–51)

The text refuses, in effect, to dwell on Irish atrocities. This is underscored by the fact that the rebellion of 1641, the most notorious instance of Irish barbarity in loyalist polemic (but see Moore's comments on Sir John Temple's narrative of the rebellion [*Captain Rock,* 92]), is dealt with by quoting from the diary of a Rock ancestor who was confined to bed for the period of the uprising and therefore only able to comment on it from a distance (81–90). At a later point, Rock's account of his father's activities as a Rightboy is interrupted by the editor, who tells us in a footnote that he has decided simply to leave out this material: "The Captain has here, in the original manuscript, entered into a long detail of his achievements at this period, under the assumed name of Captain RIGHT: but, as there is but little variety in his manner of relating these feats, and the public has long been acquainted with the nature of them, I have thought it best to omit the narration altogether" (294). This is the only time the editor censors Rock in this way.

The image of the community as an enormous extended family has important implications for the text's optimistic conception of resistance as ongoing and irrepressible. (According to an anecdote related in the journal *Captain Rock in London,* when one of Rock's ancestors was shown the head of his son fixed on a pole opposite the gate of Dublin Castle, he said, "My son has many heads.")[98] The present Captain Rock is himself his father's tenth son, showing the fecundity and, therefore, the indestructibility of the Rocks. Decimus (the Latin name for "tenth," indicating the status of a title in a long succession) Rock begins his life in 1763 on the very day the English hanged Father Nicholas Sheehy of Clogheen—"one of those *coups d'état* of the Irish authorities," as Rock says, "which saves them the trouble of further atrocities for some time to come" (155). (In fact, Sheehy's execution took place in 1766.) What was widely regarded as the judicial murder of Sheehy horrified Irish Catholics; in this text, the act is seemingly revenged by the birth of another troublemaker. It is as if violence—also called noise, fun, and sport (3, 9, 154)—is an almost biological response, on the part of Nature itself, to injustice and political folly. This is the logic, or rather "the blessed miracle," which ensures that the *real* Irish, "though exterminated under every succeeding Lord-lieutenant, are still as good as new, and ready to be exterminated again" (243). Since the sixteenth century, when England tried to pacify Ireland by exterminating the Irish, the natives have not only survived, but they have always been unruly. With the recent agrarian campaign no doubt in mind, the captain declares:

> Hibernia pacified! alas, alas, could the shade of Sir G. Carew but once more hover over his own region of Munster, he would find that a new edition of his work on Pacification is much wanted—he would find that though the same peace-makers, slaughter and persecution, have been tried under almost every government since his time, the grand object is still unaccomplished—the Temple of the Anglo-Irish Janus (that "forma biceps") lies as open as ever. (51)[99]

Moore mentions that the career of Captain Rock began "under the various names of *Mere Irish, Rapparees, Whiteboys,* &c." (12), and that a "full account of these heroes has been given in an interesting work called 'the History of the Irish Rogues and Rapparees'" (120)—a book that later turns up in the hedge-school library, alongside "Memoirs of Jack the Batchelor, a notorious smuggler, and of Freney, a celebrated highwayman" (187).[100] In this, Moore runs together the agrarian secret societies of his own day with an earlier tradition of individual banditry or crime. The tories and rapparees were dispossessed members of the Gaelic aristocracy, who had conducted "a guerrilla campaign in their own country against the new order." But this tradition of social banditry or brigandage seems to have died by the mid–eighteenth century, and with its end "also comes the demise of the individual personality as the focus of rebellion: the disturbances of the future take place under the cloak of anonymity and collective responsibility, the peasant communities seeking to provide for their own defence."[101]

However, according to W. E. H. Lecky, "the tradition of the original tories . . . had a very mischievous effect in removing the stigma from agrarian crime."[102] Novelists, such as Anna Maria Hall and William Carleton, seek to explain this Irish tolerance of lawbreakers in their fiction; Moore, in contrast, exploits it.[103]

By personifying Captain Rock and placing him in a tradition of Irish banditry, Moore reinvests nineteenth-century agrarian insurgency with the force of individual personality in a version of the story of Robin Hood. Cornewall Lewis noted in the 1830s that agrarian crime did indeed have a different character from normal crime, as it might have been understood in England. It was neither banditry, usually considered the preserve of those permanently excluded from settled society, nor was it crime carried out for the purpose of personal gain. The Whiteboys fall into neither of these categories:

> But instead of forming distinct and separate bodies, they are taken almost indiscriminately, like jurymen, from the mass of the population, into which, when their work is done, they melt again, undistinguishable from their friends and neighbours. . . . The criminal . . . is as it were an executioner, who carries into effect the verdict of an uncertain and non-apparent tribunal; and it usually happens that others profit more by his offence than he himself who committed it.[104]

It is difficult to determine when such personifications of Whiteboy authority as Queen Sive or Captain Rock are understood by peasant communities to be actual and when as allegorical.[105] Perhaps, like Robin Hood, who tends to be invented where there is a need for him, such figures are reminders of the good sovereign who, as E. J. Hobsbawm writes, cannot ever die and who will come back one day to restore justice. For the poor "can live without justice, and generally must, but they cannot live without hope."[106] By creating both a single hero, Captain Rock, and his enormous, fertile family, Moore offers us an analogous myth, one which preserves both the psychologically important idea of the individual rebel ("men who prove that even the poor and weak can be terrible")[107] as well as registering the historical fact of communal, but clandestine, resistance.

This may explain the anger of such a reader as Sir Jonah Barrington, for example, who alleges that Moore writes for "distracted cottagers" rather than for the proprietors and legislators of Ireland.[108] It might be

more accurate, however, to say that Moore seeks to render those cottagers more significant and fearful in the eyes of what Barrington regards
as the "higher orders" (just as the peasants did on their own behalf, on
occasion, through the medium of the anonymous letter or notice). In this,
we might contend that Moore attends more to an elite *perception* of the
meaning of agrarian violence rather than to its real local complexities. He
lends to it a national, rather than a regional, basis (Captain Rock's "fun"
stirs through Leinster, Ulster, Connaught and Munster [9]), and attaches
to it a consistently anticolonial politics as the latest manifestation of an
Irish rebelliousness that has been evident since the twelfth century. For as
agrarian campaigns had various characters and purposes, and as they were
directed at different social groups at different times, "it is not possible . . .
to understand the agrarian disturbances of the pre-Famine period simply
through invoking anti-colonial antagonisms"; but as far as the administration was concerned, no matter how local or how limited the demands of
the protestors, "the threat they represented was from the outset perceived
to be to the state as a whole," demanding, for instance, the creation of a
new, centralized police force.[109] Moore's text plays on such fears, but in a
minatory and even gleeful way.

But this should not be taken to imply that Moore furnishes yet another
example of an author more interested in incorporating agrarian movements
into a more significant narrative of national improvement, one that would
lead to the restoration of national pride and therefore to the calming of
Irish turbulence, than in attending to the cultural or political significance
of the secret societies and the Whiteboys. Certainly, there are moments in
the text when Captain Rock is presented, in an apparently negative light,
as collusive with—as opposed to merely reacting against—tyranny and
oppression: "Law, peace and justice, at our feet shall fall, /And *the white-shirted
race* be lords o'er all" (129). But more often, the violence of the "white-
shirted ones" is presented as merely making manifest the truth about supposedly legitimate government. In book 1, chapter 8, for example, Rock
comments on the career of Lord Strafford in Ireland in the seventeenth
century, whose actions were described by David Hume as "innocent, and
even laudable" (75). Rock says, if violating solemn pledges, robbery, plunder, and the corruption of the law can be so regarded,

then let Humes's own "Sceptic" take the world into his hands, and remove all those landmarks of right and wrong, of justice and injustice, by which honest men have hitherto steered; let tyranny and turbulence, perfidy and plunder, be the order of the day among rulers and their subjects; and let Captain ROCK and the Czar of Russia divide the world between them. I shall not complain of my share in the arrangement, and I will answer for the magnanimous Alexander being equally satisfied with his. (78)

If the point of the satire is to make clear the case for reform, then the appalling monotony of the history that Rock narrates, which presents no hope of amelioration, ensures that the possibility of moderate, rational politics will recede during the course of the text, which records a series of abuses that would turn "Job himself into a Rockite" (309). At least Rock, who glories in chaos and violence, speaks the truth, in contrast to the hypocrisy and lies of historians and politicians.

And so *Memoirs of Captain Rock* oscillates between a mordant retelling of official history and a carnivalesque descent into the unruly and the subversive. Ireland is a place where narratives (whether national or familial) do not move forward toward any definite resolution. Rather, narrators, such as Rock senior and junior, take a perverse delight in the failure of such linear stories because that failure is a rebuke to the official and, in Ireland at least, entirely discredited narrative of progress. Christopher Morash states that in writers on the Irish Famine, such as John Mitchel, we witness "the power of the Famine to disrupt the metanarrative of progress, revealing to us progress's Other." Mitchel, for example, concentrates on horrific anecdotes that resist assimilation into longer narratives, and especially into the scientific narrative of the Famine as the inevitable Malthusian check on excessive population growth. In Moore's pre-Famine text, I would argue, we can read a similar disruption of the nineteenth-century master-narrative of progress, but one which allows us to dwell not only on the "horror and desolation" of Irish experience[110] but also on the possibility of incorporating this into an *alternative* metanarrative.

Throughout *Captain Rock*, the narrator asserts that, in Ireland, history is never forgotten, for in the present, the Irish merely relive a horrible past.

In his first conversation with the missionary, the captain gestures toward the ruin of a great house and comments:

> It is melancholy to think, that while in almost all other countries, we find historical names of heroes and benefactors, familiarly on the lips of the common people, and handed down with blessings from generation to generation, in Ireland, the only remarkable names of the last six hundred years, that have survived in the popular traditions of the country, are become words of ill-omen, and are remembered only to be cursed. Among those favourites of hate, the haughty nobleman [Lord Strafford] who built that mansion, is to this day, with a tenacity that does honour even to hate, recorded; and, under the name of Black Tom, still haunts the imagination of the peasant, as one of those dark and evil beings who tormented the land in former days, and with whom, in the bitterness of his heart, he compares his more modern tormentors. The Babylonians, we are told by Herodotus, buried their dead in honey—but it is in the very gall of the heart that the memory of Ireland's rulers is embalmed. (vii–viii)

Much later, we are told more about the formation of Irish historical memory. The captain recalls from his own childhood how, after a dinner of potatoes and his father's lectures on Irish history, "the grandams of our family would wind up with such frightful stories, of the massacres committed by Black Tom and old Oliver [Cromwell], such have often sent me to bed with the dark faces of these terrible persons flitting before my eyes" (243–44). Such a passage would not be out of place in many nineteenth-century Irish texts. But what is distinctive in Moore's text is the way in which this understanding of history and memory is contextualized and indeed *justified*.

The specters of history are not invoked here in order to be laid to rest. These are not abuses that belong to earlier eras only, kept alive merely by the unfortunate predilection of Irish peasants for ghoulish tales. For there is little sense in the text of the possibility, or even the hope, of the dawn of a benign English administration in Ireland, in the style of at least the early works of a Morgan or an Edgeworth. Is it then the case that in

Moore's narrative there emerges an understanding of Irish history as the product of both English and Irish agency—a "dialectic of English misrule and Irish misdeeds"—which "was a novelty in 1824 when the historiographical scene was dominated by simplistic sectarian denunciations back and forth"?[111] We might question whether Moore delivers an even-handed denunciation of both sides, or whether instead we encounter here "a rebel view of Irish history," the narrative "pretending that the Rocks have only been able to sustain its ancestral violence as agrarian rebels because of the co-operation of the British government's spectacularly cruel policies."[112] But the historical dialectic that is outlined by *Captain Rock* is perhaps more complex still.

England has created Ireland as an exotic, even a tropical zone, through colonization and "modernization." Violence is the secret history of "civility"; the "secret" of the secret societies is also the secret of respectable, civil society. In Ireland, the supposedly rational discourse of liberal modernity has been betrayed. Contracts, for example, made in Ireland by the English are no better than "marriage vows, false as dicers' oaths" (111) or "to be read, like witches' prayers, backwards" (116). But, strangely, the Ascendancy and the Established Church in Ireland have had to avoid the methods of modern demography, including the census and the map, in calculating the mass of its "Catholic 'Enemy' (as the laws called their own manufacture)" (217).[113] Modernity creates the "primitive" and then witnesses its irruption into its own scientific records. As the editor reports in a footnote:

> Seneca tells us that when a proposition was once made to the Roman Senate, that slaves should be distinguished by a particular dress from freemen, it was instantly felt what danger might arise, if the slaves should by this means be enabled to number their master. . . . That the same sort of alarm is felt among our Orange masters, appears by the following extract from a letter written by the late Catholic Archbishop of Dublin in the year 1811:—"A complete enumeration of the inhabitants of Ireland, distinguishing their respective religious creeds, cannot be effected without the sanction or permission of Government, *which the present Administration will not permit.* The partial enumeration referred to by Mr. Newenham, *excited uneasiness in the minds of the*

Ascendancy and Orange partisans, who represented them as records of Catholic numbers to threaten the smaller numbers of Protestants. A similar enumeration even in a single parish must be conducted with caution and delicacy." (263–64)

The Ascendancy fears not just the disclosure of the truth about how small the Protestant population is, but also about its vast wealth: "Dr. Beaufort, one of their body, having at first intended, in his Ecclesiastical Map of Ireland, to mark with a particular colour the lands belonging to the Church, found the space through which this sacred line meandered so vast, that thinking it wiser, like Dogberry, to 'give God thanks and make no boast,' he cancelled this betraying line altogether, and published his Ecclesiastical Map without it" (267).

English rule in Ireland has created the vast, unruly population of the oppressed, who have never been counted as real subjects of the British crown:

> It seemed, indeed, as if these wise legislators had really succeeded in persuading themselves, that Catholics not only went for cyphers in the census of a population, but, like the devils in Milton's Pandemonium, took no room. For, while in every direction this enslaved race was multiplying (contrary to the noble example of the elephant, which refuses to propagate its race in bondage), we find the Parliament in such fear of a deficiency of population, as to encourage the importation of Palatines, Hugonots, and even Jews, by every inducement that not only full toleration, but the most lavish grant of privileges could furnish. (218)

This "enslaved race" Moore describes as "a force of nature"; he explains political history in terms of a comic "natural history," to paraphrase Ranajit Guha. The Irish inhabit a political hot zone, one which is imagined as geologically hot as well. Captain Rock, for example, tells the missionary that "Ireland like one of those fair cities on the side of Vesuvius, 'a tenant at will to the volcano on which she is placed!'" (ix). The people themselves *are* this uncontrollable substrate of the landscape: "[They] went on increasing in silence and in darkness, like that fire which some French philosophers suppose to exist at the centre of the earth,—working its way upward in secret, till it will at last make the surface too hot to hold us" (217–18).

Dreadful as the oppression of the Irish poor might be—in a country where, for example, the starving are taxed to pay for the sacramental bread and wine of the rich (284)—rage does not entirely predominate over an exultant sense that the very elements conspire with the politically power-less. As the captain speculates:

> But what will such haughty Ecclesiastics say, when, by the operation of causes, which seem as progressive as time itself, this people of Catho-lics whom they insult so wantonly,—whose number is at this moment as great as that of the Protestants of England in 1688, and who are, in spite of misery and Malthus, every hour increasing—shall, like the disloyal waves crashing round the feet of Canute, encroach still fur-ther on their sacred precincts. . . . The rapidity, indeed, with which the proportion of Protestants to Catholics has diminished and is still diminishing, seems nothing less than a judgement—a judgement of insulted Nature upon the perverse and vicious policy, which dares to set itself in array against the wants and wishes of a whole nation, and, like the absurd people mentioned by Ælian, who opposed the coming-in of the sea with shields and swords, thinks to stop the great current of nature by means of penal statutes and bayonets. (256–57)

We find here a conversion of peasant violence (and the forms of resis-tance that preceded it) into "a force of nature," yet this is not subordinated to the ends of counterinsurgence—as Guha analyzes it—in a project of dehumanizing the common people or subordinating them to "modern" politics. It is a vision of the power of the masses (or of "those prostrate giants, the People" [*Captain Rock*, 308]) that is hard to reincorporate into any vision of a harmonious, hierarchically ordered society. As the proph-ecy handed down in the Rock family states:

> As long as Ireland shall pretend,
> Like sugar-loaf, turn'd upside down,
> To stand upon its smaller end,

So long shall Old ROCK's renown.
As long as Popish spade and scythe
Shall dig and cut the Sassanagh's tithe;
And Popish purses pay the tolls,
On heaven's road, for Sassanagh souls—
As long as millions shall kneel down
To ask of Thousands for their own,
While Thousands proudly turn away,
And to the Millions answer "nay"—
So long the merry reign shall be
Of Captain ROCK and his Family. (157)

These lines represent a more polite counterpart to the Pastorini-inspired verses, which were current in the days of Rockite unrest. This is a Limerick ballad of 1821:

Now the year 21 is drawing by degrees,
In the year 22 the locusts will weep,
But in the year 23 we'll begin to reap.
Good people, take courage, don't perish in fright,
For notes will be nothing in the year 25;
As I am O'Healy, we'll drink daily beer.[114]

Both prophecy and ballad draw on the incantatory power of even bad verse; like threatening letters, these lines exploit rhyme, rhythm, and the primitive power of language as it might be understood by people for whom blasphemy and cursing are still potent and terrifying.[115] (In this context, we may recall the diction of the *Melodies* and their avoidance of ballad or popular forms.) Moreover, the threat of an undisciplined oral culture (this prophecy has been passed down in the Rock family, and Rock's father was particularly fond of it) is not simply sanitized by being translated into a higher literary style. The prophecy declares that the ordinary constitution of class society (where thousands rule over millions) is an inversion of nature. Therefore the realm of popular protest (the liminal zone of folk culture, ritual, cross-dressing, disguise, and so on) is at one and the same time a zone of carnivalesque distortion, and one which has escaped the distortions of official culture.

For the sources of his most positive images, Moore seizes on precisely those aspects of Irish peasant life that most appalled so many contemporary observers. We can turn once again to the review of Moore in *Blackwood's Magazine* to gain a sense of how the spectacle of Irish hyperfertility is more usually regarded: "On the soil which we have described are each day springing up new shoots of human life, extracting from the same unhealthy ground their scant nourishment, and exposed for ever to the droppings of the parent tree, which, in their turn, they taint and impoverish."[116]

In his *Sketches in Ireland*(1827), Caesar Otway comments how he was reminded of Malthus's "convincing but gloomy book" during his travels in Munster: "war, pestilence, and famine, 'terribles visu formae,' rose up in necessary association, as summoned to feast and make prey in future, of this teeming population."[117] Such sentiments are echoed in the *Edinburgh Review*. This writer attributes the woes of the country directly to the increasing population:

> The actual state of Ireland—the magnitude, misery, fierceness, and desperation of her population, the violence of their leaders, and the fury of the contending factions to which she is a prey—ought, if anything can, to excite the earnest and anxious attention of the people of Britain. . . . Nor will this frightful progression [of population] cease, if left to itself, until the whole country has been parcelled into potato gardens, capital been annihilated, and the curse of poverty rendered universal. There is not, therefore, a moment to be lost. If the whole energies of Government are not speedily set in motion and steadily directed, to check the torrent of pauperism, it will prove too strong for them, and the reign of filth, beggary, and outrage will forever be secured.[118]

Morash has observed that, in nineteenth-century writing on Ireland, the catastrophe of the Famine is often attributed to the extravagance of two classes: the aristocracy, reckless in their monetary expenditure, and the peasantry, reckless in the number of children they produce. "In both instances," Morash writes, "the Famine acts as a Malthusian 'check' upon extravagance, moderating the two extremes of society, making them both more like the middle class."[119] Moore, however, delivers his critique of the exploitative greed of the Ascendancy and the Church of Ireland, including their reliance on famine as an instrument of policy in Ireland (*Captain Rock,* 56), without any corresponding rebuke of the peasants for their excessive numbers.

There are moments in *Captain Rock* when Moore asserts that the wildness of the Irish is simply the consequence of their brutalization, and he repeats a familiar Burkean rhetoric concerning the essential docility and loyalty of Catholics (330). This is particularly stressed in relation to 1798; indeed, throughout book 2, chapters 11 and 12, a more recognizably elite Moore is heard much more frequently than elsewhere (e.g., in his disdain for the mob of forty-shilling freeholders [336]). But the fact that Captain Rock is still thriving, occupied with "the great press of political business" that the Union brought upon him (367), is indeed significant in the context of the early nineteenth century in Ireland. For all this follows the "phlebotomy" of 1798 (352), which enabled the British government "to cool down the temperament of the country, into a state tame enough for the reception of a Union" (355). Even in those circumstances, to hear the fun beginning to stir again is important, for it means that the people are still answering the charivari of government policy (325) with their own "rough music."[120] To have, like Rock, an ear for "discordant politics" (33) and "a love of riot"(9) is a great advantage at such time. It prepares for another "paroxysm of 'wild justice' that is denominated an 'odious and unnatural rebellion'" (92). Ireland is still a hot zone, not just an exhausted province. It has not been civilized by the contract of Union, with its false exchange of the "fairy money of Hope, which seems gold to the eye, but will turn into dust in the hand" (365). Moore does not depict the decades since the rebellion as a depressing vacancy, and he does not assert that any new era—either better or worse than earlier ones—has dawned.

Carnival, Rebellion, and the Irish Novel: Moore and Griffin

Carlo Ginzburg regards the new genre of the "imaginary biography" in the nineteenth century as occupying a point somewhere between traditional biography and the slowly emerging theoretical categories of social history. By exploring the stories of such imaginary figures as Jacques Bonhomme (the hero of Augustin Thierry's *Essai sur l'histoire de la formation et du progrès du Tiers Etat* [1850]) in the context of real history, writers such as Thierry and Michelet overcame the problem of the irrelevance, according to traditional historiographic criteria, of suppressed groups such as peasants or witches, and created new stylistic models for the writing of "history from below."[121] We can see how Captain Rock similarly offered Moore the opportunity to break out of the political impasse created by his fixation on heroes, such as Lord Edward and Emmet in his other works. The narrative that Rock relates concerning English government in Ireland is so dreadful that it can hardly be recuperated by the liberal Whiggism with which we more usually associate this author.

Moore stumbles on a profoundly productive insight when he identifies Rock, the much-feared leader of agrarian outrage, with this transindividual subject whose history is offered as the key to the history of the nation. The idea of such a figure as Rock as an expression of communal identity is part of a submerged folk tradition, one that contemporary scholars of rural Ireland are only beginning to reconstruct and understand. Moore entirely breaks with the elite fears of an agitator from outside the ranks of the peasantry, which would have been more typical of the fictional narratives of his day, from such writers as Charlotte Elizabeth to William Carleton. But at the same time he does not depict Rock as an anthropological exhibit to be explained to outsiders. Rock's immediate family history is merely sketched for us, but by these means Moore at least gestures toward the actual living conditions of the mass of Irish people in a way that would be unthinkable in the *Melodies*. Captain Rock relates such details with humor and is entirely devoid of sentimental self-pity. In this way, Moore's devotion to literary politeness lends itself well to the re-creation of a popular resilience and wit.

As I have argued, the text may in some ways appropriate the image of the peasantry for the political purposes of Moore's own class, but against this must be set its depiction of a comic, life-affirming dimension to rural unrest, rather than the more usual classification of such forms of protest as symptoms of cultural degeneration. Instead of detailing the rapes, the maimings, and the killings, Rock scandalously insists on the recreational or even the artistic nature of insurrection; terrorism (which is what most of his readers would have understood Whiteboyism to be) is here treated as joyful self-expression, or as a great "harvest of riot" (59). Thus, Captain Rock, who was confined to bed during the great Rebellion of 1641, consequently "could not share in the pastime that was going on" (81). Rock recounts of another ancestor how he was "personally engaged in no less than forty rebellions—making within five of the number of years that good Queen Bess (as well he might call her) reigned—to say nothing of a multitude of episodical insurrections, of a lighter nature, with which he amused his summer months" (59)—and remarks on how "the contemplation of even an old Irish rebellion is as gratifying as the study of a real *cinque-cento* to a connoisseur—the skills with which the Government has always furnished the materials for the work, being only equalled by the *con-spirito* style in which the people have always executed it" (80).

While Moore remains aloof from the attempts of pioneering folklorists, such as Thomas Crofton Croker, to know the people of rural Ireland, those elements in his depiction of Rock that suggest the traces of the green man of folk ritual also shed light on the larger politics of the text. In the popular festivals of many cultures, an inversion of the accepted order is dramatized and celebrated—announcing the temporary ascendancy of women over men, children over parents, the poor over the rich. Mikhail Bakhtin is the most important modern theorist of this culture of carnival.[122] It could be argued that Whiteboyism itself bears some of the features of the Bahktinian carnivalesque, not least of which are the disguises and the women's clothing that the participants adopted on their nighttime missions. They inhabit a dreamworld, where social repression is released and the usual order of things reversed. As one special commission judge exclaims of the Whiteboys, "Can it be endured that those peasants who labouring by day, should be legislating by night?" Or, as Daniel O'Connell puts it, "the spirit which is curbed by day walks abroad by night."[123] And even outside the pages of *Captain Rock*, Moore clearly had some appreciation of the exuberantly subversive nature of Whiteboy rituals. This is indicated in a letter from Tipperary in 1815, which compares the painted bodies of the Shanavests (members of another agrarian secret society) to those of Native Americans:

The only *stimulants* we have here are the Shanavests, who enter the house here at noonday for arms, and start out, by twenties and thirties, upon the tithe-proctors in the fields, stark naked, and smeared all over with paint like the Catabaros [Catabaw Indians]. The good people of Tipperary will have a bloody winter of it. . . . The rector of this place has just passed the windows on a tithe-hunting expedition, with a large gun in his gig. This is one of the ministers of peace on earth![124]

Moore's tone (however conventional his own politics may have been) could not be more different from, say, John Banim's pained apologies for "these rustic depredations, so utterly disgraceful to the county in which they take place."[125] The peasant writer John Keegan of Abbeyleix balks even at describing the full horror of a Whiteboy meeting, informing us, in one of his "Tales of the Rockites," that "the scene of confusion and blasphemy which the carouse of these midnight legislators presented is too revolting for detail."[126] These views of Whiteboyism go hand-in-hand with a more general anxiety about lower-class popular culture. Keegan tells us that "never did I dream of human debasement until I went to Donnybrook [Fair]," and argues that "the lower orders of Irishmen" are more violent and blood-thirsty than even "the painted and tatooed native of the Pacific Islands" or the "wild savages of the American woods."[127] Moore's humor in treating of such matters may appear to correspond more closely to the shocking levity of the peasants themselves than to the attitudes we might expect from an inhabitant of his social *milieu*. Banim indeed finds the laughter of these "rustic Lycurguses" to represent the most singular feature of the Irish character, and one that almost threatens to destroy our faith in "the common tendencies of human nature":

The local reformer of the mountain, the bog, or the desert; the legislator for an almost uncultivated tract of impoverished country; the desperate neck-or-nothing leader of a throng of desperate and sanguinary men, disguised his identity in a humourous ideal; wrote his threatening notices in the tone of an April-day hoax . . . and performed his whole part as if he were Tom-fool to a corps of Christian mummers. (*Peep O'Day; Crohoore*, 26–27)

The fiction of Gerald Griffin offers a useful foil for Moore's innovative deployment of at least the idea of an attractive, lively, and rebellious peasant culture in *Captain Rock*. The works of both writers can also be understood in relation to a larger history, that of the suppression of popular carnival in modern Europe by a newly dominant bourgeoisie. Stallybrass and White relate that, from the seventeenth to the twentieth century,

> [T]here were literally thousand of acts of legislation introduced to eliminate carnival and popular festivity from European life. In different areas of Europe the pace varied, depending upon religious, class, and economic factors. But everywhere . . . a fundamental ritual order of Western culture came under attack—its feasting, violence, drinking, processions, fairs, wakes, rowdy spectacles, and outrageous clamour were subject to surveillance and repressive control . . . In 1855 the great Donnybrook Fair of Dublin was abolished and in the very same year Saint Bartholomew's Fair in London finally succumbed to the determined attack of the London City Missions Society.[128]

But carnival does not simply go away. As a symbol of communality that the bourgeoisie had had to deny in order to emerge as a distinct class, its images and rituals were, in effect, displaced into bourgeois discourses such as art and psychoanalysis. There, the *"disjecta membra* of the grotesque body of carnival"* reappeared as terrifying threats to a pure individual subjectivity.[129]

And if this is true of middle-class identity formation in general, we can appreciate the particular strains that may have been experienced by the rising Catholic Irish middle class. Their political case was based on the claim that they were to be distinguished from their half-civilized fellow countrymen and women, but that the disciplining of this unruly mass could safely be entrusted to them. Hence the enormous stress on self-repression in Catholic propaganda—and not only on the repression of sinful desires (especially the thirst for alcohol)[130] but also of violent language and spontaneous protest. Thus Bishop James Warren Doyle (a Catholic polemicist much admired by Moore, and referred to in *Captain Rock*) preached to his flock: "Let this truth sink deep into your souls. Tell it to your children in your huts and cabins; and, if turned forth to starve and die, tell it amid the darkness of the night, in the storm and rain, in your hunger and raggedness, still ever, ever repeat, 'Revenge is God's alone.'"[131]

In his 1823 pamphlet on the Catholic question, Doyle advised the authorities that "It is not . . . in the character or dispositions of the Irish people, that we are to seek a reason why hundreds of families would submit to perish with hunger in the midst of plenty, rather than infringe on the rights of property. No! such sacrifices could only be the fruit of religion pushed to an extreme extension by the influence and exhortations of a pious priesthood."[132] Such was the apparent success of teaching self-restraint to the peasants that John O'Connell, son of the Liberator, boasted in 1847: "I thank God I live among a people who would rather die of hunger than defraud their landlords of the rent!" And, as Michael Davitt remarks, "He was not even hissed by his audience; so dead to every sense and right of manhood were the Irish people reduced in these black years of hopeless life and of a fetid pestilence of perverted morality."[133]

But the repression of the primitive, of the instinctual, and of the realm of communal celebration can never be total. Bourgeois identity, indeed, is defined not merely by fear and loathing of the "lower bodily stratum" and of the lower parts of the social body with which it is identified, but also by desire for, and even envy of, that Other in relation to which a pure civilized identity has been constructed.[134] There is an intense debate in Gerald Griffin's novels, for example, between "spontaneity" and "civility." The "bloody longing[s]"[135] of gentlemen and landlords such as Hardress Cregan in *The Collegians* and Abel Tracy in *Tracy's Ambition* are scarcely even consciously acknowledged by these characters but yet eventuate in horrible crimes committed by lower-class characters, who are in effect merely acting out their masters' secret wishes. (And in the actual murder case on which Griffin based his plot, John Scanlon, the real life Hardress Cregan, had no lesser an advocate in court than Daniel O'Connell, who argued that Scanlon's servant should bear sole responsibility for the murder of Ellen Hanley.)[136] And for all Griffin's self-conscious respectability and piety, the image of the peasant who is pleased that he does not have "to be watching [himself], an' spake Englified, an' not to ate half [his] 'nough at dinner"[137] is almost as powerful in these texts as the image of peasant deprivation and suffering. Maybe, as some alarmed contemporary commentators also noted, the Irish peasant does not really want to rise in the world: "Other countries only become populous when they have the means of comfortably supporting a large population; but Ireland is populous without wealth—she is populous because her inhabitants are satisfied with the merest pittance that can support existence—because they are contented to divide among *three*, food and clothing not sufficient for *one!*"[138]

Griffin's most exemplary middle-class hero, Kyrle Daly in *The Collegians*, proved to be an artistic failure. The author was deeply upset that readers preferred Hardress, the dissolute son of the squirearchy, to the tediously correct Kyrle, and this contributed to a major moral crisis for Griffin, who gave up writing fiction altogether shortly afterward. And if the rational but bloodless Daly was the *ideal* product of the civilizing process, what of, for example, the lethargy and disillusion of a character such as Ulick Regan in *Tracy's Ambition*? Regan tells his brother-in-law Tracy, after the latter has destroyed his family in the failed pursuit of wealth and social position, that he in fact regrets that his immense fortune has condemned him to a merely "secondary species of enjoyment":

> As I entered this inn, last night, I saw a stout fellow, without shoes or stockings, seated at a table in the landlord's kitchen, with a mountain of laughing, mealy potatoes, and a wooden piggin of thick milk before him. . . . and his whole face was lighted up with such a keen sense of enjoyment, that, if I were to look no further than this world (I have hitherto seldom looked further), I would gladly have changed persons with the boor. (*Rivals; Tracy* 3:131)

In Griffin's preoccupation with food, appetite, and the body, we uncover elements of the grotesque body, which accord very well with White's account of the terrifying nature of those elements of carnival that return in private, bourgeois fantasy. While the communal carnival represents a celebration of food, drink, sex, and laughter, here the "body of the people" is disturbing and repulsive. At one point in *Tracy's Ambition*, Tracy scours the country for his arch-enemy Dalton, a corrupt magistrate who has stolen his money and betrayed his trust. (When he eventually finds Dalton, Tracy puts his hands around Dalton's throat but finds that he is—mercifully, according to his own Christian principles—physically unable to throttle him.) At the Limerick fair, Tracy observes two ancient hags wrestling in the mud, one of whom is the mother of his tenant, Morty Shanahan (who will soon take his own violent revenge on Dalton for the killing of his Whiteboy brother). In this scene, we find the most extraordinary concatenation of anxieties about women, sexuality, and dirt, about the superstitious Irish mother who stifles the life of her own sons, and even about the land itself and the potato as a means of subsistence. The two women, who are no more than walking skeletons, are squabbling about their youthful charms:

> "Where! ye tawny-faced hag!" said one, "where would you get a white skin, that hadn't the price of a ha'p'orth o' soap to wash the black o' ye'r yellow cheeks on a Saturday night, afther wiping your withered paws on them, for want of a rubber the whole week before?" . . .
>
> "I washed them in potato-wather and a grain o' male, a thing that was far wholesomer than soap suds, as them will tell you as has a right to know. Tawny-face, inagh? My face then or now is fairer than yours, leather-browed hound; if I had a setting stick, I might stick [plant] skillanes [seed-potatoes] in the ridges o' your face, an' ax no manure to make 'em grow aither." (3:16–17)[139]

Griffin's writing bears eloquent testimony to the strains involved in iden-tity formation. The purification of social identity creates fears that are transferred from the repudiated parts of the bourgeois body itself to other distasteful places in society—to the slum, to the sewer, to the gutter,[140] and to what Thomas Moore called, in his journal of 1823, Ireland's "naked swarm of wretchedness."[141] In *Tracy's Ambition*, Dalton, who has an intimate knowledge of the family histories and of the customs of the people he persecutes, describes Irish country people as "bloody in their inclinations, debauched and sensual in their pleasures, beasts in their cunning and beasts in their appetites" (2:189). We may understand this character as Griffin's own mouthpiece in this passage.[142]

At first sight, it may appear absurd to turn to Moore for any alternative conception of the grotesque body given all those coy, moist-eyed lovers of the *Melodies*. (Tears are the only substance produced by the body that can be mentioned in modern polite society.)[143] Certainly, the kind of "nocturnal excesses" at stake in *Memoirs of Captain Rock* fall short of Rabelaisian revelry,[144] but Moore does linger on precisely those aspects of peasant culture—excessive fertility, spontaneous violence, a long historical memory—which so disturbed many of his contemporaries. Griffin concludes *Tracy's Ambition* with the warning that "the vengeance of an Irish peasant is not to be despised" (3:280), but Moore delivers the same message in a very different spirit. The invocation of Rock as a character who is bigger than the bourgeois self, who belongs to the whole community, surely represents a different model of middle-class identity formation, one which is not so dependent on fearing, loving, or hating the people.

Another way of conceptualizing the difference between *Captain Rock* and the fiction of Griffin and the Banims is in terms of narrative form. The novelists experienced great difficulty in combining their initially folklorist impulse to record the "traits and stories" of the Irish people with their attempt to emulate the progressivist, individualistic forms of English realist fiction. They are, in effect, attempting to marry the cyclical narratives of festivity, custom, and anecdote with the linear narrative of the typical realist novel. In his study of narratives of the Famine, Morash does cites a solitary example of a novel, Margaret Brew's *The Chronicles of Castle Cloyne* (1885), which portrays its female protagonist, an Irish peasant, as successfully entering the world of commerce, or the bourgeois world, against the backdrop of the terrible crisis of the 1840s. The early part of the text describes the colorful, traditional characters of pre-Famine Ireland in an episodic, anecdotal style. As Morash recounts, such storytelling gives way to a more progressive, novelistic style as the heroine's efforts to better her lot become the main focus of attention.[145] But is clear that such realist, individualist plots do not tend to evolve, in any organic way, from the stories of the earlier, traditional society—especially when that society is in the process of being destroyed in the most traumatic way imaginable. Much more typical of Irish Famine writing is, for example, William Carleton's fiction of the 1840s which, Morash argues, breaks down into incoherence and the grotesque when confronted with the devastation wreaked by hunger and disease. This is despite the fact Carleton himself would not have been ideologically hostile to the processes of modernization, which would inevitably sweep away the world of landless migrants, "prophecy men," and the rest, which he had recorded in his early work. But the face of a colonial, Irish modernity proved too ugly for him to contemplate with any equanimity.[146] In *Captain Rock*, in contrast, Moore superimposes a narrative of natural cyclical recurrence and resurgence on an otherwise depressing history of recurrent corruption and violence. In this way, despite his ignorance of the Irish language and of much of Irish rural culture, Moore offers us not necessarily a truer account of popular resistance than that offered by his peers, but potentially a much more suggestive one. It indicates how, after the debacle of the rebellion, there could reemerge, in the literary imagination at least, the kind of alliance between the intellectual and the common people of which the leaders of 1798 had always dreamed.

2

The Irish National Novel

The National Novel in the 1820s

During the 1820s, the Irish novel became established "as a separate generic category in the British literary sphere."[1] *The Tales of the O'Hara Family* (1825), co-written by John and Michael Banim, was the first Catholic-authored contribution to this emerging genre; Gerald Griffin's *The Collegians* (1829) is considered to have been the most successful.[2] But from the outset, the works of the Banims and of Griffin were criticized as aesthetically uneven and politically ambiguous—not least by the authors themselves. These new Irish Catholic novelists were profoundly anxious about how they might render the truth of Irish conditions in fiction without giving offense to either their Irish or their English audiences. They faced the task of exposing Ireland's misery while demonstrating that the country's problems did not stem from any irredeemable flaw in the national character. Nevertheless, the novels' accounts of the Irish Catholic home and family would have surely posed difficulties for anyone promoting the notion that Ireland had the potential to be an orderly and modern political economy.

Thus, the Banims and Griffin hoped to attract curious readers with dramatic and even sensational plots, but they strove for inauthentic happy endings that cast the Irish problem in constitutional and reformist terms. When they depicted a lurid Irish actuality, they tended to stray far from the sober conventions of English realism; when they remained faithful to their O'Connellite program, they produced saccharine and predictable resolutions. As Thomas Flanagan puts it, these pioneering Irish novelists repeatedly fell from the high road of serious fiction in English (defined in this era by Walter Scott) into the "conventions of the shilling shocker."[3] Hence these novels are more often invoked as illustrations of the inappropriateness of realist protocols for Irish subject matter, rather than as literary artifacts that merit any detailed analysis as such.[4] For example, Eagleton's comments on the "psychic dislocations" that "play havoc with realist figuration and narrative continuity"[5] in the novels of the Banims offer a compelling insight into the stories, but they do not suggest how we might read the precise nature of these distortions and discontinuities in relation to the history that generates them. Can the texts be read as saying more about Irish conditions other than that they are "disturbed"? Or is their mode of saying even this itself so disturbed and incoherent that it cannot effectively analyze, or creatively transform, the material with which it deals?[6]

I have explored the implications of Moore's essentially comic treatment of Irish agrarian violence and of his departures from his favored poetic modes (particularly that of the *Irish Melodies*) and from the Irish national tale (as represented by Morgan's *The Wild Irish Girl* [1806]). In *Captain Rock,* Moore produces a view of the peasant underworld and of the realm of popular spontaneity, sexuality, and the instinctual that is entirely different to that of his Catholic contemporaries who were so anxious to show how open Ireland was to modernity. However, it is hard to measure the impact of this wily narrative on the presiding ambitions that governed the new Irish Catholic public sphere, which Moore himself had helped to create. Moore was, of course, a vital role model for aspiring Irish Catholic authors. But more specifically, I will argue that *Captain Rock* is an important precursor of the earliest Irish realist novels produced by Catholic writers in the 1820s. The significance of this goes well beyond the contrasting portrayals of the peasantry in Moore and Griffin. Although Griffin's depictions of the crimes of servants or dependants certainly raise questions about the bad faith and guilt of the rising middle class, John (1798–1842) and Michael Banim (1796–1874), from a rather lower social class than Griffin (their father was a shopkeeper in Kilkenny), provide an account of the peasantry and violence that is even more revealing.

It is often suggested that the Banims must disguise their passionate emotional identification with peasant Ireland as they assiduously go about the task of explaining this strange world to their metropolitan readers. To a much greater extent than Griffin, they dwell on the intricacies of plots involving Whiteboys, Rockites, and, in their historical fiction, Rapparees.

Michael Banim informs us in a note to the two title stories in *The Peep O'Day, or John Doe; Crohoore of the Billhook* (1825) that his brother had originally intended the first story, *The Peep O'Day*, to be entitled "Captain Rock," "when a book appeared from our great national poet, Moore, bearing the name of the rustic hero of the day." Although Banim disavows any "similarity of purpose or design between the two publications," he suggests that the title had to be changed in order "to avoid the apparent presumption of even identity of designation" (*Peep O'Day; Crohoore*, 186). Despite this denial, at least one crucial scene in the story *The Peep O'Day* closely echoes Moore's framing narrative in *Captain Rock*. The English hero enjoys an illuminating encounter with an Irish priest, whom he first mistakes for a Captain Rock (or John Doe). Like Moore's Rock, this figure is outlandish in appearance, wearing a wig resembling that of a man of the law, and notable for the "self-assured twinkle" of his eyes and his "mixed character of severity and humour" (*Peep O'Day; Crohoore*, 33). The idea that the leader of the Irish rebels might be a charming and cultivated eccentric clearly owes a great deal to Moore. In a later novel, *The Anglo-Irish of the Nineteenth Century* (1828), another visitor from England has an extraordinary conversation with a stranger during a journey on a stagecoach by night. As we shall see, this friendly although somewhat menacing figure articulates the most direct expression of John Banim's nationalist convictions in any of his works. But beyond providing the direct inspiration at these key moments, Moore's account of Irish turbulence also casts light on the Banims' wider treatment of violence: as a principle of historical continuity; as an expression of wildness, which is opposed to, but never overcome by, a modern civility that the texts cannot wholeheartedly sponsor; and as a feature of national character that is particularly associated with femininity, mobility, and duplicity. Inevitably, the domestic intrigues of the novels, so preoccupied with sexuality, marriage, and the proper Catholic family, are greatly intensified by the saturating effects of such highly gendered and politically governed assumptions. Their fiction provides an ideal opportunity to consider David Lloyd's claim that the widely canvassed "crisis of representation" in the nineteenth-century Irish novel is the inevitable result of Irish writers' inability to make sense of agrarian violence, in particular by encoding it within the conciliatory agendas typical of English realist fiction.[7]

The suppressed and subversive plots of the early Irish novel need to be seen in relation to the more domestically focused stories of *Crohoore of the Billhook* and *The Nowlans*(from the Banims' *Tales by the O'Hara Family*) before it can be shown how they complicate the Banims' later experiments with the Anglo-Irish national tale and the historical novel. But their operation might first be illustrated by reference to one of Griffin's tales, *The Rivals*, which demonstrates how the early Irish Catholic novel attempted to digest other forms of storytelling, and the politics associated with them, in early-nineteenth-century Ireland.[8] The Irish novel certainly did this less well than its metropolitan counterparts. But I intend to de-emphasize the social alienation and the lack of personal and cultural self-confidence that are often understood as shaping (or rather deforming) these authors' texts, and thus as explaining their doomed pursuit of politeness, their narrative incoherence, and their failure to create the range of emotional intensities appropriate either to comedies about peasants or tragic tales of virtuous heroes. The task was certainly a delicate one. Nationalist programs may, in any event, only be interested in highly selective and sanitized versions of their original native cultures, which these novels fail to supply. This fiction does indeed experiment with the characteristic forms of the realist novel through repetition and imitation. But such mimicry should not merely be interpreted in terms of colonial deference and slavishness, for it can also be read as parody and critique—and indeed as *self*-critique, on the part of the rising native bourgeoisie.[9]

Disappearing Whiteboys: Griffin's *The Rivals*

Griffin's *The Collegians* (1829) is the most notable novel by a Catholic author in this era. The story is set in the 1770s, during the era of Grattan's parliament and of the first concessions to Catholics, and ends with a mention of one of O'Connell's great victories, the Clare election of 1828. Yet the major events of the intervening half-century are elided. There is no reference, for example, to the Rebellion of 1798 or to ongoing Whiteboy campaigns, which are central to the other less-celebrated stories of the same year, *The Rivals* and *Tracy's Ambition*. But Griffin's strategies in the least regarded of these texts, *The Rivals*, may help us better to understand both him and the Banims, and in particular, the ways in which these writers attempted to accommodate the inescapable theme of popular political resistance and violence within the conventions of English realism.

Francis Riordain, the hero of *The Rivals*, is a young Catholic radical whose idealism and enthusiasm are derided by the narrator of the story. He is a "sensitive mope" who would disgust any man of common sense; he has fallen into the erroneous belief that "it was not his business to fit society, but the business of society to fit him" (*Rivals*; Tracy 1:19, 26–27). But Riordain, the darling of the local peasantry in Wicklow, is not merely a political orator but also a leader of Whiteboy activities in the district (or so we are led to believe). He is driven out of Ireland by Richard Lacy, a corrupt magistrate, who is also Francis's rival for the affections of his sweetheart, Esther. Francis fights for liberty with the patriots in Colombia but eventually returns to Ireland and is exonerated from all suggestion of past criminality. He is also reunited with Esther and lovingly embraced by her staunchly Protestant and loyalist family.

It is hardly surprising that critics have decried the melodramatic incoherence of such a plot; Flanagan even goes so far as to call the story "disingenuous."[10] He presumably refers to the extraordinary dissonance between the narrator's judgments and the fate of the main character in the text. While the narrator, for example, tells us that the Irish who fought with the patriots were "a legion of unfortunates," Riordain exults in having seen "tyranny struck to the dust" (*Rivals*; Tracy 1:47, 122). In addition, Griffin's happy ending is achieved at the expense of some major breaches of verisimilitude. We might particularly mention the scene in which Francis rescues Esther's dead body from the family vault, only to discover that she is still breathing. Such incredible incidents have their counterparts in the political realm as well. Francis's courtroom declaration of innocence (although he does admit to having once rescued a falsely accused cottager from custody) is simply impossible to square with all we know about him and his involvement with the grievances of the local people. Yet it alone makes possible the implausible fantasy of the text's concluding chapters, with their vision of "blameless peasants, chivalrous patriots and virtuous landlords."[11] In all of these respects, we can see how Griffin struggles to subordinate what Moretti calls the various social realms or "language-spaces" depicted in the novel to the authority of the "informal, impersonal, common" style of the centralizing, modernizing nineteenth-century novel.[12]

Critics' objections to *The Rivals* encapsulate the case more often made against the Banims: A loss of nerve, as well as a failure of artistry, lead them away from authenticity and intensity and toward the "easy path of evasions" that popular fiction left open to them.[13] But in what follows here, I will consider in greater detail the relationships *between* different realms in these novels—and especially that between the domestic milieu of the respectable Catholic family and the underground world of the outlawed Whiteboys. The intention is not to prove that Irish Catholic novelists were secretly in favor of Captain Rock. Nevertheless, agrarian insurgents and primitive rebels feature prominently in the national allegories they wrote, and such shadowy actors parallel the upper-class heroes and heroines in significant ways—even forming aspects of their identities, as with Francis Riordain in Griffin's novel.

William Carleton commented approvingly that John Banim was "always to the foremost to inculcate obedience to the law, whilst it is a law, and in no instance is found to defend him who, by an act of moral guilt, ventures to violate it."[14] However, it is an outward conformity to the law of the land in these works that plays havoc with the "laws" of writing novels. A gap opens up between what can be said to be true and what can be acknowledged as real. Riordain is a rebel, but he cannot be openly recognized as such. Rather, his United Irish radicalism, Whiteboy connections, and his sanctioning of liberation achieved by physical force in Colombia are surreptitiously ratified in the novel, precisely because he never undergoes the disenchantment typically in store for the hero of a *bildungsroman*.[15] The transformations and reversals that bring about the politically acceptable, official resolutions of these novels are so unconvincing precisely because they cannot erase the other meanings of the stories. The latter operate as a threatening background noise that occasionally drowns out the message of the foreground story. The political continues to adhere to the world of the unrealistic. The Whiteboys of the Banims, although always liable to vanish into thin air, do not go away—not entirely. They constantly reappear in the day-lit world of romance and adventure as "semi-comic and semi-threatening."[16] This takes the harm out of them, to some extent, but simultaneously indicates the disfiguring danger.

Violence and Domestic Fiction:
The Nowlans and *Crohoore of the Billhook*

In two of the best-known of the O'Hara family tales by the Banims, *The Nowlans* and *Crohoore of the Billhook*, the brothers employed the allegorical modes embedded in realist fiction in an attempt to give a proleptic account of the emergence of a new Irish Catholic citizenry. The Banims concentrate in these instances on the microcosmic world of the family, and their chief anxiety in that regard is how best to protect and regulate the private realm of the home and of the domestic woman.[17] But in this fiction, it is never possible to effectively insulate domestic space from the appeal of premodern forms of community, or from the shocks of communal violence. It also proves to be exceedingly difficult for the Banims to slot either their male or female characters into the standard gender roles of the modern nuclear family. Crucial issues urgently in need of clarification in the familial and social worlds, such as the regulation of sexuality, and legitimate birth and succession, are never worked out in these texts. One index of this is the fate of the two main male protagonists of these novels, each the only male heir in their respective families.[18] Neither is able to marry and to continue his line: John Nowlan because he is a Catholic priest and the eponymous Crohoore because he is a hideous dwarf.

The Nowlans is a narrative about a family, rather than about any particular individual (appropriately enough for a novel supposedly authored by a family). Yet only its portrayal of the tragic John Nowlan has won critical praise. In his representation of Father John, John Banim (to whom the story is usually attributed) is regarded as having achieved a rare degree of psychological insight. But in the second half of the book, or so critics have asserted, the story lapses into tedious and incoherent melodrama as Banim swerves away from the horror of John Nowlan's plight and instead concentrates on the priest's younger sister, the unlucky but otherwise conventional Peggy Nowlan.[19]

John is the son of a reasonably comfortable tenant father in Tipperary, who fulfills his parents' wishes in deciding to become a priest. As an adolescent he is sent to live in the disorderly household of his uncle Aby, which is shared by his uncle's various mistresses and their offspring. Here John undergoes a painful sexual awakening in the company of his spirited illegitimate cousin Maggy. He manages to rededicate himself to his religious vocation and is close to taking his final vows when he encounters another woman, Letty, the niece of a local Protestant landowner. He eventually elopes with Letty, and they live miserably in Dublin until her death in childbirth. John's sister, meanwhile, has been forced into marriage with Letty's reprobate brother Frank. She has various adventures in pursuit of John in Dublin, but eventually, after the death of her child and rather fortuitous suicide of her dreadful husband, she returns home to be courted by an inoffensive local man, David Shearman. At the very beginning of the text, the narrator (Abel O'Hara) relates how he first encounters the Nowlans while seeking shelter as a traveler in their neighborhood, at the point when the young priest is newly returned to his family and is gravely ill. By the time we return to this framing narrative at the end of the text, John has recovered his health and Peggy is married. Ostensibly, domestic normality has been restored.

The most extraordinary feature of *The Nowlans* is its representation of the claustrophobic, hypersexual intensity of what might otherwise appear to be the cottage idyll of the family (small wonder that an embarrassed Banim was obliged to agree with his publisher that parts of the text were "too warm and impure").[20]

From the outset, Peggy Nowlan is an object of desire for the narrator, O'Hara; at the conclusion of the text, he tells us that he is hoping for greater romantic success with her younger sister. When O'Hara returns to the house after getting soaked in a shower of rain, he is stripped "almost by main force" by the women of the house, until he begins "to entertain some alarm as to the eventual result of the proceedings."[21] He is left with the command that he should "instantly peel off my Russia-ducks and my inner garment, drop them at the bedside, and then retiring between the sheets, call out to have them removed" (11). A maid in whose face he reads a "most provoking merriment" arrives to attend on him, but he is offered only a "female shirt" of Peggy's to wear (12). Although the narrator is as yet unaware of John Nowlan's doomed affair, this scene also closely resembles John's first encounter with his lover, Letty. She too first enters the Nowlans' house to escape the rain and is obliged to undress in John's bedchamber (the family evidently aspires to segregated privacy for men and women but is defeated by the size of its house). Letty leaves behind her glove and her ring, which John later caresses in erotic anguish:

> Something moved on the cover of the bed; he stopped, and picked up a lady's glove: a very small one; a very soft, slight kind of one; in short, a real "Limerick glove." It was so curious an article, that he could not help peering at it with eager scrutiny; and then, half smiling, he tried how only two or three of his fingers could make way into the opening at the wrist; and again, as the velvet feel of the interior reminded him of the small and still more velvet hand that had often worn it, he caught himself inclined to a respiration like a sigh. . . .
>
> He touched [Letty's ring] all round, and tried to put it on the tip of his little finger, just to ascertain if it was so very small as the owner of the very small glove might wear. With quick association, Letty's taper, rosy-tipped finger was presented to his mind, instead of his own; then her whole person again; then her sun-shiny face, her bewitching smile, her blushes, her glances: from this he ran on to the mystery of her having made her toilet in his chamber, and to some of the mysteries of that toilet, too: of her sitting on that very bed; and of his holding that moment, on the tip of his finger, her ring in that very bed; and in fact, more sorely beset than ever, John found himself straying once more, and hastily sat up, made the sign of the cross, and prayed to be delivered from temptation. (72–73)

Banim seems to be drawn to an almost pornographic representation of the family and of domestic space in this novel. Nowlan is first attracted to the "finery and dirt" (52) of his cousin ("according to the discipline of his church, not, without a heinous sin, to be regarded in any other light than that of a sister" [46]). Even after he falls in love with Letty, he endures dreams during which this image of her is confused with that of the unruly

Maggy: "In his dreams she [Maggy] was the chief tempter too, while sometimes the meeting with her ended in a fantastic encounter with her new rival; or, as his arms clasped her, she changed her identity" (73). Later, an impostor attempts to violate John's younger sister, Anty, in her bedroom by posing as her lost brother. (Sibling relationships and the threat of incest remain a veritable obsession for the Banims.) John's ill-fated quest for sexual purity eventually leads him to insist that his sister gets married to the villain Frank (for he believes that Peggy has already lost her virtue). It is cruelly emphasized that Frank finally enjoys what he describes as his "fancy and revenge" (172) after the woman of the house, the "good dame herself led Peggy to her nuptial chamber" (173).

Here Banim dwells on the horror at the heart of a religiously sanctioned union: Peggy was married by a renegade Catholic priest and therefore respects her vows, despite the fact that such a marriage would not have been legal. She is released from her bond to Frank only after his death, even though he has, in the meantime, attempted to poison her and to abort their child. Her brother John, by contrast, although legally married by a minister of the Church of Ireland, believes that he and Frank's apparently virtuous sister Letty are engaged only in mutually degrading fornication:

> It was a miserably happy nuptial day; a day and evening of delightful anguish; of terrible enjoyment. . . . He felt the joy of frenzy, the secret of despair, that sends the poor suicide to the bed destined to be drenched in his blood, smiling upon the hard-crammed pistol, which, at a certain hour, is to give him his supposed triumph over misery. . . . Immolate himself as he might, he believed he dared never call her his wife; and his blood curdled at the thought. (145–46).

As he tells Letty, his vow of priestly celibacy can only be broken, not forsworn (123).

Surveillance and discipline are the hallmarks of the new Catholic dispensation in which John Nowlan believed he had found his vocation. As one member of the Anglo-Irish gentry in this novel observes in alarm: "We see those priests becoming more numerous, more enlightened, more combined, more *watchful* than ever, headed by a body of their bishops still more enlightened and more *watchful*, and powerfully aided by popular speakers, by popular newspapers and tracts,—the whole forming against us such an array of zeal, talent, reflectiveness, caution, and even denunciation, such as our utmost efforts cannot counteract . . . " (117; my emphasis). Thus, while those priests pursue their watchful crusade, Nowlan, a bright and earnest scholar and in every way the pride of his humble family, pursues a connected but lonelier project: the inauguration of a new sexual discipline, just as watchful, but confined to the policing of the body as such, and particularly his own body and those of his kin. But the project of (in effect) instituting a general repression of sexual instinct in the name of a thoroughgoing discipline that would patrol the intimacies of private life as well as the organization of communal life proves to be drastically self-defeating.

What Nowlan discovers is that others appear to have greater liberty and capacity for self-creation than he can permit himself. His mother, for instance, has converted from the Church of Ireland to Catholicism without any soul-searching whatsoever; one of the self-styled "Mrs. Nowlans" at his uncle's house (none of whom are actually married to his uncle Aby) simply takes herself from one chapel to another after she is denounced from the altar. John's commitment to chastity is derided by the libertine Frank: "Do you think the Author of true religion would ever have given us, first, wishes, impulses, and capabilities for virtuous happiness, and, next, a tyrant and unnatural code to shackle those wishes, paralyze those impulses and capabilities, and cheat us of that happiness?" (91).

Even Letty cannot share John's scruples, for in her world, "Virtue was not taught as chiefly dependent on prayer, watchfulness, self-knowledge, but rather on instinctive feeling" (81). Nowlan's (and Banim's) preoccupation with decency in fact produces an image of an unreformed traditional culture as obscene, disgusting, and even criminal (as well as powerfully alluring). It is interesting, in this regard, that a close association is established between John's uncle Aby and members of the corrupt quasi-aristocratic Ascendancy. In fact, we are informed that between Aby and the "half-genteel" family of Frank Adams and his brothers, "scarce a virtuous girl or woman could be found in the neighbourhood" (100, 102). Frank seduces Aby's daughter,

Maggy, "child of crime and of nature" (46), before turning his attention to John's sister. Clearly, this Tipperary has serious need of a well-behaved middle-class. But yet an even more negative image of family life is provided by the "pinching economy" and "cold, heartless, worthless independence" (149–50) of the respectable Protestant family in Phibsborough, where John lodges after his elopement. The failure of *any* of the alternative homes in the novel to provide an acceptable balance between instinct and its civilized restraint dramatizes the importance of the problem for Banim and the difficulty of its resolution. This illustrates the contradictory nature of the new Catholic subject: supposedly liberated into civility, but the object of a savage and now self-inflicted repression.

John's follies and errors impel Peggy into the criminal underworld of the second half of the novel. (She has various grisly adventures on her journey to Dublin and in the city itself, including witnessing a bloody murder and narrowly escaping being forced into prostitution.) But the realism of the text and its notorious melodrama are intimately related, although they cannot be reconciled by Banim and persist as distinct modes.

Ultimately, John's suffering intensifies so greatly that it can only be described by external observers. This is how he appears to the gentlemen who discover him, keeping vigil over the bodies of Letty and their newborn child in a disused hovel by the roadside:

> The door of the cabin, which they had supposed to have been stolen, lay, supported by four large stones, on the wet floor; upon it lay the corpse of a beautiful young woman, of which the arms clasped a newborn babe, also dead, to the breast; a rushlight, stuck in a lump of yellow clay, flickered by their side; and at their feet, kneeling on one knee, while the raised knee propped his arm, and the arm his head, appeared a young man, his face as white as theirs, except where a black beard, long unshorn, covered it. . . .
>
> "It's as I tould you," resumed Will; "he's mad, and neither hears us, nor heeds the sight before him."
>
> "Do I not?" cried John, springing up and darting to them, his right hand still plunged into his breast; "mad I may be—mad I am—but do I not heed nor feel! Look at that!" He tore the hand from under his

shirt, and with it a portion of the mangled muscle of his breast. "Look at that! there's the way I was trying to keep it down." (166)

The reader never again has access to John's private thoughts—not even after he seems to have recovered his poise in the healing embrace of the Church. Banim suggests that bodily gesture, even paroxysm, is the only resource left to John, who here tears at his own flesh. This fierceness of feeling, which is, by implication, beyond the power of literary convention to represent, becomes almost hopelessly staged and extravagant, rather like an actor in a silent movie who, robbed of language, overcompensates by gestures that are both emphatic and generic. These are the standard features of the empathetic moment in melodrama.[22]

Moreover, John Nowlan's voice, and with that his consciousness, are significantly absent from the cozy ending; we never hear in any detail what at that critical point he thinks in retrospect about his "early crime and sorrow" (271). However, we have the pantomime frenzy of the Peggy and Frank plot, which also testifies to the violence unwittingly unleashed by John onto his loved ones. The relentless action of the final portion of the book in part disguises, in part reveals the author's inability to bring the story to any more natural or convincing conclusion. The novel is consumed in the sheer velocity of its events. The innocent victims of all this—the infant children of John and Peggy—are eliminated, presumably in preparation for the arrival of more appropriate grandchildren for the elderly patriarch and his devoted wife. But the relative peacefulness of the family at the end of the story is not the result of enterprise or economy, nor of any of the commercial-ethical virtues the Banims might have wished to inculcate in their Irish readers. It is simply the quiet of exhaustion.

Another noteworthy character, Peery Connolly, is credited by the family with having rescued Peggy and her sister Anty from ruin in Dublin. At the beginning, the narrator notes that the Nowlans have accepted Peery as a perpetual dependent, although he does little useful work. With his thick brogue, his chanting rhymes, his physical deformities (which appear to come and go at will), and his patter about the Mayboys, Peery is a version of a character encountered throughout the Banims' works. These rogues or tricksters combine elements of the "bocchoch," or professional beggar, and of the Whiteboy. (A magistrate in Dublin asks Peery whether he has "Deserted from Captain Rock" [269], which he of course denies.) Unlike John Nowlan, Peery apparently has no rich individuality or inner life, but he can disguise himself successfully, survive in the city, and save the honor of the Nowlan daughters. Clearly, he is no mere remnant of an antique world. In him, the melodrama of popular fiction meets the melodrama of folk tradition and of underground political resistance. (Sir William Wilde noted that the Ribbon societies in Connaught were characterized by "a spirit of rude enterprise and adventure" with much dressing up and "melo-dramatic exhibition.")[23] The story illustrates the somewhat uncomfortable domestication of Peery, who was in love with Peggy but was rejected. He cannot seek admission to the family through marriage, but still he lingers as a changeling at the family hearth.

This is a position occupied in another household by the most bizarre of all the Banims' many grotesques, Crohoore of the billhook. A repulsive, flame-haired goblin, Crohoore is discovered as a young baby in a field and taken in and raised by a fairly prosperous tenant farmer, Anthony Dool-ing. One Christmas Eve, Dooling angrily reprimands Crohoore, who is sharpening his billhook against a whetstone as a piper is entertaining the company. The next morning, the farmer, his wife, and a female servant are found hacked to death; the billhook is stained with blood. The creature himself has fled and has taken with him the only child of the house, the beautiful Alley Dooling.

Alley's betrothed, Pierce Shea, leads the hunt for the presumed mur-derer and ravisher. The local people, who had always suspected Crohoore of belonging to the "good people" (or fairies), refuse to assist. Although there are many sightings of the fugitive all over the locality, he appears to have a supernatural immunity to injury or capture. Shea is assisted by Rhiah Doran, a thoroughly villainous robber-bandit figure who entirely lacks what Michael Banim (in his later notes to this novel, which was largely his work) describes as the "aura of chivalry" of the famous Captain Freney of Kilkenny (401), who was the historical model for this character. Doran is also the leader of the local band of Whiteboys, and he inducts Shea into their secret society in return for the boys' help in searching for

Crohoore and Alley. Shea is involved in a Whiteboy attack on a local tithe proctor and is condemned to death.

Eventually, and largely through the agency of the mysterious Crohoore, the full extent of Doran's crimes become known; it is also revealed that it was Doran who killed the Doolings and attempted to abduct their daughter. Crohoore was in fact Alley's savior, and he has kept her hidden in the lair of an ancient crone, the wife of a bocchoch, Garodhe Donohoe (who, like so many others in this novel, has another identity as Lheeum-na-Sheeog, and in that incarnation is revered by the common people as a powerful intermediary with the fairy world). Shea, who has now (incidentally) been pardoned and thus escaped from the gallows, reclaims his sweetheart Alley. The old woman then hastens the *promesse de bonheur* by announcing that Crohoore (also known as "Crohoore-na-bilhoge" and "Cornelius Field") is really Anthony Dooling, the only son of the dead couple. She had stolen him from his cradle more than twenty years earlier, leaving her own dead child in his place, but returned him to his family when she gave up begging. So despite all appearances to the contrary, Crohoore is not merely a mortal man, but respectable, chaste, and honest as well. (The chastity is an especially timely virtue, since it turns out that Alley is his sister.) But this is no tale of Beauty and the Beast. Whatever spell fell on Crohoore, to make his external appearance so contrary to his inner nature, is not to be lifted—although right at the end of the text he is granted what we are told is a "steady and not unmelodious voice" (381), as if to compensate him for being so ugly in every other way. He remains impossible as a candidate for any legitimate sexual relationship.

The names and identities of Crohoore, and of some of the other key people in this novel, change according to the different and conflicting worlds in which they dwell. It is no wonder that themes of conversion or transformation dominate the narrative, as Banim tries to bring these identities into convergence within one single world—that of modern realism. But can Crohoore and his ilk enter the domestic world of the realist novel? Can the peasantry become a citizenry or at least some version of the modern political subject? Banim cannot understand how the communal world to which Crohoore belongs can become political except by being supplanted by the regime of the civil individual subject: Crohoore represents an obviously strained compromise between the two. The narrative bears the stress of the attempt toward convergence most obviously in relation to the two key issues of superstition and violence, which had been targeted by the improvers as central to the redemption of Ireland as a modern culture.

Crohoore of the Billhook is set in the 1770s, some fifty years before the novel was written. In his later notes, Michael Banim emphasizes that many features of the rural society he describes, from highwaymen to drunken wakes, are now on the point of disappearance. Banim mourns the passing of some of these things. For example, "burrowing archaeologists" may have disproven folk beliefs about the supernatural origins of fairy forts, or raths (raised mounds that were regarded as the home of the fairies in Ireland and left undisturbed by farmers), but he still "clings to the popular faith of rath proprietorship," against those scientists who would "depopulate our rural solitudes" (404). While some nostalgia about the recent past is to be expected even from a modernizer such as Banim, this image of depopulation is particularly suggestive.

Willa Murphy has pointed out that communal life in the Banims' fiction is usually depicted as dense and complex, and that this is reflected at the level of narrative form. The narrator of Crohoore is a cultural insider; the story "moves along by hearsay, gossip, and rumor, bits of information pieced together by the whisperings of servants and tenants."[24] Folk belief is at the heart of this communal solidarity. Despite the fact that the country people are terrified of Crohoore and of the fairy host that they imagine he has at his back, the effects of their credulousness are entirely benign. Even the bocchochs (here associated with the fairies through Garodhe or Lheeum), who are ostensibly no more than exploitative liars ("artists in counterfeiting every malady that 'flesh is heir to'" [410]), in the end do only good: They protect the innocent Crohoore, and preserve Alley from harm.[25] Indeed, what Banim regrets is perhaps not so much the old faith itself as the forms of community that it fostered. But can a traditional society retain its solidarity and lose the systems of belief that helped produce that solidarity? For those who regarded the belief and the solidarity with suspicion, the two were indissolubly related; thus rebelliousness (the only form of solidarity of interest to the authorities) and superstition were near allied. But for the Banims, it was not so simple, especially as the sectarian state was all too ready to identify Catholicism with superstition. They wanted to retain Catholicism, free it from superstition, overcome the bigotry it faced and, at the same time, connect it with a modernity that would not dissolve the communal bonds of a group that could claim access to the franchise on democratic grounds.

The difficulty of this mission accounts for the haunting but ambiguous nature of some key scenes in the novel. None of the characters, incidentally, seems to have any great investment in orthodox Christianity. The most significant sacred place in their locality is not the chapel but the great Cave of Dunmore (which in his later notes Michael Banim claims was visited by Walter Scott shortly after the original publication of *Crohoore* [*Peep O'Day; Crohoore*, 406]). Dunmore, a portal to the world of the supernatural, contains the fairies' great Market-Cross, where they hold their biggest gatherings. After Crohoore is seen disappearing into the recesses of the cavern, a crowd of people materialize from the countryside around to regale the waiting Pierce Shea with "many a frightful anecdote of the cave, and of the inhabitants of the cave" (260). This is not just a supernatural underground, but one that is a counterpart of the modern world above: Banim reports that the subterranean Market-Cross lies directly underneath the man-made Market-Cross of the city of Kilkenny, six miles away from the mouth of the cave (407). The fairies are also associated with the bustle and variety of the town in other ways. The bocchochs thrive in the city, especially enjoying the fair days when they can practice their arts of disguise and deception to the utmost. Even the narrator is sorry not to be free to describe all the wonderful distractions of the fair: "We regret that now, when we have not rehearsed the hundredth part of its novelties, pleasures, and incidents, we are no longer free to indulge our teeming garrulity: but the story to which we have yoked ourselves requires immediate attention" (327). The world of superstition is not just archaic, but filled with the pleasures and promises of the commercial and the modern. The country folk are preoccupied with tales of fairy abduction and changelings. But in these tales, the stolen people do not go—as W. B. Yeats would have it—to the "waters and the wild"; the fairy raths are brilliantly illuminated palaces, filled with revelry,

music, and sweet food and drink. These are images of a very material utopia, typical of the collective fantasies of any peasant society.[26]

Some of the imagery associated with the mythical leaders of agrarian
protest becomes attached to Crohoore during the course of the story. The
country people fear him, but they also feel awe and admiration for him
(and, of course, any fugitive from the official law in nineteenth-century
Ireland might expect some popular sympathy). Crohoore's indestructibility, his ability to break his followers out of jail, and his defiant speech
from the dock ("'I stand here to listen to your sentence: nothing have I
to say against it; my time to spake is not yet come. You will tell me that
I must hang like a dog upon the gallows; but—' a grim smile crossed his
features—'the skibbeeah's [hangman's] fingers will never be laid on my
neck'" [381])—illustrate that he has been endowed with the traits of a
Captain Rock, although without any of the latter's more festive attributes.
This partly balances Banim's demystification and condemnation of actual
Whiteboyism in the novel: "Neglected, galled, and hard-driven, in poverty, bitterness, and ignorance, without competent advisers, without leaders a step above themselves, and scarcely with an object, [the peasants]
wildly endeavoured to wreak vengeance upon, rather than obtain redress
from, the local agents of some of the most immediate hardships that maddened them" (234).

The attack on the tithe-proctor Clancy is frenzied and chaotic, presenting a thoroughly negative account of the community's "rough music":
"The inmates of the hovels, at their doors, or lying on their straw, joined
the uproar; and even the shrill scream of the women, and the tiny pipes
of the children, could be distinguished" (285). The violence of this episode, during which Clancy's ears are cut off and he is left buried up to his
neck, is far exceeded by the later violence of a party of dragoons who fire
on a crowd of peasants, killing thirty of them. When violence is inflicted
by the disciplined army of the state it is less horrendous than that of the
mob—or at least, evidently less worthy of extended novelistic treatment.
This is partly because the idea of military discipline and order—no matter how bloody its effects—is consolidated with the idea of the modern
disciplined community from which the vengeful saturnalia of the Irish had
to be exorcized.

But Banim's representation of the insurgents is significantly inconsistent. Terence Delaney, for example (the only one of the Whiteboy band who wants to take the tithe-proctor's life), simply seems to occupy an entirely different emotional and moral universe to that of the villain Rhiah Doran or the drunken, rabble-rousing schoolmaster Mourteen. The latter is by day the schoolmaster of the district and by night the "writer of notices, regulations, and resolutions, and, to crown all, the orator in general to the reformers of Clarah" (270). We hear a number of Mourteen's bitter and inflammatory speeches: "Hasn't the Sassenach Clargy, I say, all Ireland to himself every tenth year, while the world is a world. Sure, if he had a conscience along wid id, *that* might be enough, an' not for to send the bloody proctor on our back, to lift the double o' that, again. To take the food from our mouths, our Christhen mouths, an' the rag o' covering from our beds an' our bodies" (275).

Unlike his comrades at the Whiteboy gathering during which Shea listens to Mourteen and takes the Whiteboy oath, Delaney does not use the English language. Instead he

> poured out a speech in his native tongue, adopting it instinctively as the most ready and powerful medium of expressing his feelings; for one who boggles, and stammers, and is ridiculous in English, becomes eloquent in Irish. We follow the speaker in translation, which will necessarily show none of the rude *patois* he must have betrayed had he attempted, as all the others did, to display his feelings in a language almost unknown to them and him. (276)

Banim translates this character's words into poetic English, quite unlike the Hiberno-English of the other peasants:

> "But look at me!"—With the fingers of one hand he pressed violently his sallow and withered cheek, and with the other tore open the scanty vesture, that, leaving him uncovered from the shoulders to the ribs, exhibited a gaunt skeleton of the human form—"I have nothing to eat, no house to sleep in. My starved body is without covering: those I loved and that loved me, the pulses of my heart, are gone.

How gone, and how am I as you see me?" . . . There is no friend, no
help, no mercy, no law for the poor Irishman. (276–77)

We have already seen the miserable tableau of Delaney and his moth-
erless children trying to eke out an existence in a filthy hovel. This is
later complemented by another tragic picture of Delaney's ancient mother
tending to her orphaned grandchildren in the corner of a barn, after their
father has been killed in the attack by the dragoons. She laments for her
son in the style of a Gaelic poet: "I nursed you at my breast; I baked your
marriage cake; I sit at your head!—Ullah!" (301). These representations of
the family's plight may be melodramatic, but they are all the more powerful for being so at odds with the sentimental representation of the central
Shea/Alley romance.

But the variation in the speech of the Whiteboys has also an ethical dimension. Pierce Shea had prevented Delaney from murdering the
tithe-proctor. Delaney later thanks him for this and tells him that he is
grateful that he can die without that stain on his soul. But when the news
of Delaney's death is conveyed to his mother, she rejoices in his message that he died with "the blood of the traitors" on him (301). The total
contradiction between this and the earlier sentiments about Christian
forbearance is not remarked on. The moral evaluation of peasant resistance seems to vary, depending on the language that is being spoken and
the regime of verisimilitude that corresponds to that language. Banim's
various modes of representing peasant speech in English and Irish in this
novel may suggest a similar division. Penny Fielding reports that in Scottish fiction of this era, "Anxiety about the behaviour of 'peasant' culture
led to a splitting of the image of the oral into a romanticized and idealized form and a demotion of popular orality as a concept to be called
'illiteracy.'"[27] But here, the purer orality of the Delaney family seems to
contain an even more powerful political threat than the more uneven
rhetoric of the other Whiteboys.

In this novel, the bocchochs too sing out their "supplications for charity in the true Hibernian tongue" (410) and are masters of the traditional
funeral lament, or Keenthecaun (318). Banim acknowledges that the
extreme grief of the Irish keener is usually assumed to be feigned, and notes

that the behavior at Irish funerals is finally becoming more restrained and discreet (189–90). But falseness—like the savagery of the Whiteboys—may be a matter of perspective. While, in common with many other Irish writers on Ireland, the Banims at times offer the likes of the bocchochs as exhibits of an incurable whimsicality that arises out of Irish character, they also offer some analysis, at least, of the economic or political conditions that breed such apparently fantastic caprice.

Captain Rock, Wild Irish Girls and the End of the National Tale

John Banim's *The Anglo-Irish of the Nineteenth Century* was published anonymously in 1828. Evidently, Banim was afraid to attach his name to this work, which contains such a ferocious attack on the "horsewhipping spirit"[28] of the Protestant Ascendancy.[29] Banim's uncompromising satire of this class strikes at a central premise of the Anglo-Irish genre of the national tale. In works such as Morgan's pioneering *The Wild Irish Girl* (1806), or Edgeworth's *The Absentee* (1812), the tacit double assumption is that the Ascendancy is capable of reform, and that its reformation is necessary for Ireland to progress. As Banim's young Anglo-Irish hero, Gerald Blount, travels by night in a stagecoach to visit his Irish estates for the first time, he falls into conversation with a shadowy figure who disabuses him of such notions. Although he introduces himself as a Protestant landlord, this gentleman (clearly modeled on Moore's Captain Rock) dismisses as historically insignificant those English-Irish who refuse to throw in their lot with the "mere" (or pure) Irish: "Whether they stay or go, their national existence will be destroyed; I do not mean by any means of annihilation directed to them, but as a matter of course, according to the nature of things" (*Anglo-Irish* 3:123). The exchange concludes with the gentleman's challenge to Gerald and the Anglo-Irish in general: "HOW WILL YOU STOP US?" (131).

Ina Ferris argues that, in this novel, Banim "directs the national tale out of the unhomely space of the hyphen into the homely space of identification," giving a central place to potent terms of belonging ("native," "real," "home").[30] But Banim does not, in fact, counter his relentlessly negative portrayal of Anglo-Ireland in this novel with any straightforwardly positive representation of the "real" Ireland. *The Anglo-Irish of the Nineteenth Century* has none of the national tale's characteristic emphasis on the country's natural beauty, or on the appeal of its folk traditions and native culture; rather the reverse: Irish violence, sexual excess, and duplicity dominate the story.

In a typical national tale, the hero's prejudices against Ireland quickly evaporate once he undertakes his Irish tour, which concludes with marriage to a beautiful native woman. Banim, however, uses the Anglo-Irish Gerald to explore more profound and far-reaching anxieties about Irishness. These are first aroused by the spectacle of the drunken, licentious, and riotous Irish inhabitants of the London ghetto of St. Giles, years before Gerald confronts Captain Rock in the heart of the Irish countryside. Although he is impressed by the architecture of Dublin and the arguments of O'Connell and the other Catholic leaders, Gerald never overcomes his fear of Irish people of all social ranks. Most of the wily country folk he encounters during his journey toward the family seat of Lower-Court are eventually revealed to be law-abiding. Yet they collude with his patriotic sister, Augusta, in constantly teasing and confusing him. He eventually discovers that his putatively renovated estate is presided over by Augusta and two of her female Irish friends. The vision of "female despotism" (3:96), which Gerald encounters in the drawing-room of Lower-Court (3:299–300), hardly seems calculated to reconcile him to residence in Ireland. The only prospective bride for Gerald appears to be his sister's best friend Rhoda Knightly—a woman whom he describes as a "rustic Amazon," who is given to wearing a riding-habit and a man's hat, and carrying a whip (2:98).

At this point the story ends "without absolutely concluding" (3:303). Banim informs us that he will tell the full story of this strange marriage in a sequel (which was never written). *The Anglo-Irish of the Nineteenth Century* lacks any appropriately seductive incarnation of Ireland to match the standard heroine of an Irish national tale. Rather its wild Irish girls are multiple, active, scarily androgynous, and well-versed in the buffoonery of the Irish banditti (3:198). Drawing partly on Moore, Banim in fact deploys images of Irish sexuality and violence in *Anglo-Irish* that ultimately contribute to a highly unflattering account of Irish national character. Gerald's loathing for all things Irish, and his failure to fall in love with an Irish woman, clearly stem from the author's own ambivalence about aspects of subaltern identity. The Banims were to use similar images to more far-reaching effect in the sequence of Irish historical novels that was to be their final and most ambitious project.

Charles Townshend proposes a triadic classification of types of violence in nineteenth-century Ireland. In ascending order of sophistication, these are the "competitive," or violence as communal recreation; the "reactive," or Whiteboyism, characterized by its local, proto-political nature; and, finally, "proactive" political violence directed toward the state.[31] One of Banim's ostensible aims in *Anglo-Irish* is to dispel English and Anglo-Irish paranoia about Captain Rock. He attempts to realize this by reducing all forms of violence in Ireland to the first of Townshend's types (which Moore in *Memoirs of Captain Rock* calls "fighting for fun"). For example, while the respectable Protestants of Dublin fear an invasion by "a fleet of turf-boats, bearing as many armed Rockites or Ribbonmen, as 'sods of turf,' from various bog-holes in the heart of wild Ireland" (2:186), they discover that the uproar which disturbs their dinner party comes from a ragged crowd of boys who "in mockery . . . of the terrors of people who ought to be wiser than they, were amusing themselves very laughably in the streets" (2:287).

Early in this novel, it is said of the Irish: "They must have fighting . . . 'tis meat, drink, and clothes to them—(indeed, sometimes they want it as a substitute for these matters)—if they can have it with an enemy, and with an Englishman above all the world, all the better; but rather than go without it, they must have it from each other" (1:41).

But how consoling does this supposedly amusing conception of the wild Irish really turn out to be? Take the scene during which it falls to the man in the coach (who most likely is Mr. Knightly, father of the bold Rhoda, in disguise) to explain the terrible "riot and panic" (1:44) of St. Giles in London to Gerald. This mysterious person accounts for that Babylon by referring to the treatment experienced by Irish emigrants (including the fact that their marriages are not legally recognized). He is neither embarrassed nor worried about the behavior of his compatriots; in fact, he announces that he doesn't care "one little harmless blow of a shillelagh about it" (3:110–11). He predicts that in any event such prancing will die out in a generation or so. But the reckless energy displayed by the lower-class Irish is also embodied by Mr. Knightly himself—in his joviality, his enormous appetite for food, and his great brood of children. It is also clearly associated with his optimistic vision of the inexorable rise of the new Irish nation. These new United Irish, as he warns Gerald, will not be satisfied with a mere "escape from the remaining fetters of the statute-book" (3:121).

As he draws near to his family's estate, Gerald's constant obsession with spying out criminals and Whiteboys is frustrated by his inability to make out the family relationships in any of the peasant households he enters; he is perpetually suspicious, hostile, and bewildered. Even that stock figure, the kind-hearted young girl who tries to help him, imposes on him strategies of evasion and pretense, which he much resents, drawn from "her knowledge of her own tribe" (3:198). But during the final volume of *Anglo-Irish*, what Gerald calls "the process of Rockism" (3:185) is yoked to the plot of comic intrigue against the hero, which is initiated by members of the social elite themselves. In *The Boyne Water* and their subsequent historical novels, the Banims instead sought to connect such stories of playful but subversive violence with the larger narrative of Irish history itself.

The Banims and the Historical Novel

Thomas Moore attributed the boom in Irish novel-writing in the mid-1820s to the example and success of Walter Scott, the "inimitable romancer of the North."[32] John Banim, in particular, longed to be the Irish Scott.[33] However, the few critics who have given sustained attention to the Banims' historical novels, of which the best-known is John Banim's *The Boyne Water* (1826), seem to regret that he ever conceived his fictional project in such terms. Indeed, the critical case concerning Banim's apparently ill-advised "imitation" of Scott is typical of the larger arguments that attempt to account for the inadequacy of the nineteenth-century Irish novel more generally. Banim evidently copies some structural features of Scott's Waverley novels in *The Boyne Water*, but he misses much that is essential to them. He models his young male protagonists, Robert Evelyn and Edmund M'Donnell, on characters such as Edward Waverley in *Waverley* (1814) and Henry Morton in *Old Mortality* (1816); these heroes' romantic entanglements, and their relationships with various father or mentor figures, are also based on Scott's stories. He also—optimistically enough, in the Irish context—repeats Scott's assurances that a deeper understanding of past conflicts will serve the cause of present-day "moderation," as opposed to "extremism." But, unlike Scott, Banim (or so the argument goes) does not succeed in depicting historical change in what Georg Lukács calls a felt relationship to the present; and, indeed, Irish history did not lend itself very readily to plots about enlightened reconciliation, or gradual but steady progress.

In his classic study, *The Historical Novel,* Lukács argues that Scott's novels affirm history as a process that is "full of contradictions, the driving force of which is the living contradiction between conflicting historical forces, the antagonisms of classes and nations. . . . This is vital for the creation of a real historical novel, i.e., one which brings the past close to us and allows us to experience its real and true being."[34]

In *Waverley* and *Old Mortality,* Scott deals with the conflicts that led to the Glorious Revolution of 1688, and with its aftermath. In *Old Mortality,* he explores the Scottish Covenanters' rebellion of the 1670s against Charles II (although the hero, Morton, ultimately finds himself in the service of William of Orange, the future king of England and guardian of its Protestant liberties). *Waverley* chronicles the final defeat of the Stuarts after the Highland revolt of 1745. So these two novels depict the threat to the modern British state from the legacy of seventeenth-century Puritanism, on the one hand, and Catholicism, Stuart absolutism, and the primitive clan society of the Scottish Highlands, on the other. Banim's *The Boyne Water* is also set at the time of the Glorious Revolution, although almost the entire story unfolds in Ireland. William had a decisive victory over James at the Battle of the Boyne in 1690, but the conclusion of the novel is concerned with the promises of religious toleration made to Irish Catholic Jacobites when they surrendered at Limerick in the following year. In contrast to Scott, Banim cannot wholeheartedly ratify the revolution because the breach of the Treaty of Limerick, and the penal code that was to follow in the eighteenth century, made it abundantly clear to him that Catholics were never truly accepted as equal subjects of the Crown.

But according, for example, to Tom Dunne, Banim's treatment of this period is distorted by its narrow polemical focus. In attempting to lend weight to the campaign for Catholic Emancipation (finally granted three years after the publication of the novel), Banim sanitizes the history of Irish resistance to the British. He suggests in the novel that Irish Catholics are inherently loyal (as they were to James II), and utterly resigned to the loss of their culture and their lands: Once the question of religious liberty has been resolved, a peaceful Irish nation will reemerge. In this, Banim reflects "the mimicries, manipulations and repressions" of Catholic fiction in the 1820s, although Dunne asserts that *The Boyne Water* is remarkable, even in that context, for "the extremes to which it took the appeal to English sympathies, and the extent to which it cloaked Irish Catholic resentment in the dominant narrative discourse of the imperial power."[35] For while Scott's views on the middle way and historical progress are in fact in harmony with the those of the Anglican church and the British ruling class, Banim's call for the toleration of supposedly docile Irish Catholics had little real historical reference or force: It merely represents one strand of O'Connell's notoriously ambiguous political rhetoric. Hence the Irish novelist, ostensibly speaking up for the historically vanquished, must actually underplay conflict and antagonism, and take the emphasis on moderation to absurd lengths. For example, Banim deals with both Catholic and Protestant bigotry (represented by the friar O'Haggerty and by George Walker) within the same novel, with contrived even-handedness. Scott had succeeded in registering both the trauma and the tragedy of the destruction of Gaelic society, in Scotland rather than Ireland—which he nonetheless regarded as necessary and inevitable. But Banim's wish to emulate Scott leads only to the loss of affect and conviction. William Carleton lamented that, in this phase of his career, Banim's "plots and characters, instead of rising naturally from the warmth of his own Irish conceptions, were projected in the cold, artificial mould of imitation"; Wolff finds something "almost comic" in Banim's fidelity to Scott in *The Boyne Water;* while Thomas Flanagan concludes that the text lacks "some ultimate sense of commitment by Banim to his material."[36]

Of course, Lukács's claims about the inherently progressive nature of Scott's historical fiction have been contested. Katie Trumpener contrasts the Waverley novels with Irish national tales such as Morgan's *Wild Irish Girl* (1806), which were an important influence on Scott. Pointing out Scott's indebtedness to the stadialism of the Scottish Enlightenment, which (in the words of Kevin Whelan) "consigned regional cultures to erasure under the sign of progress," Trumpener argues that the movement of the national tale is geographical rather than historical, mapping "developmental stages topographically, as adjacent worlds," rather than demonstrating "the collapse and transfiguration of place."[37] So Morgan, for example, does not depict native Irish culture as a merely picturesque anachronism, which might safely be enjoyed as aesthetic spectacle once the political threat with which it was associated has been put down (we think of the large and spirited painting of Edward Waverley and Fergus Mac-Ivor in their Highland dress, in *Waverley*, which is hung at Tully-Veolan after Mac-Ivor's execution). This is signaled, according to Trumpener, by Morgan's refusal of a totalizing narrative voice, which Trumpener interprets as a more appropriate response to Ireland's painful colonial history than Scott's suppression of alternative stories of the future. Morgan's more complex view may also be registered in what Leerssen describes as the unspeakable and indescribable, in *The Wild Irish Girl*'s "almost infatuated fascination with what is exotic and interesting in Ireland," particularly its music and song.[38]

No comparable claims have been advanced on Banim's behalf. But we should perhaps review the question of Banim's relationship with Scott—which may, at least, result in a more sympathetic account of this immensely long and ambitious text. More significantly, we may also open up the larger question of the dependence of early Irish Catholic national novelists, such as the Banims and Gerald Griffin, on metropolitan models, to which their own works may appear as little more than inadequate approximations. For example, if Scott's fiction represents the viewpoint of the historically victorious, recording their sentimental tribute to their defeated enemies, then clearly its premises cannot comfortably be adopted by such authors as Banim, so concerned with Catholic *recovery* in this period. The absence of a tragic sensibility in *The Boyne Water*, so regretted by Flanagan and Cahalan, is in part due to Banim's sense that the Irish future, at least, is still open. Indeed, Banim's revision of historical fiction may take the form precisely of failing properly to reproduce its motifs.

The Boyne Water is primarily concerned with the intertwined stories of Robert Evelyn and Edmund M'Donnell, who meet for the first time in

Antrim shortly after the succession of James II, and fall in love with each other's sisters, Esther and Eva. Here we immediately perceive the outlines of love affairs which promise to eventuate in not one but two national marriages of the kind that conclude *The Wild Irish Girl* and *Waverley*. In those novels, of course, the marriages are between English men (Mortimer and Waverley) and women who embody a softened version of their native Gaelic culture (Glorvina, Rose), and they are offered as optimistic allegories of a closer union between the respective countries of the husbands and wives. The British state, which facilitates such personal and political relationships, is also thereby ratified. In Banim's case, the prospective alliances are between Irish Protestants and Irish Catholics but, regardless of this variation, the way in which he plots the love stories also diverges significantly from the paradigms established by the national tale and the historical novel.

In Scott's novels, those significant marital unions that symbolize a happier political future come at the conclusion of long narratives. For example, Waverley discovers in the course of his adventures that his personal destiny lies not in the Highlands with Flora Mac-Ivor, but in Hanoverian Britain with Rose Bradwardine. Rose proves to be much better suited to the quiet domestic life that he now yearns for than the brilliant but excessively zealous Flora, whose clan and way of life are doomed to historical eclipse. The couples in *The Boyne Water*, by contrast, meet and agree to marry in advance of the political events that separate them. While Robert Evelyn, in particular, rather fussily complains throughout the novel that he detests "politics, and political movements and persons" for their intrusion into his "private feelings and arrangements,"[39] in fact the only period of contentment that the lovers ever enjoy is while they remain in the idyllic seclusion of the M'Donnells' ancestral home, the Strip of Burne in Antrim. Although the M'Donnells have lost their lands, they inhabit this Gaelic enclave under the protection of Lord Antrim, the only Catholic magnate in Ulster to have held on to his estates through the Cromwellian settlement and the Restoration. This historical anomaly allows Banim to preserve Scott's topographical divide between an English south and a Gaelic north, which is otherwise inapplicable to Ireland.[40] So at the very beginning of the text, we follow the Evelyns as they travel northwards from Belfast toward the glens of Antrim, which feature as a kind microcosmic version of the Highlands in this novel—Edmund M'Donnell even appears in a Scottish kilt during the siege of Derry. (This imported topography competes with a more familiar Irish one later on the novel, with the introduction of the band of vagrant Rapparees: While these outlaws are found all over Ireland, they speak in a distinctive southern brogue, and when one of their women, Moya, tries to seduce Robert, she calls him away from the "black north, an' from all its roads an' towns, into the green country" [368]). The realm of romantic happiness, then, is located not so much in the private sphere, as Robert would understand it, but in a society under threat: in a haven that is irretrievably lost when Edmund and Eva's father and his followers are slaughtered during the war. Unlike Inismore in *The Wild Irish Girl* or Tully-Veolan in *Waverley*, this place is never available for remodeling under new ownership. Indeed, in various ways, Banim breaks with the conventions of the exploration of "the non-contemporaneity of European countries"[41] so characteristic of historical fiction. Here there is no sustained *Waverley*-like journey back (or northwards) into the remote past: Banim's commitment to vindicating nineteenth-century Catholics necessitates a depiction of the M'Donnells as civil and modern, rather than strange and barbaric. Although according to Scott's scheme of things, these Irish Highlanders should really be exotic primitives (and some traces of this do remain in *The Boyne Water*), this role is largely taken over by the Rapparees, together with their "athletic, broad-shouldered, sunburnt, wildly habited" women (214). And as we shall see, Banim's modification of the paradigm of the historical novel has some interesting consequences. So, too, the goal of defining and vindicating marriage and the domestic life, absolutely central to the novel in this period (even the historical novel, set in a generally masculine public world), is greatly complicated in Banim.[42] Robert and Eva do ultimately live together as husband and wife and have children, but Eva's journey toward this settlement is tortuous indeed. Her reluctance to fulfill the role of the domestic woman has some far-reaching political implications, not least for the light it sheds on the notion of Catholic docility in the novel. By contrast, Esther, the quiet and gentle heroine (the modern woman), does not survive the war: She dies of starvation during the siege of Derry.

As Dunne asserts, there is certainly a good deal of insistence, in the early part of the text at least, that the Catholic Irish do not resent their political condition, but instead desire only to live in peace and practice their religion. This reaches almost a parodic pitch when Carolan (the character is based on the renowned Irish harper) responds to the following speech by Edmund:

> Irish we are, in feeling, and I will say, in generosity;—Irish enough to forgive and forget all the wanton cruelties that have been practiced upon us;—to forget the rank we have lost, and be content with that which we sweat and toil to earn, if, indeed, that poor privilege of humanity be left to us. I would not draw a sword this moment, for the recovery of my old right, when blood and convulsion must be the consequence. Sensible of my father's loss I must be, and prompt to speak of it warmly. But I find myself born under a new order of things; the voice of law, and of a king, have sounded in my infantine ears, to command obedience to that new order; and I say to myself—as my ancestors gained my lands, so I forfeit them. It is the chance of the world, and I am content. (74)

Carolan lists his own even greater privations with relish: "'I am poor, and I am blind,' he continued, 'and, worst of all, I have lost a friend [his old master]. But come!—I will try to be merry. Edmund, put the cup in my hand'" (75).

But to accept "the chance of the world" is a rather different thing than to bow gracefully to a grand historical necessity, and it is surely questionable whether Banim's novel persuades English readers of the willingness of the Irish to forgive and forget in quite the craven (and disingenuous) fashion that Dunne suggests. For in the cases of Edmund, Eva, and the bizarre wild woman Oonagh, a period of real or feigned insanity followed by an almost deathly resignation seems to be the usual pattern of response to grief or loss in the novel. Indeed, each of these characters temporarily sheds his or her real identity in mourning; this is why Edmund and Eva in effect go missing for much of the action, and why we only discover Oonagh's true identity at the end of the story. This is perhaps fitting for a novel in which (although extremist demagogues like O'Haggerty and Walker are killed off) many of the principals are historical losers who nevertheless survive into the new era, while not necessarily becoming reconciled to the new dispensation. There is nothing in Banim to support Scott's view that the defeat of Jacobitism was inevitable, or that it was in any case destroyed as much by its own inner weaknesses and anachronisms as by any external force. In fact, throughout *The Boyne Water*, Banim depicts "the war of the two kings" as a rather close-run thing. And does the story in fact demonstrate that the Catholic Irish were really only suffering from frustrated loyalty to a whole series of English monarchs, as eager to serve George IV as they were to fight for James II? How is the fact that loyalty can be "transferred" any proof of its sincerity? The British, certainly, believed that it was impossible to honor the Treaty of Limerick precisely because of the depth of the Irish attachment to the Stuarts. The Pope continued to regard James as the legitimate king of England and Ireland, and as Mortimer O'Sullivan asks: "If the Roman Catholics of Ireland were honest men, could they be faithful to the new government of England?"[43] The Jacobites in *The Boyne Water* offer no recantation of their spiritual or political faiths, and the novel ends with the surviving males of the M'Donnell family leaving for France to join the exiled prince. The very last line of the text tells of the birth of a child, to be named James, to Robert and Eva. So while Banim's novel, in some ways, corresponds well enough to what Eamon Ó Ciardha describes as the "dejacobitisation" of the Irish political tradition by accommodationist Irish Catholic political interest after the late eighteenth century, it also points to the embarrassing absence of any Catholic cult of loyalty to the house of Hanover.[44]

The presence of the Rapparees in the text also provides an oblique commentary on the theme of dispossession. For although Banim never mentions it, the popular belief in Ireland was that these bands of primitive rebels (to borrow E. J. Hobsbawm's term) were the descendants of those who had been thrown off their lands by Cromwell. Savage, violent, cunning, and pleasure-loving, the Rapparees, although helpful to the Jacobites at key points, do not form part of any regular military force in the novel. They did, however, indeed play an important role in the conflict, and as one contemporary commentator put it, caused far more damage to the

Williamite forces during the winter of 1690–91 than "anything that had the face of an army could pretend to."[45] Yet as Patrick Sarsfield (the commander of James's forces during the siege of Limerick) says in Banim's text, "these rascals have ever their own interests in whatever they do" (*Boyne Water*, 489). They can seduce maidens, matrons and even loyalist dogs (214); their wrong-doing often takes the form of carousing or mischief. Rory-na-chopple, one of their number, has already survived hanging, escaping from the gallows with only a twist in his neck (132). This is a close echo of Michael Banim's description of Captain Rock, the mythical agrarian leader, in his notes to an earlier novel about the 1820s, *The Peep O'Day*:

> Hang him up "by the neck" to-day "until he is dead"—his select and general mode of exit from this world—when, lo and behold! to-morrow or the next day, he is again on *terra firma*, even more strong and vigorous than he was before becoming a pendant for the gallows-tree. It would appear as if, by becoming defunct for a day or so, vampire-like, his powers and his energies received additional stimulus. . . . And so he has been hanged and been revivified almost time immemorial. (*Peep O'Day; Crohoore*, 185)

We are also told in *The Peep O'Day* that the "escapes, disguises and movements" of Captain Rock (or John Doe) "equalled if they did not surpass, the subtlety and wonderful finesse of the whole corps of primitive Irish Rapparees, with Redmond O'Hanlon at their head, and Cahier-na-chopple bringing up the reserve" (*Peep O'Day; Crohoore*, 28). This is how the so-called primitive manages to survive, and indeed thrive, when its proper historical period is over. Through the Rapparees, Banim inscribes in *The Boyne Water* a view of seventeenth-century history, and of his own time in the 1820s, that represents an alternative to the pronouncements of the genteel and pious M'Donnells. For these unruly subaltern rebels provide more than a mirror-image of the various armies—both Williamite and occasionally Jacobite—that they attack (and Banim's novel has often been criticized for its overly neat symmetries), standing instead for a cultural force that is much more elusive and unreadable. Moretti has noted that in Scott, as in the historical novel more generally, comic characters (such as

Bradwardine) tend to occupy border zones, which can generally be easily incorporated by the central power, while tragic ones (such as Fergus) lie beyond the border in the spaces of strongest resistance, which must be ruthlessly crushed.[46] Yet in this text, the most effective and inexhaustible resistance is embodied by these comic characters, who are at once less loyal (less committed to James) and more national (apparently ubiquitous, but steeped in local geography, and with all the cunning and "sly civility" of the native under colonial eyes)[47] than the rest of the Irish that Banim depicts. But the Rapparees, in relation to questions of sexuality, wildness, and marriage in the text, provide a critical commentary on the allegories of historical fiction.[48]

It is ironic that Banim, who aspired to write respectable and polite fiction, was constantly accused of vulgarity. Despite his best intentions to the contrary, he frequently introduces improper material in his narratives. (An instance of this in *The Boyne Water* would be his failed attempt to suppress the famous epithet attached to James II after his retreat from the Boyne, "Seamus-a-chaca" or "shitty James." Banim assures us that he will omit the "vulgar, cruel and unmerited Irish expletive, recollected to this day, but rather unsuited to our pages," and so has Rory-na-chopple repeat, "Shamus-a- . . . Shamus-a- is gone, sure enough" [477]. The text reminds us of what it would wish us to forget.) Even before their double-wedding ceremony at Antrim Castle is interrupted by the news that William of Orange has arrived in England to claim the throne, the air of gloom and foreboding that surrounds the nuptials of Edmund and Esther, and Robert and Eva, seems very much connected to that event which ordinarily would form no part of public discussion of the marriages: the consummation. Robert, for example, dreamed that he had just been married and "that he had entered the bridal chamber, and just pressed the bridal couch, when a skein was plunged into his breast" (144); and the women, as the wedding preparations proceed in the castle, "explored each other's destined anteroom, sitting-room, nay, bridal-chamber; never having courage, however, to bestow more than one glance at a time on the progressive furnishing of this last-mentioned terrible apartment" (159).

When Eva and Esther have their first disagreement, about the religious education of their future children, neither can bear to allude to the fact that "wives generally become mothers" (166) without much blushing. (Although no doubt Esther's apprehensions about the nuptials are greatly intensified when she visits the cave of the hag Oonagh, who shows her a vision of a skeleton wearing a bridal chaplet on its bony brow [165].) The wedding day itself begins ominously enough, with a violent storm raging. The plan is for both ceremonies to be performed first by a Catholic priest and then by Walker. But by the time the Protestant clergyman arrives, late in the evening, to announce triumphantly that William has landed, (Catholic) Eva and (Protestant) Robert have been married only according to the Catholic rite, and (Protestant) Esther and (Catholic) Edmund not married at all. And even with the howling of the wind and the shouting inside the church, Oonagh makes her gothic presence felt: "While her pallid face appeared now at one window, now at another, and her 'Never! never!' rising above the roof of the chapel, seemed to be a tongue of the tempest" (179).

During the siege of Derry, Edmund again tries to marry Esther, who is now gravely ill. But she dies shortly after this second failed wedding, still a maiden, seeing and hearing only the ghastly Oonagh as the ships that will relieve the city finally appear (349).

I would suggest that there is more to these scenes than the lesson (as Robert Evelyn rather anachronistically puts it) that politics interferes with people's private lives. Oonagh's motivations, of course, remain obscure until the end of the novel, yet despite the M'Donnells' brisk dismissal of superstition (on behalf of enlightened Catholicism), all of this woman's prophecies regarding the unfortunate Esther come true. The prominence and specific nature of these marital difficulties in a text that is at a political level chiefly concerned with a broken contract (Treaty of Limerick) is in itself significant. Carole Pateman has pointed out the anomalous nature of the traditional contract of marriage. She argues that although marriage is treated as the equivalent in the private sphere to the foundational social contract in the public sphere, it contracts women *into* civil society but *out* of legal personhood—creating a relationship of permanent insubordination that presents a difficulty for any liberal notion of contract. Moreover, unlike any other contract, marriage involves two steps: first the public exchange of vows, and then the private act of sexual consumption, without which the public contract is invalid.[49] Given the

preponderance of marital metaphors in the discourse of Anglo-Irish relations, especially after the Act of Union, it is surely worth attending to the
fact that the Irish Catholic heroine in this text spends most of the time
in the extraordinary position of a virgin wife, or half-contracted woman.
During the war, she begs her husband not to force her into "the wretched,
half-trusting, half-devoted intercourse which, if we at present meet, must
ensue between us" (270). Indeed, during her angry speech to James, after
his flight from the Boyne to Dublin, she makes a special virtue of her
virginity, declaring herself to be an Irishwoman "who has in her veins the
kindred blood already lavished to do you service—the blood that still
throbs to flow, maiden as she is, in your righteous cause" (482).

Of course, it could be argued that Eva is simply torn between her loyalty to one set of patriarchal values (based on the authority of her father,
the old king, and the Catholic Church) and an opposing one (her duty to
her husband). She does, after all, only very briefly refuse to acknowledge
that Robert is her husband at all (when her servant responds to Robert's
pleading letter to his wife by informing him that "no such person as Mrs.
Evelyn was known by the family" [184]). In the end she consents to stay
with him in Ireland, rather than leave with her brothers for France. Even
then she takes some persuading:

> "And do you, indeed, leave me, with but this mocking symbol of an
> eternal fate, once solemnly sworn at the altar?" asked Evelyn, catch-
> ing her arm, as, blinded with tears, she also put her foot on the boat,
> and *he showed her the marriage ring.* . . .
>
> Her husband grasped her hand, and replaced, unseen by any, the
> ring on her finger. Her brothers, not displeased, nor, on her account,
> sorry, saw which way God and woman's nature at last swayed her.
> They embraced their sister; she clung, sobbing, and almost shrieking,
> to them. The boat was about to move; *her husband caught her in his arms.*
> (549 and 551; emphasis mine)

However, in her rejection of Robert's insistence that it is more natural
for a woman to remain neutral in war than a man (269), and in his conviction, from the outset, that her "career," independent of him, is bound to be

"improper" (417), there is in the depiction of Eva something that goes well beyond the stereotypical image of the spirited Irish girl (as opposed to her gentler and more "English" friend Esther). This is reinforced by Robert's sense that when Eva assumes martial dress or, later, male attire, her new garments reveal rather than hide her true nature, which he at times fears is "coarse, masculine and vindictive" (187; see also, for example, 330).

It has always been regarded as a major weakness of *The Boyne Water* that Banim believed that it would be more acceptable for his English readers to make the liberal Protestant, Robert, both the main witness to events as they unfold and the mouthpiece for the novel's pro-Emancipation rhetoric. But this view underestimates the significance of the enigma that attaches to both of the M'Donnell siblings as they in effect disappear into a political and cultural underground for most of the novel: turned by their suffering and rage into Rapparees. Their stories cannot be narrated in any straightforward way but rather reach Robert in the form of shocking and scandalous rumors. Edmund finds an alter-ego in the shape of Yamen-ac-knunk, the Rapparee chief, although he eventually reemerges from the ranks of the outlaws chastened and subdued. Reports of Eva's progress are even more disturbing to Robert. At one time he believes that she has been raped and murdered, or has perhaps died for the loss of her virtue, but later he catches glimpses of her at the Battle of the Boyne, and at Kensington Palace, poised to assassinate King William. Finally, a mysterious friend informs him that his wife, now lost to shame, she has become a "ridin' Rapparee . . . a thrapsin' throllap that turns her back on him to go wid the Rapparee captains" (424).

But as Tom Moore wrote of another of Banim's stories: "[A] train of wonders is laid which explode in nothing, and the only solution given of all the marvels that have happened, is one still more marvellous and insoluble than any."[50] This is equally true of *The Boyne Water*. In fact, I suggest that what Moore identifies here as the disappearing plots and improbable anticlimaxes of Banim's novels would surely be central to any theory about the "structural compromises" that must be made in what we might call colonial realist fiction.[51] In this case, it is ultimately revealed that Eva has spent the war as a lady-in-waiting at King James's court in Dublin Castle. Robert has been misled by her resemblance to a long-lost brother who has conveniently reappeared, and by the incredible machinations of the jealous Moya, who is herself in love with Eva's husband. Eva's sojourn to a place beyond "God and woman's nature," and beyond the customary location of a woman in historical or domestic fiction, is abruptly ended; or rather, we are informed that in fact it never happened at all. The only problem is that this restoration of novelistic propriety actually involves a greater offense against realist *vraisemblance* than the more subversive story itself. In this way, perhaps, this novel—like the Banims' fiction more generally—remains at some distance from the epistemological and ethical norms that it nonetheless struggles to ratify. But the ultimately censored subtexts of *The Boyne Water* still retain some significant critical force in the context of Banim's commitment to producing an Irish version of Scott's historical novel.

In the introduction to *The Boyne Water*, Abel O'Hara tells his brother Barnes (the Banims' original pseudonyms) that he is confident that this novel will portray a more faithful likeness of those—meaning, primarily, William and James—whose identities have been "disguised according to the musty fanaticism prevailing two centuries ago" (14). Like Scott, they would wish to live in enlightened times, but their confidence that they do is frail. How exactly the revelation that there was political intrigue and personal fallibility on both sides in "the war of the two kings" is going to enable Irish people to recognize each other "as belonging to a common country" (13) is not worked out at all in the exchange between the O'Haras. But rather we can say that Banim's novel fails to subdue the difficulty of the Irish question. The concluding declaration of Robert Evelyn that "Englishmen will keep yet pay their fathers' debt of faith to Ireland" (553) has to be read in the light of his own great difficulties in his private contract of national reconciliation. (The novel ends with Robert's letter to Edmund; although Edmund is informed that Eva will be writing for herself, we never read her words.) But even after Eva has come back to her senses and her husband, she still has a bit part to play in Irish history as it is narrated in the novel.

As Patrick Sarsfield reluctantly prepares to sign the Treaty of Limerick in Ginkle's tent, he is interrupted by uproar and tumult outside, and by the cries of a "haggard and agitated" figure, who implores him to wait and listen to her. A bystander orders the mad woman to be put aside (546). The scene may be reminiscent of Oonagh's past appearances, but this is Eva M'Donnell, who much earlier on had similarly dismissed the prophecies of that "impostor" or "mad woman" (161). Eva has information about the imminent arrival of a ship from France, which would relieve the Jacobites. Sarsfield immediately regrets signing the document but is taunted by the accusation that, in breaking the treaty in the very hour as he had made it, he resembles all "perfidious Papists" who never keep their word (547). He later dies stricken with "rage, shame, remorse, and despair," praying in his final moments that, as Ireland was now "degraded and wretched, and he unable to assist her, he might no longer live" (551). Eva, the woman who initially left her marriage in the hour in which it was made, takes on the role of a Cassandra: Ireland is to be violated, not truly wed; like Oonagh, Eva's screams, too, "foresee and foretell" (543). In turn, Oonagh's torture of the unfortunate Esther is explained at the end of the text. She is Grace Nowlan, lover of another long-lost M'Donnell brother and the mother of his illegitimate child. She became mad after witnessing Donald M'Donnell and the baby being burned to death by her brothers in a black bog near his house: "And when the curious neighbors went to scrape among the ashes of the turf, they found two buttons of a man's coat, half melted away. That was all" (542).

She takes her revenge on M'Donnell's family by trying to ensure that no brother of his enjoys the wedding day she was denied. Although she apologizes for the trouble she caused Esther and the others, her madness no longer has the meaningless malevolence of a natural force, which she had ascribed to it:

> But you ask me for reasons—and reasons I cannot give. As well may you ask the sea why it crushes the ribs of the strong ship against the rock; or the wind why it tears up the stately tree; or the fire why it burns; or the water why it drowns. My mind was then without a reason for any thing, most of all for that; it dashed like the sea; roared like the wind; burned like the fire; all with that upon it. (540)

The traditional Irish unruliness of wild women and Rapparees (that also evokes the agrarian violence of the nineteenth century) has been deployed in this text to highlight the past crimes and the class position of the M'Donnells. Yet neither they nor other high-born families like them are the only or indeed the primary historical agents on the Irish side. Issues concerning violence, sexual violation, legality, and justice haunt the text's exploration of national marriage, the making and keeping of treaties, and the Banims' optimistic attempt to disperse "the mist that hangs over Irish ground" (13). In these ways, *The Boyne Water* disturbs and complicates the Scottian paradigm on which it was based, and the framework of a cowed, O'Connellite politics in which it has been interpreted in Ireland. If, as Moretti argues, the ultimate aim of the historical novel is to narrate the incorporation of the internal periphery into the larger unit of the state, a process that involves consent *and* coercion, then we might counter that Banim has problematized both love and war as the means to this end. Marriage as "the mutual desire of the more 'civilized spaces,'" and the achievement on the part of the state of "a monopoly of legitimate violence"[52] are put into question by this plot, which exposes the difficult conditions under which the (fictional) marriage and the (actual) treaty were contracted and instantly regretted by the subordinate or defeated parties. Banim may consciously have sought to illustrate that (in the words of one of Moore's melodies) "on *our* side is Virtue and Erin," or to plead alongside O'Connell:

> When, O when! will justice be rendered to thy sons, O loved fatherland! When, O when! will mankind recognise the just title of the Irish to preeminence in the most glorious virtues? to morality of the purest order, domestic and public? Temperance of the extensive and practical utility? Tenacious religious fidelity, beyond the example of all, or any of the countries on the face of Christendom?[53]

But while the text ostensibly preaches the necessity of submission to imposed forms of civility and counsels the oppressed to suffer virtuously, it also explores the formation of the underground resistance that was central to popular Irish consciousness, and to Irish Jacobite culture. Banim embraces the form of the historical novel, developed as the counterpart of an ideology of improvement and modernization, but balks at the celebration of that modern condition itself. He instead shows how progress had created a wildness—neither passive nor patient, but rather unruly, carnivalesque and often cruel—that persisted, unsubdued, into his own time.

Two years after *The Boyne Water*, Michael Banim wrote *The Croppy* (1828), the first full-scale historical novel about the Wexford Rebellion of 1798.[54] In it, he tries in various ways to depict and account for the "wild outbreak of the Irish peasant in 1798."[55] He lays particular emphasis on the absence of adequate leadership for the cruelly oppressed peasants and implicitly suggests that such leadership is precisely what his own class was to provide during the campaign for Catholic Emancipation. John Banim returned to further explorations of passive and violent resistance in two novels about the era of the Penal Laws, published together in 1830 under the general title of *The Denounced*. Daniel Darcy, the central figure of *The Conformists*, provides an image of a degenerate and utterly demoralized Catholic yeoman class that had become poor and indolent as a consequence of the legal restrictions on education and industry. Banim here, in effect, faces the wellnigh impossible task of writing about the historical significance of a class that was ruined to such a degree that its most typical representative is the young Daniel Darcy, a pathetic individual who cannot even get out of bed in the morning.[56] Daniel's sole achievements in the novel are his successful resistance of the sexual temptation offered by the voluptuous country girl Jinny, and his decision *not* to convert to Protestantism, which would have enabled him to disinherit his elder brother and turn his aged parents out of their house. *The Last Baron of Crana*, by contrast, is a final return to some of the motifs of *The Boyne Water*, with the underworld of peasant resistance again allegorized as the hidden face of Catholic accommodationism in the eighteenth century.

In *The Croppy* Michael Banim does not depict any upper-class Catholic families at all. This may reflect his grim view of the decay of Catholic society during the previous century, although the absence of any member of this class contributes to the sense of ethical and political confusion in the novel. We are not presented with a single character whose personal virtue or good judgment might help us to interpret the conflict that convulsed Wexford in the summer of 1798. Instead, all the various relationships between members of the elite household of Hartley Court (which is the focus of much of the plot of *The Croppy*) and the terrorized people are shown to be in some way corrupt or exploitative.

The scene in which the peasants gather in front of Hartley Court to entreat Sir Thomas Hartley to lead them into battle is both threatening and poignant, given the later sad fate of the rebel army. Sir Thomas is a liberal landlord and a former Irish Volunteer, but he shrinks from the "vortex" of 1798 (*Croppy* 1:276). His daughter Eliza is caught between two rivals for her hand in marriage: Sir William Judkin, who appears to be sympathetic to the croppies and eventually conducts their attack on Enniscorthy, and Henry Talbot, the leader of the local Yeomanry corps. But Sir William is a villain who wants to enter Enniscorthy only to gain possession of Eliza despite the fact that he is married to another woman. Talbot is a man of honor and ultimately becomes Eliza's husband. However, we are never granted access to his consciousness during the story; Banim cannot, it seems, represent the thoughts of a virtuous *loyalist* soldier. Belinda, Eliza's schoolfriend, has a strange affinity with the rebels. Her nocturnal rambles are associated by the Hartleys' servants with the "roarin' work at the anvil" (1:109) in the local blacksmith's forge, where pikes and other weapons are being made by night, in preparation for the approaching conflagration; later, Belinda moves about, apparently at will, among the rebel forces. All this is eventually explained by the revelation that she is Judkin's abandoned wife, seeking vengeance for his murder of their unborn child. Belinda also has an unexpected biological link with the most malign representative of the lower-class Irish depicted in the novel. Although her mother is a lady, her father is Rattlin' Bill Nate, a mountebank and conjurer, who swears many rebels into the United Irish "Waxford army o' freedom" (2:15). Nate's corruption is ultimately demonstrated not by his sedition but by his treachery toward his own people: he is an informer, an agent of the Crown forces.

Certainly, there is little indication in *The Croppy* that the peasant mobilization has any autonomous logic or strategy (and it is interesting to note that while the title promises an analysis of some particular rebel, maybe even a romantic version of such a figure, we never meet any obvious candidate for such a role). In this it is at odds with some of the other Banim novels, especially those written by John. The opening chapters of the third volume of *The Croppy* dwell on the atrocities committed by the inebriated, vengeful mob at the height of the rebels' campaign. Banim comments on the "ribald mirth" (3:263) of the pikemen, but this carnivalesque element in the rebellion is regarded as entirely enigmatic and sinister. The Irish peasant, Banim tells us, conceals the terrible secrets of his "inner heart" not only from his oppressor, but also from the "friends who, if they knew him better, could better serve him" (3:7). There is a nervous footnote about the massacre at Scullabogue, suggesting that the sectarian violence should not be attributed to the "general body of the armed peasants," but rather to the "cowardly who had fled the battle," or those who were "maddened into revenge by burnings or torturings inflicted on themselves or upon their relatives" (3:233–34).

Banim's condemnation of the rebels' ferocity lacks the terrible detail of, for example, his description of the attack on Shawn-na-Gow's forge and the torture and murder of the blacksmith's son in the second volume. None of the rebels' victims are individualized in this way. Banim is here preoccupied by finding the means adequately to represent bodily suffering and the emotional effects it produces (this leads him to be somewhat dismissive of the distress suffered by the romantic heroine Eliza as she undergoes abduction, or what Banim calls the "customary calamity of novels" [3:162]). He appeals to the patience of his English readers, whose "privileged persons" have never experienced "a touch of Despotism's most darling mode of coercion— bodily torture" (2:37); the behavior of the military in Wexford, he argues, made "open insurrection . . . almost necessary" (2:38–39). Father Rourke, the priest who goes over to the peasant army, first asks himself: "Which is it better for a man—to die on his own green sod, fighting against his cruel enemies; or stay at home, to be flogged like a negro, or strung up by the blaze of his own cabin?" (2:85).

Peter Rooney, a dapper little tailor and a United Irish organizer, who appears to be a rather absurd figure when we first encounter him, later bears "hundreds of lashes" rather than inform on his comrades; thus he achieves "what would be called heroism in another cause" (2:204). When Shawn-na-Gow, the blacksmith, discovers Bill Nate's treachery, he calls not to heaven to witness his vengeance but to his murdered son: "Tom, my boy, can you see us?" (3:309). The final sentence of the novel is concerned not with the public business of the national marriage of Britain and Ireland, nor even with Eliza's happier union with Talbot, but with the priest's executed body. This is how the torturer, Smyly, who was responsible for the death of the blacksmith's son and who drove the priest to arms, is deprived of the pleasure of witnessing his final victory over Rourke: "Father Rourke was hanged upon the bridge of Wexford; the weight of his colossal body having broken the rope, however, before Saunders Smyly saw him pending to his heart's content" (3:318).

The Last Baron of Crana is set in the immediate aftermath of the Battle of Aughrim with which *The Boyne Water* ends. In the opening scene, a dying Jacobite, Sir Redmond O'Burke, begs his Williamite opponent, Miles Prendergast, to find and protect his only surviving son, Philip, who will now inherit the ancient Irish title of Baron of Crana. Prendergast finds the son very much reconciled to William's victory and with no nostalgia for "hard knocks and short commons in the service of old Shamus."[57] However, we eventually learn that that Philip has an elder brother, Patrick, who is still living. He is Randal Oge O'Hagan, the infamous Rapparee. Because the elder son had forfeited his inheritance for rebellion, Philip discovers that not only is he *not* the true baron, but that the title and the estate are lost to his family forever.

This is how Philip describes his brother, who is hiding near the ruins of Dunluce Castle in Ulster, when Patrick's true identity is revealed: "There, upon that rock—among these ruins—like himself and his name—begirt with the savage sea at one side and with common thief catchers at the other—there, a common thief—and the surrendered prisoner of those blood-money men—there, good boy, skulks the real and last Baron of Crana!" (*Last Baron*, 185).

These *two* last barons seem to embody the most intense conflict in the novel, between the various possible responses to the shipwreck of Irish Catholics after the Battle of Aughrim, in which the secret baron eventually (although unwittingly) destroys his brother's attempt to live with the new political settlement. The final undoing of Philip, the law-abiding baron, is accomplished by the lust of yet another wild-eyed madwoman, who turns out to be his own niece, born and abandoned while his brother Patrick was in political exile in Spain. This woman, Louise, is initially tolerated by Philip's family as an unfortunate guest and an object of their charity, but ultimately stands revealed as a true daughter of Castle Crana. She represents, in other words, another version of the "bold carelessness of mind" (224) that her Rapparee father also displays in his criminal career. Such behavior, although presented as inescapably inherited, is nonetheless also presented as the more blamable and unseemly in a young woman of marriageable age. The image of the last remnant of an ancient clan or race is, of course, a powerfully romantic one in Scott, as in other historical novels (most famously, James Fenimore Cooper's *The Last of the Mohicans* [1826]). Banim, though, offers no sense of a glorious sunset for these last remnants of the Gaelic order. Instead, a rather suspiciously cheerful attempt at compromise is completely destroyed by the fateful reappearance of an heir who had not been safely killed off. At the end of the novel all but the reprobate brother must leave Ireland and go abroad. Even though Patrick swears that he will cause no further trouble, there seems to be little reason to believe him.

For here, the vision of reconciliation in Ireland is rooted in the imagined acceptance of the Williamite settlement, which itself had been the basis of and stimulus for rebellion and resentment ever since the 1690s. This Rapparee's promise would frequently be broken, according to the Banimian version of the Irish political world. In the conventional realist novel, the ethical imperative of such a promise would effectively be detached from the political conditions that enforced the making of it in the first place. The fiction of the Banims ostensibly sponsors the ethical values of the private, individual character, but their stories also explore the history and significance of the usually violent behavior that is regarded as the preserve of the extremist. It is precisely such extremism that turns out to be the key to understanding the collective and political life represented in these novels.

Afterword: William Carleton's "Wildgoose Lodge"

W. B. Yeats declared that the novelist William Carleton (1794–1869) was "the creator of a new imaginative world, the demiurge of a new tradition."[58] By this Yeats meant that it was Carleton, rather than Edgeworth or the Banims, who had successfully depicted Irish peasant culture through the medium of English for the first time. Only Carleton, "born and bred a peasant, was able to give us the vast multitude of grotesque, pathetic, humorous persons, misers, pig-drivers, drunkards, schoolmasters, labourers, priests, madmen, and to fill them all with an abounding vitality."[59]

The Banims, too, were familiar with the world of ordinary folk, but "unlike him, they covered the peasant life they knew with a melodramatic horde of pirates and wealthy libertines whom they did not know." In contrast to Griffin or his successor Kickham, Yeats judged that Carleton was mercifully free of the middle-class tendency to "moralise with ease."[60]

Yeats's view that Carleton is the first significant native Irish writer of fiction in English remains generally accepted (for example, he is the earliest author in this line discussed by Declan Kiberd in his comprehensive historical study, *Irish Classics*).[61] Following Yeats, authenticity is frequently mentioned as the key feature of Carleton's writing. Carleton's early *Traits and Stories of the Irish Peasantry* (1830–33), in particular, appears to offer direct description of characters and scenes from the author's own childhood in the bilingual and largely preliterate society of rural Ulster; his depiction of the wild, boisterous energy of the people is all the more poignant given the imminence of the Great Famine of the late 1840s.

But authenticity, especially when identified by a member of one class and sect as the recognizable feature of another, is always a suspect category. Indeed, the political and ideological significance of Carleton's much-praised truthfulness has proved remarkably difficult to gauge.[62] Over the course of his long career, Carleton apparently adopted a range of political opinions, attacking both Catholic superstition and Orange supremacy in his novels. Kiberd suggests that the chronic "instability" of Carleton's writing merely reflects the "maimed and enfeebled" culture on which he reported; the Irish people had surrendered their language and many of their customs in a bid for the benefits of modernity, and had been rewarded by devastation.[63] Morash argues that ultimately Carleton found consistent moral value only in the "family of the prosperous small farmer," especially after his faith in any general social improvement was shaken by the horror of famine.[64]

But if for no other reason than that nationalism would have been the most obvious affiliation for a member of an emerging class—or for what Antonio Gramsci called an organic intellectual—the question of Carleton's resistance to it merits further attention. The transformation of the "Catholic question" into the "national question" in the decades after Emancipation was inevitable, yet complicated.[65] O'Connell's campaign for the Repeal of the Act of Union was not as successful as his earlier mobilization of the Irish masses; in 1846 the more radical leaders of the Young Ireland movement withdrew from his Repeal Association, staging their own abortive insurrection two years later. But Carleton's reluctance to embrace his inherited cultural identity is not really explicable by reference to this political context.

In an autobiographical sketch, Carleton comments caustically on the assumption of his parents and neighbors that he was destined to become a Catholic priest, simply because they were so impressed by the "pedantic bombast"[66] that came out of his mouth. He states that in fact he was "as great a young literary coxcomb as ever lived" (*Traits* 1:xv), a typical if precocious student of the hedge-school educational system, which was by Carleton's time associated with a stylized, prolix autodidacticism. Carleton evidently abandoned any thought of a religious vocation, together with his faith in Catholicism when, at the age of about nineteen, he undertook a pilgrimage to St. Patrick's Purgatory in Donegal. This trip was the inspiration for a story, "The Lough Derg Pilgrim," which was much admired by his early patron, the evangelical Caesar Otway, and represented for Carleton his *"début* in literature" (*Traits* 1:xvi). Clearly, acceding to independent manhood, turning his back on "superstition," and the discovery of a serviceable and marketable style of writing are all closely associated in the mind of this author. A similar trajectory can be observed in Carleton's relationship with the agrarian secret societies. He tells us that he was inducted into the Ribbonmen's conspiracy "before I had time to pause or reflect on the consequences."[67] Later, in the tale "Wildgoose Lodge," Carleton produces the most celebrated work about agrarian crime in nineteenth-century Irish literature, one of the salient features of which is the total contrast between the first-person narrator's formal, disciplined literary language and his own speech as he reports it:

> "Well," said I, "I'll jist trust to God and the consequences, for the cowld, Paddy, ma bouchal; but a blessed dhrop of it won't be crossin' my lips, avick; so no more ghosther about it;—dhrink it yourself, if

you like. Maybe you want it as much as I do; wherein I've the patthern of a good big-coat upon me, so thick, your sowl, that if it was rainin' bullocks, a dhrop wouldn't get undher the nap of it."

He gave me a calm, but keen glance, as I spoke. (*Traits* 2:352)[68]

It is no coincidence that the protagonist is here declining the whiskey offered by the ringleader of the Ribbon gang, just as he will later hold back from participation in the atrocious deeds that the men commit. He pulls his thick, protective coat around him and reveals his subtlety to the reader by showing, in the detailed attentiveness to "authentic" dialect here, how he affects to be without it. The narrator adopts this self-consciously accented speech to show how well he is performing the role of the innocent. This makes the authenticity question even more barbed than usual.

Of course, even a writer who describes himself as "the son of a man who was one of the people" (*Traits* 1:xi) will necessarily have to find some vantage point outside that culture if he is to seek "a position in Irish literature" (2:xv). Carleton's early conversion to Protestantism meant that he was inclined to understand the distinction between himself and his community of origin primarily in religious rather than in class terms. While the Banims and other novelists depict a vertical cross-section of Irish society (however inexpertly, as Yeats complains), Carleton displaces larger class distinctions onto differences between particular rural families in his novels. It is true that the peasantry was not a homogenous social group, and that Carleton believed that the Irish poor were indeed the victims of a cruelly oppressive system. But in "The Lough Derg Pilgrim," he had described looking to the south toward Lough Erne, seeing

> the Protestant city of Enniskillen rising amidst its waters, like the island queen of all the loyalty, and industry, and reasonable worship that have made her sons the admiration of past and present time; and before me, to the north, Lough Derg, with its far-famed isle, reposing there as the monstrous birth of a dreary and degraded superstition, the enemy of mental cultivation, and destined to keep the human understanding in the same dark unproductive state as the moorland waste that lay outstretched around. (*Traits* 1:238)

Although Carleton toned down the anti-Catholic polemic of his early works, he consistently dwells on the key social contrast between the productive and the rational, on the one hand, and "complacent volubility"[69] on the other. This can often be mapped onto a purely sectarian division. In *The Emigrants of Ahadarra* (1848), for example, he suggests that if emigration to the colonies could clear the "great mass of pauperism which lies like an incubus on the energies of the country" (*Emigrants,* 153), it would be no bad thing. Instead, "the prudent, the industrious, and the respectable" (281) flee from Ireland, attempting to escape that "loose and unsettled population" that possesses within itself "a fearful facility of reproduction" (283).[70] It is not difficult to deduce that "paupers" are usually papists.[71]

Some elements in Carleton's writing were open for recuperation by a Catholic nationalist ideology of improvement and modernization.[72] But in general, the absence of any interest in Catholic leadership in Carleton means that he never ventures beyond liberal Unionism, the aesthetic as well as the political shortcomings of which had been grasped even by Edgeworth and Morgan by the end of the first decade of the nineteenth century. Curiously, it is precisely this feature of Carleton that makes him so attractive to the fin de siècle Yeats, who was then developing his own version of an antimodern, aristocratic nationalism. Carleton's account of the vitality of the folk and their endless capacity for superstitious belief sits very well with Yeats's critique of what he took to be the modern, anemic, and secularizing spirit. All these people needed was a leadership that was sympathetic to their wildness, even participated to some degree in it, but was distinct from it—a cultural officer corps or "a company of leading men." A conversion like that of Carleton's has for such an ideology a wonderful symbolic value; it retains wildness and Irish authenticity but brings with it a measure of control. This is why Yeats sniffs at the works of those middle-class Catholic authors in which he hears "the accent of people who have not the recklessness of the landowning class, nor the violent passions of the peasantry, nor the good frankness of either."[73]

But the limitations of Carleton's representational strategies are evident in "Wildgoose Lodge." This story is based on a notorious raid on a well-to-do Catholic household in Co. Louth in 1818, during which numerous members of the Lynch family were burned to death; the attack was a punishment for one family member's testimony against some local Ribbonmen. Although Carleton offers an analysis of the causes of agrarian crime in his introduction to *Traits and Stories of the Irish Peasantry,* he omits any such contextualizing discourse from "Wildgoose Lodge." Indeed, the story has been highly rated for its supposed aesthetic qualities of vividness and concentration, which seem to be further enhanced by its avoidance of the lengthy historical and polemical asides that, in their formal delinquency, are so typical of nineteenth-century Irish fiction in general. But Carleton's exclusive commitment to the viewpoint of an individual participant/eyewitness, together with his overreliance on conventional Gothic tropes of sublimity and horror, actually weaken any attempt to throw light on the phenomenon of communal violence.[74]

The narrator recounts how he is summoned to a meeting of the Ribbonmen in the Catholic chapel, where they drink and take oaths of loyalty to the society. Carleton emphasizes the eerie beauty of the scene as the band makes its way toward the house of their intended victims: "There we stood, about a hundred and thirty in number, our dark forms bent forward, peering into the dusky expanse of water, with its dim gleams of reflected light, broken by the weltering of the mimic waves into a thousand fragments, whilst the few stars that overhung it in the firmament appeared to shoot through it in broken lines, and be multiplied fifty-fold in the gloomy mirror on which we gazed" (2:357).

He notes how the faces of the captain (later named as Patrick Devann) and of the men in his inner circle are transformed during their contemplation of their evil plans. In such passages as the following, Carleton strains to produce the appropriately Gothic flourishes:

His lips were half open, and the corners of his mouth a little brought back on each side, *like those* of a man expressing intense hatred and triumph over an enemy who is the death-struggle under his grasp. His eyes blazed from beneath his knit eyebrows with a fire that *seemed* to be lighted up in the infernal pit itself. It is unnecessary, and only painful, to describe the rest of his gang; demons *might have been proud* of such horrible visages as they exhibited; for they worked under all the power of hatred, revenge, and joy; and these passions blended into one terrible scowl, *enough almost* to blast any human eye that would venture to look upon it. (2:358; emphasis mine)

The violence perpetrated by the Ribbon men, especially against the women and children of Wildgoose Lodge, is described in horrific detail. After the house has been completely destroyed and the attackers disperse, Carleton offers us two endings to this "tale of terror." First we conclude with what is presumably the voice of the narrator, who reports on the executions of the leading insurgents and the exhibition of their bodies outside the cabins of their families. This, he informs us, illustrates the central political and religious lesson of the tale: "I thought in my heart how seldom, even in this world, justice fails to overtake the murderer, and to enforce the righteous judgment of God—that 'whoso sheddeth man's blood, by man shall his blood be shed.'" But in a postscript we are told (presumably by Carleton writing in his own voice):

Devann, the ringleader, hung for some months in chains, within about a hundred yards of his own house, and about half a mile from Wildgoose Lodge. His mother could neither go into nor out of her cabin, without seeing his body swinging from the gibbet. Her usual exclamation on looking at him was—"God be good to the sowl of my poor martyr!" The peasantry, too, frequently exclaimed, on seeing him, "Poor Paddy!" A gloomy fact that speaks volumes! (2:362)[75]

The two endings are entirely dissonant. Clearly, official violence has not produced the appropriate effect on those who contemplate the decaying bodies (although perhaps it did on the narrator). Nothing in the story has prepared us to consider Devann and the others as members of a family or community. Hence, we are likely to dismiss this mother and her neighbors as merely degenerate. Alternatively, we can suggest that any explanation of the systematic violence of their world—the violence of the militarized state as well as of the protean and often feeble secret societies that oppose its depredations—will involve modes other than the Gothic. The Banims had inaugurated such a fictional exploration of Irish conditions years before.

3

Irish Pastoral

Griffin's *The Collegians* as National Allegory

Gerald Griffin's *The Collegians* (1829) and Charles J. Kickham's *Knocknagow* (1873) are generally recognized as the novels in which an Irish Catholic sensibility achieves its earliest definition. Like Moore's *Melodies*, both are marked by a "peculiar blend of politeness and sentimentality"[1] and appear to owe little to the more subversive and uneven line in nineteenth-century Irish writing that I have traced to Moore's *Memoirs of Captain Rock*. *Knocknagow* in particular, the most popular Irish novel of the nineteenth century, is the outstanding Irish example of what Doris Sommer has described in the context of Latin America as a "foundational fiction," or romantic novel of national consolidation.[2] Both Griffin and Kickham forecast a rosy and secure future for Irish Catholics. Their optimism requires a suppression of much of the actuality of Irish historical experience, which is accompanied by the rendering of Irish customs as immemorial. This was an important step in the mutation of history into "traditional" culture, a suitably sanitized version of which would eventually become official in Catholic-dominated independent Ireland.

Although Griffin's plot is borrowed from a sensational murder case of his own day, *The Collegians* is set some fifty years earlier. The 1770s were a relatively promising time for Irish Catholics, and we are told at the end of the novel that one of the characters, Lowry Looby, lived long enough to vote (presumably for O'Connell) in the Clare election of 1828. By framing his story in this way, Griffin avoids any engagement with 1798 or with the vicissitudes of the struggle for Catholic Emancipation. Charles Kickham (1826–82) was a prominent Fenian and a former political prisoner, but *Knocknagow* reflects little of this radical and eventful career. The novel is a chronicle of village life in Tipperary. Although the community has known famine, mass evictions, and emigration, Kickham's tone is generally nostalgic rather than angry. At the end of the story, the surviving country folk look forward quite sanguinely to the imminent liberation of the country by its Irish American sons; in the final scene, as James Cahalan puts it, "[T]he remaining characters sit happily and incongruously listening to flute music, surrounded by rural devastation."[3]

To be sure, the repressed often returns in these stories. For instance, it is ironic that Griffin, who set out to provide "a softening corollary" to the "passionate romance"[4] of the Banims, was inspired on this occasion by the brutal killing of an innocent peasant girl. *The Collegians* tells the story of Kyrle Daly and Hardress Cregan, two young graduates of Trinity College, Dublin. Kyrle is from a well-to-do Catholic family in Co. Limerick; Hardress is a son of the dissolute local gentry. (However, the Cregans are apparently Catholics; toward the conclusion of the novel, Hardress attends Mass with his mother in Listowel [*Collegians*, 192].) They are rivals for the affections of the heiress Anne Chute, who is more drawn to the energetic, reckless Hardress than to the sober, reasonable Kyrle. However, Hardress has already cast his eye on Eily O'Connor, the daughter of a poor tradesman. He seduces Eily into a clandestine marriage but soon grows tired of his bride's simple charms and hides her away in the mountains of Kerry. But before the long-anticipated wedding of Hardress and Anne can take place, Eily's body is discovered. She has been killed by Hardress's servant, Danny Mann, in the belief that he was following his master's command to get rid of his abandoned wife. Hardress is found guilty of murder and dies on board the ship that is carrying him away from Ireland. The way is now clear for Kyrle to be united with Anne. Yet *The Collegians* is seriously weakened by the fact that this couple's courtship is so lacking in "passionate romance." This is one indication of the degree of stress that these novels undergo in their formulaic attempts to produce an Irish counterpart to an emerging Victorian domestic ideology. They had no easily available, persuasive alternatives to the sexual and class alliances that generally offered such satisfying resolutions of the issues central to the English novel since Richardson's *Pamela* (1740).

The plots of many English novelists, from Richardson to Jane Austen or Charlotte Brontë, are concerned with strong-minded but impeccably virtuous women from humble backgrounds, who eventually succeed in reforming and marrying dashing aristocrats. This might be read as reflecting the historical condition of the English bourgeoisie after the Glorious Revolution, which preferred compromise with the old ruling order to revolutionary war against it. Franco Moretti suggests that this in part accounts for the Cinderella-like fairy-tale quality of the English novel, compared to the more radical continental tradition.[5] Nancy Armstrong, however, has more recently commented on the extraordinary reluctance of Victorian novelists to depict any impressive middle-class men at all. This too is part of the explanation for bourgeois women's attraction to upper-class partners. The shortage of acceptable middle-class males in Victorian novels illustrates a telling problem for bourgeois sexual arrangements: The "competitive masculinity required for economic success is evidently not at all that 'agreeable' to women" and does not foster the affective bond necessary for the creation of an adequate home.[6] How then might such issues of class and gender play out in the Irish context, where the situation of the rising middle class was complicated by sectarian conflict and the struggle for national autonomy?

The Irish novel of middle-class courtship and marriage is also afflicted by what Armstrong calls a "crisis of masculinity." In the case of the national tale, a hero such as Mortimer in Morgan's *The Wild Irish Girl* has cultural legitimacy bestowed on him by marrying the impoverished Gaelic princess, Glorvina. What would the equivalent be in the cozy Catholic-bourgeois world of the Daly family in *The Collegians* (a milieu successfully realized here for the first time in Irish fiction)? A union between Kyrle Daly and the beautiful but lowly Eily, daughter of a Garryowen rope-maker, might seem to have offered the best allegory of O'Connell's (and Griffin's) hopes for Ireland after Emancipation: national progress under responsible and educated native leadership. But this is an impossible prospect because, as Kyrle tells Hardress, he favors elegance over simplicity (*Collegians*, 83). Kyrle prefers Anne to any colleen he could pluck from "the wild orchard of nature" (83); in effect, he chooses wealth and respectability over beauty and folk culture. But the novel remains haunted by its betrayed national heroine, Eily, who had her first fatal encounter with Hardress on St. Patrick's Day, her birthday. Modern rationality (represented by the Dalys) can evidently not be wedded to what Deane refers to as the "delinquent nationality" (represented by Eily and the other colorful rural characters)[7] with which *The Collegians* is otherwise so obsessed, and the alternative national marriage of Kyrle and Anne is thoroughly unconvincing. Eily, in contrast, falls for the charming Hardress, who is presented not only as a charismatic feudal hero much loved by the common people but as a Catholic to boot. In other words, Eily is in love with a gentleman, for all that the likes of Kyrle might imagine themselves to be the champions of her class.

A number of historical conditions help to explain Kyrle's lack of charisma. To begin with, he is not even a "successful competitive male," having merely inherited a comfortable class position from his father. Mr. Daly, in turn, was passively promoted to the status of middleman when "the country was deserted by its gentry" (25). He is, in other words, a beneficiary of absentee landlordism. But even if the Dalys had not been so fortunate, there is apparently no active way, in the society that Griffin depicts, to advance one's position, other than through corruption and exploiting the poor. This is made explicit by the hero of *Tracy's Ambition*, who laments that he ever experienced the thirst for wealth and influence, wishing only that he "were still contented to let my desires keep pace with the even course of Nature herself" (*Rivals; Tracy*, 244). In Defoe's *Robinson Crusoe* (1719), for example, such rhetoric is contradicted by the protagonist's success and prosperity. But, as Kiberd puts it, during the heroic phase of the bourgeoisie elsewhere in Europe, "Ireland produced not so much a middle class as its caricature: the middlemen, the consumerist parasites."[8]

The sociologist Max Weber famously coupled the Protestant work ethic with "the spirit of capitalism."[9] Ian Watt, in turn, explored the connections between Protestant, middle-class individualism and English literary realism in his hugely influential *The Rise of the Novel* (1957);[10] two years later, Flanagan regretted that the "power and range" of early Irish fiction was limited by the fact that questions such as those of creed and nationality overshadowed the issues of "personal morality" with which the English novelist was primarily concerned.[11] But we might say more accurately that personal morality is determined by a different set of historical conflicts in the Irish novel. In Griffin, for example, we have a Catholic modernizer who nonetheless clearly doubts whether, in Weber's terms, virtue and worldly reward can ever go together. For this novelist, true Christianity and literature were ultimately in contradiction with each other, and he eventually dedicated himself to the former, burning his manuscripts before becoming a Christian Brother. But even while he was still writing novels, he articulates a moral critique of modern luxury that scarcely seems demanded by the conditions in which the mass of Irish people actually subsisted in this era. Eily's uncle, the gentle Father Edward, may speak for Griffin himself when he exclaims: "Oh, world! world! world! You are a great stage coach with fools for outside passengers; a huge round lump of earth, on the surface of which men seek for peace, but find it only when they sink beneath" (*Collegians*, 159).

Such tensions and even contradictions in Griffin's ideological position mean that *The Collegians* cannot work as a straightforward fable about the creation of a satisfactory world of either middle-class enterprise or respectable conjugal bliss. Neither is it a particularly happy allegory of Catholic-nationalist emergence. But at the same time, an appreciation of Griffin's difficulties helps us to account for the text's characteristic atmosphere and appeal. Some of its more striking formal features also facilitated its adaptation to stage melodrama and opera.

Throughout the novel, public as well as private space is curiously foreshortened and intimate. After the vivid narrative of the "rise and fall of Garryowen" at the beginning of the book, the scenes introducing the Daly family also show us a thickly populated and lively rural landscape, now glimpsed through the open windows of the dining room where they are eating their substantial breakfast. When Hardress's pleasure boat, the *Nora Creina*, passes by on the river, the Dalys can see every detail of its green hull "and white sails and beautiful green colors flying over her peak and gaff-topsail" (16) through their handy telescope; they even speculate about the identity of the mysterious woman in the blue cloak who is sitting aboard with Hardress and Danny Mann. Shortly afterwards, as Kyrle goes to visit Anne Chute to ask for her hand in marriage, he sees the *Nora Creina*'s green flag lowered in greeting as she glides past Castle-Chute. Kyrle again observes the blue-hooded figure, as the boat is nearly destroyed by a storm just before Hardress arrives at Dairy Cottage where he has a crucial conversation with his old college friend (72). At the end of the novel, as Hardress is being carried away from Ireland in punishment for his crime, he enjoys a panoramic yet—once again—microscopically detailed view of Garryowen, the Daly house, and Castle-Chute. Limerick already feels like a theatrical set: All Dion Boucicault had to do when he based the wildly popular melodrama *The Colleen Bawn* (1860) on Griffin's novel was to move all the action to the even more picturesque location of the Lakes of Killarney.[12]

The woman on the *Nora Creina* is of course Eily, whom Hardress is bringing to her ruin. Her garment recalls images of the Virgin Mary, and in her passivity she is an emblem of long-suffering, devoted Irish Catholics. Her blue cloak is last seen in a boghole when her body is discovered by a pack of hunting dogs. The corpse is covered by a "large blue mantle, drenched in wet and mire" (225), which reveals only a pair of small feet in Spanish-leather shoes and a mass of fair hair. As Hardress watches the discovery of the remains of his murdered young wife, it "astonished him to find that all emotion came upon the instant to a dead pause within his breast" (226). Certainly, the dreamlike recurrence of the blue cloak, and Hardress's experience of blank shock, seem of a piece with Griffin's disjunctive style in the novel more generally as he narrates a tale of crime and atrocity in a tone of casual and irrepressible good humor. Eagleton ascribes the self-indulgent "narrative buoyancy" of *The Collegians* to the fact that Griffin is a member of a rising rather than a falling class, but we should also account for the way in which what Eagleton somewhat dismissively calls the novel's "theatrical anguish" is nonetheless historically determined.[13] Inevitably, the formal techniques characteristic of this variety of realist fiction are quite different to those we find in other kinds of realism.

Siobhán Kilfeather has analyzed Griffin's treatment of simultaneity in the novel, noting how often different plots and subplots unfold in adjacent spaces at the same time, or even in different rooms of the same house.[14] We might further suggest that Griffin's elaborate construction of social unity—the busy *tableaux*, the backdrop of natural sublimity, the anecdotes and fragments of superstition, the overheard songs—are a substitute for a more organic notion of social totality, conventionally associated with a mature realist aesthetic. Lukács, for example, understood realism as a form in which key social forces are embodied by typical individuals. Here, by contrast, individuals take up parts in a hectic performance of nationality. The color and energy of this display serve to disguise underlying difficulties and divisions, as in the case of Catholic Ireland's bad conscience about the common people in this novel. Although she is an obedient Catholic, Eily also belongs to the exuberant world of Garryowen and its popular festivity. In her time of greatest trouble, she turns to her uncle, Father Edward, who is an idealized example of a humble country priest. These were the kind of images of Irish Catholicism cherished by liberal Catholics throughout Europe and especially in France; Montalembert, the leader of the French liberals, pointed to Daniel O'Connell as proof that Catholicism could be on the side of popular democracy.[15] But the destruction of Eily in *The Collegians* may suggest that official Irish Catholicism would have difficulties allying itself with the folk. Over the course of the nineteenth century, pro-Vatican centralizers led by Cardinal Cullen, Archbishop of Armagh and later of Dublin, were to completely outflank nationalist Church leaders such as Archbishop MacHale of Tuam.

Eily O'Connor's death was written out of Boucicault's *The Colleen Bawn* and the later operetta by Julius Benedict, *The Lily of Killarney* (1862). At the end of *The Colleen Bawn*, Eily reappears and is embraced by her repentant husband. She is even invited to "spake" in her own natural and "national" accent.[16] The problem of national vivacity or unruliness, of course, did not loom so large in the later nineteenth century; the catastrophe of the Famine had seen to that. But it could be argued that Boucicault and later artists simply repressed any anxieties about all that Eily O'Connor stands for more successfully than Griffin managed to do. For in one form or another, the Colleen Bawn had to be revived again and again in Irish art.

When Kickham renews the project of the Irish national novel fifty years after *The Collegians*, he chooses as the central hero of *Knocknagow* another example of a nonbourgeois male, the laborer Mat the Thrasher. But before the "rollickingest, rovingest blade in all Tipperary"[17] can become a family man, Mat has a definite task to perform. He must win his sweetheart Bessy back from the temptations and dangers of modern life beyond the little village. For this national romance to succeed, the lovers (especially the woman) must recommit themselves to their native place.[18] The attempt to elaborate a vision of a happy future for Mat, Bessy, and Knocknagow involves Kickham in an innovative fictional treatment of historical trauma and the forms of collective identity it produces. For long stretches of the novel, Mat and Bessy's protracted courtship is sidelined as a large cast of secondary characters occupies our attention. In this way, Kickham experiments with the depiction of village life against the horizon of a national community-to-be.

The "Dead Past" and the "Living Present":
Keeping Time in Kickham's *Knocknagow*

Fredric Jameson has suggested that allegory is an especially significant literary mode for writers from the colonized or "third world," in whose texts "the telling of the individual story and the individual experience cannot but ultimately involve the whole laborious telling of the experience of the collectivity itself."[19] While it could be countered that such allegorization is characteristic of virtually all realist texts to some degree, Jameson's remarks seem to have a remarkable relevance to many of the Irish novels I have discussed here. Kickham's *Knocknagow*, in contrast, offers a model of a rather different style of national allegory.

The most extraordinary feature of this novel for many of its readers is the *disjunction* between its depiction of an Irish rural idyll and historical actuality. This is all the more surprising given Kickham's public, political affiliations. Between the 1840s and 1870s, he had progressed from a fairly standard middle-class enthusiasm for O'Connell (he came from a family of relatively prosperous shopkeepers in Mullinahone, Co. Tipperary) to an outright rejection of constitutional and parliamentary politics. He was sworn into the Fenian Irish Republican Brotherhood in 1861 and attended its first convention in Chicago two years later. He spent several years as a political prisoner in British jails. On his release as a semi-invalid, he remained an important figurehead within the movement, and in Fenian theory was president of the Irish Republic for many years.[20] But in his fiction, often dismissed as blandly pastoral, Kickham endeavors to preserve a notion of an Irish sacred space of endearing "home affections" that not even the worst of British imperialism could penetrate. For the most part, *Knocknagow* relies on anecdote and repetition; the realm of local color and unique personal experience that it depicts is largely autonomous, without any allegorical or other attachments or implications.[21]

Some commentators on Kickham, however, might suggest that there is in truth no real contradiction between his politics and his aesthetic. For his biographer R. V. Comerford, the idealizing haze through which Kickham views his Tipperary peasants is typical of the mindset of Irish nationalism (and it seems peculiarly appropriate for this view of the author that Kickham himself ended up almost completely deaf and blind as the result of a childhood accident). *Knocknagow*, which Comerford describes as the national epic of the rural-oriented majority that dominated independent Ireland until the middle of the twentieth century, shows the inherent conservatism even of radical republicans, who were mostly, in the end, satisfied with having created a stable rural bourgeoisie.[22] By avoiding any representation of nationalist struggle in his fiction, Kickham could also be charged with drawing a veil over the violence that nationalists were prepared to unleash in pursuit of their ends.[23] But the question of what we might call "selective perception" in Kickham is much more intricate than these readings imply.

The strangest thing about *Knocknagow* is how representations of atrocity alternate with fond portrayals of young lovers, sturdy infants, and cozy homesteads (and these contrasts are just as pronounced in Kickham's first novel, *Sally Cavanagh* [1869]). It is noteworthy that crucial incidents of cruelty, eviction, or forced emigration are often narrated primarily through the consciousness of observers who witness or recall the suffering of other members of their community, usually neighbors. But multiple points of view are always brought to bear on such events, some of which may have taken place years earlier. As we shall see, the transitions between one point of view and another (especially between the perspective of the observer and that of the victim) are carefully managed. The narratives constantly return to these traumatic moments. Yet the stress on grief and pain does not lead to the cultivation of a communal memory of the kind that would directly inspire rage or political violence; nor does it cause a swerve away from the norms of realist representation into the surreal or the Gothic (although elements of both are certainly present in Kickham). If anything, the juxtaposition of disaster and sentiment seems designed to place a check on either reactive violence or the loss of any secure sense of external reality. Jane Tompkins reminds us that sentimental fiction is designed to produce specific worldly effects through manipulating the emotional responses of its readers.[24] But in addition, the work of a novel such as *Knocknagow* may involve the exploration and *rejection* of alternative responses to historical experience.

Music is the most important vehicle for the conversion of individual and communal loss into shared feeling in *Knocknagow*. Moore's *Melodies* are discussed and performed on numerous occasions by people from all levels of the social hierarchy; there are also many allusions to traditional Irish songs such as "Nora Creena" (reminding us of the name of Hardress's boat in *The Collegians*) and "The Coulin." For instance, toward the end of *Knocknagow*, Mrs. Kearney recounts a nightmare that was full of "uproar and confusion," but declares "the 'Coulin' could be heard through it all; and that's what makes me think it was not a bad dream, at any rate" (560). Such songs evidently play a particularly significant role in redeeming bad memories. James H. Murphy proposes that two conflicting worlds are presented in the novel, and that the first (filled with grief and conflict) is simply dispelled when the characters are performing music or being entertained.[25] This, however, is to underplay the self-consciousness of Kickham's work, in which the therapeutic but sometimes delusory effects of music and sentimentalism are explicitly thematized.

There is no more abject victim of the Irish social system in Kickham's fiction than the eponymous heroine of *Sally Cavanagh or, The Untenanted Graves: A Tale of Tipperary*. The text presents a horrifying vision of the miseries of Irish peasant life, and many elements of this tragic story recur in *Knocknagow*. Sally is a vivacious and attractive young woman when her husband and oldest son leave Ireland for America, after their rent is unjustly increased. Her situation deteriorates and she is forced to enter a workhouse where, separated from their mother, her five younger children die of fever and their bodies are taken away. Driven insane by grief, Sally goes away from the workhouse and fashions five empty grave mounds in the old village churchyard, which she then refuses to leave. On her husband's return, he desires only that his wife might at least know who he is before her own inevitable death. Their remaining son grows up in America and loses an arm fighting for his adopted land. At the end of the story, he returns to Tipperary and announces, "I have an arm left—for Ireland!"[26]

Two subplots deal with the vicissitudes of romantic love. Sally's husband, Connor, has a great friend, Brian Purcell, who helplessly watches the family's decline; in the meantime, he reencounters his first love, Jane Evans, who, educated in the city, rejected him and the simple life of the countryside. Brian also hears from the local schoolmaster, who has traveled to the United States to pursue a young woman who was once in love with him, only to discover that she has become a prostitute, a "lost, polluted thing" (*Sally,* 89).

What is of most interest here is the style in which this sorry sequence of events is related. One important dimension of this is Kickham's preoccupation with temporality, particularly the contrast between objectively measured time and time as it is experienced by those who are in severe distress. In framing scenes at the beginning and the end of the text, Brian repeatedly glances at his watch as he contemplates Sally and Connor's cottage, scarcely able to believe that "reality is not a hideous dream" (*Sally,* 198). He later has a dispute with the local doctor about whose watch tells the time correctly, which is ended by the doctor pronouncing that as they are standing side by side, so "now, at this identical moment" (61), it is five minutes past eleven. The phrase "this identical moment" is later used in *Knocknagow* to structure long descriptive passages about what the different inhabitants of the village are doing at any particular time (for example, see *Knocknagow,* 423). The references to clock time and the concern with allowing us to coordinate the daily activities of individuals who cannot see each other point to Kickham's interest in recalling both characters and readers to a stable, shared temporality. But as in the case of Sally, this "real" time may well be a construction or an illusion. Her husband Connor and their neighbors do not seek to help Sally by enabling her to come to terms with her present. Instead they gather her long-dispersed household possessions together in order to trick her into believing she is a newly married woman whose children have not yet been born, never mind perished. These familiar, humble objects have the desired effect on Sally, and she eventually acknowledges Connor, who addresses her in the language of their courtship, *"A gradh geal mo croidhe"* (197). In fact, we could say that the real truth of her situation lies in the graveyard and the lonely "untenanted graves" of the novel's subtitle, rather than at her artificially reconstructed hearth. This is what the community insists on repressing, for the purpose of its own survival as well as that of the victim. Kickham's extremely leisurely, even repetitive narratives and his constant lapses into the present tense are bound up with his supposedly ahistorical obsession with legendary or idyllic time (as John Kelly points out, even the exact date of the setting of *Knocknagow* is "curiously elusive").[27] But it will become clear from the later fiction that Kickham also deploys the same techniques to help us to apprehend the peculiarly nonprogressive temporality of trauma. Kai Erikson has noted that in communities absorbing a traumatic experience, the "moment becomes a season, the event becomes a condition."[28] Thanks to his sensitivity to this phenomenon of the freezing of time, Kickham offers us a version of Bergsonian "temps durée" (inadequately translated as "lived time"). Of course, James Joyce (born in the year of Kickham's death) is the twentieth-century writer most closely associated with the investigation of the modern "time-mind";[29] more recently, Irish commentators on Kickham's more illustrious successor have linked Joyce's refusal of linear, progressive time to the historical experience of colonialism. But unlike Kickham, Joyce appears initially to surrender to what Erikson calls the "centrifugal" rather than the "centripetal" tendencies of trauma; as we shall see, he eventually depicts a radically different kind of therapeutic community.[30]

Another characteristic motif in *Sally Cavanagh* is Kickham's recurrent references to certain landmarks as what we could call "sites of memory,"[31] which help to map both the life stories of individuals and the broader history of his Tipperary villagers; his treatment of the collective consciousness connected to familiar landscapes also evolves in significant directions in *Knocknagow*. As with much else in Kickham, these places often have romantic associations in what appears to be a standard sentimental way. Both Brian Purcell and Jane Evans, for example, often remember the grey rock on which they sat one St. John's Eve as young lovers. There Brian reads Jane the story of the schoolmaster and his lost sweetheart, the ending of which Brian eventually finds out about in a letter from the schoolmaster in America as he sits alone in the same place. But Miss Evans's memories of that day, which constantly interrupt her present thoughts, are in the end not strong enough to return her to the Jane Evans that she had been when the schoolmaster's story made her shed tears. "What a comment on her life since then!" she reflects (*Sally*, 73). Nonetheless, she betrays the affections of her girlhood. In this, she evidently resembles Kickham's own lost love, Bessy Blunden, but not her namesake, Bessy Morris of *Knocknagow*, whose memories of Mat throwing cherries over the hedge to her eventually recall her to her earliest and supposedly best self.

But remembrance cannot simply be controlled by the individual will. As Jane Evans finds, the "chords of the heart" may "vibrate unbidden" in "well-remembered" scenes (27). Nor is it determined only by individual stories. Like Sally herself, these individuals must be reminded of a version of their pasts in order to survive communal catastrophe (Shawn Gow, by contrast, is described as one of those "not-to-be-trusted individuals" who is not "transported" by music or any "concord of sweet sounds" [100]). Brian and Miss Evans's grey rock, for example, also evokes America through the story of the schoolmaster and his pitiful letter. The fingerpost on the mountain road, where the crowds who are preparing to emigrate gather, recalls the "little tributaries of bruised and broken hearts" that flow into the "melancholy stream" toward the sea (26). So Brian is often distracted from his romantic travails: "[His thoughts] turned neither to the right nor to the left of the fingerpost to follow the faithless idol of his youth, or the gentle little maiden whom, something whispered to him, he had not prized at her real worth, but up the Gap, and on with that sorrowful caval-cade, on to the sea" (29). The emigrants' *via dolorosa* is constantly recalled in Kickham's fiction (and *Knocknagow* is unusual among Irish novels of the time in featuring scenes set in the United States as well as in Ireland). Irish men must go to America if Ireland's strength is ever to be rebuilt, but at the same time, America evidently represents a horrible, sexual threat to young Irish women and families. America is the land of the free, but Ireland's achievement of liberty must be projected into the next generation. Like Connor Shea's son, its children are physically mutilated rather than emo-tionally paralyzed like their mothers and fathers (two of the young men at the end of *Knocknagow*, like young Shea, are lacking limbs). In the same way, the Fenians had counted on the veterans of the American Civil War for their eventual revolution. But the interval on which Kickham concentrates is the aftermath of the Famine; in his novels, if not in his own political life, he simply defers the question of insurrection.

In *Knocknagow*, we find Kickham's experiments with representing time, memory, and place elaborated at epic length. His descriptions of domesticity are almost absurdly overextended (when a reviewer commented kindly that Kickham was like "Dickens without his exaggeration," he responded that "Dickens with his exaggeration is exactly what I would strive to be").[32] In a single sentence of over two hundred words, Kickham describes how two gusts of wind come into the kitchen of the house where Mat Donovan lives with his mother:

> A gust of wind rushed in after [Judy], and was met by another gust that rushed down the chimney; and both gusts joining together, whirled round and round Mat Donovan's kitchen, extinguishing both the candle which Billy Heffernan had laid on the end of the bench upon which he sat, and blowing the ashes and some sparks of fire into Mrs Donovan's lap, causing the good woman to spring to her feet and beat her apron as if it were in a blaze about her; and not content with this mischief, the two gusts of winds whirled up to the thatched roof, and so jostled Nelly Donovan's hens about, on the roost over the door, and their querulous screams at thus being rudely and unseasonably awakened from their repose were piteous to listen to; and then, by way of finishing their frolic, the intruders swept the old cock himself from the collar-beam, where he reposed in solitary dignity, bringing him down straight upon Phil Lahy's head, who had just risen to his feet and was making an ineffectual effort to comprehend the state of affairs, and upon whom the sudden assault had such an effect that he staggered backwards and was coming down into a sitting posture upon the fire, when Billy Heffernan caught him in his arms in time to prevent the unpleasant catastrophe. (*Knocknagow*, 160)

Kickham likes to "prevent catastrophes"; a pattern of anticlimax in the novel is often evident both at the level of the individual sentence and that of the narrative as a whole. But when this is applied to matters of greater moment than the disturbance of Mrs. Donovan's hens, some interesting tendencies become evident.

By Kickham's time, his native county had long had the reputation as a center, first of agrarian insurgency, and later of Fenian activity. By the 1870s the very term *Fenian* had become a byword for Irish criminality and degeneration in Britain; Angela Bourke discusses perceptions of country people in this region as "Hottentots" in the context of a notorious murder case of 1895.[33] As the Ulsterman William Carleton had lamented, "If Tipperary and some of the adjoining parts of Munster were blotted from the moral map of the country, we would stand in a far higher position than that which we occupy in the opinion of our neighbours" (*Traits* 1: xxi). It is certainly a long way from *that* Tipperary to Knocknagow. Some of Kickham's energy in the novel is devoted to demystifying Ireland and giving a corrective to earlier fictional representations of the sensational by both English and Irish writers who had an eye on their English readers. So *Knocknagow* opens with a young Anglo-Irish man, Henry Lowe, observing life in an Irish village for the first time. But the plot involving this nephew of the local landlord quickly peters out; the response given to his mother's anxieties about his safety among the wild Whiteboys of Ireland is the assurance that the only evidence of the existence of any such bandits in this part of Ireland is a solitary "threatening letter found nailed to a door seven or eight miles from here" (*Knocknagow*, 126). In part to distinguish himself from his precursors in Irish fiction, Kickham works hard to avoid disturbing "the equanimity of [his] readers . . . by anything that might bear even the faintest resemblance to a surprise" (439). Toward the end, some of the characters comment that the story of Mary Kearney's secret love has everything requisite for a drama or a novel "except the sensational," but that "nothing is easier than the sensational" for the lazy artist (572–73). Kickham's avoidance of sensation and shock is all the more noteworthy as the novel makes it clear that he understands very well the violence that is inscribed on the Irish landscape and the traces that it leaves in the consciousness of his characters.

Late in *Knocknagow*, Kickham describes how, as the priest at Mass reads the long list of the week's dead to his congregation, "Some faces were quite white, and others almost *black*" (549). These furious black faces recall the blackened faces of Whiteboys. But when a woman hears her husband's name being read out and realizes that he has become another victim of the workhouse, she begins to shriek in agony. This incident, as Mary Kearney reports, turns the anger of the people into pity, "though one would think it ought only to incense them all the more against their rulers" (549). In the central section of the text, from chapters 32 to 49, Kickham offers a particularly involved dramatization of how a key group of villagers in Knocknagow responds to appalling events in the community, past and present. These characters take their places along a continuum that stretches from the unrepentant old croppy, Phil Morris, who has killed a soldier; to Mick Brien, whose family is homeless and starving, and who skulks in the dark moor at night contemplating murder; to Phil Lahy and the other men of the neighborhood, incessantly discussing Ireland's problems and how to solve them; to Norah Lahy, the saintly invalid whose role in life is to sit at her window and give hope to everyone that there is a better world beyond this one.[34] In a number of crucial scenes, Kickham cuts from the consciousness of one character to another as their individual lines of vision converge on a series of flash images, each of which has an iconic force for the whole community: the vision of Norah saying her prayers, the light at Mat the Thrasher's window every night, the three poplar trees on Phil Morris's deserted farm. As with the vivid but simple picture of the white and black faces in the church, Kickham often describes horror in a way that tames or domesticate its force. So the story of the judicial murder of Father Nicholas Sheehy in 1766—one of the most notorious incidents in the history of Tipperary—is introduced by a reference to Clonmel as "the big town with the cloud over it" (259), a phrase that indicates how much the murder had become embedded in folk memory and that also provides a typical instance of Kickham's tendency to pastoralize atrocity, to turn it into the rhetoric of a children's story. Later, Billy Heffernan explains that "Clo'mel was never wudout a cloud over id since the day Father Sheehy was hung" and tells how the priest's blood was sprinkled on the door of the bishop who had refused to testify to his innocence (265).

At times, Kickham's almost whimsical tones are provoked by someone or something that has become especially endearing because its familiarity is taken to be a natural feature of the social world. For instance, when he recounts how Mrs. Donovan, Mat's mother, got what is referred to as her sad face, the history of her bereaved expression is shocking. However, the brutality of the episode is deflected by the tone that transforms it into an anecdote:

> For poor Mrs Donovan got that sad face of her one bright summer day in the year '98, when her father's house was surrounded by soldiers and yeomen, and her only brother, a bright-eyed boy of seventeen, was torn from the arms of his mother, and shot dead outside the door. . . . the gallant officer hacked away at the poor boy's head in fury, and was in so great a passion, that when the trunk fell down at last, leaving the head in his hand, he flung it on the ground, and kicked it like a foot-ball; and when it rolled against the feet of the horrified young girl, who stood as if she were turned to stone near the door, she fell down senseless without cry or moan, and they all thought she too was dead. (376)

The shadow on her features becomes indelible when the earlier memory is reactivated by soldiers approaching her house again years later:

> But the sad look was in her face, and never wholly left it from that hour. It was beginning to clear away in after years; till once again the house was surrounded by soldiers. . . . That fatal summer day in '98 came back with such strange vividness that she thought she felt her brother's head strike against her foot; and again she fell down senseless without cry or moan. After that the sad look became fixed and permanent, and she was destined to carry it with her into the coffin. It was the shadow of a curse. (376)

In that last sentence, Kickham throws the actual and historical sequence into a legendary, fairy-tale perspective. The memory simply becomes part of the daily reality of the household; it is not a matter of historical record any more, but a matter of wonder. So Kickham has his cake and eats it; he keeps the history intact but mystifies it into an affectionate tale about the oddness of memory. For example, the story explains why Mat's mother is so upset when he tries to improve his literacy to become more worthy of Bessy. Mrs. Donovan is simply frightened that he might want to become a policeman, for she would rather he were murdered than become one of the state's murderers: "So Mat Donovan's slate and pencil made the sad look on his mother's face a shade sadder, lest by any chance he should be qualifying himself for the 'peelers.' She would rather a thousand times to see him dragged out and shot like the bright-eyed boy whose head rolled against her foot in '98, or hanged from the old cherry tree in the garden" (376). The novelist's apparently idiosyncratic treatment of such experiences may in fact illustrate with some sensitivity how they are narrated and absorbed by both the individuals directly affected and those around them.

The most visible reminders of the eviction of the Morris family, which led to the death of Bessy's mother and her father's flight to America, are three tall poplar trees, which can be glimpsed from all over the village (for example, note how Grace remarks on those "lonely-looking trees," as Bessy tells her that "their shadow is now on the house where I was born" [318]; and the "remarkable coincidence" that Mat, Bessy, and Attorney Hanly were "all looking towards the three poplar trees at the same time" before all turn round and look toward "the whitethorns at the foot of the hill" [333]). In the chapter entitled "An Old Croppy's Notions of Security of Tenure," we learn that Phil, Bessy's grandfather, believes that it is only the "dread of assassination" (230) that has prevented any new tenant from taking his son's farm. Severely admonished by the priest and told to "hold his tongue," he mutters resentfully under his breath "Ay, that's the way always. 'Howld your tongue' settles it" (230). But while old Phil's logic seems sound enough, Kickham is in general committed to defusing the emotions that might lead to random, individual acts of vengeance, although the possibility of a manly fight like the Rebellion of 1798 remains (229).

On one particular night, three characters are recalled from "The Dead Past" to "The Living Present" (even though the author comments, "We hold that the Past is the more living of the two, sometimes" [382]) by one of the most familiar sights in the village—the lighted window of the Donovan house (chapters 48–49). Two of these characters, Mat and Mary Kearney, turn away from their melancholic thoughts of lost love, but the last, Mick Brien, is saved by the ordinary sights of communal life from committing a deed of blood. When he enters the Donovan house, the gaunt and ragged man alarms the inhabitants:

> The fire, being covered with a large griddle, did not afford sufficient light to enable them to recognise the new-comer; and the candle being behind his back only showed the outline of his figure, in which Nelly fancied she saw something wild; and she felt and looked somewhat frightened as she thought of the "gang" which, according to common report, were just then prowling nightly about the neighbourhood. (387–88)

The light of the fire is only briefly dimmed by the griddle used to bake bread, which the Donovans then share with the famished Brien. The fear that the visitor is a wild bandit or an outlaw turns out to be a quickly dispelled illusion.

There is one other noteworthy instance of illusory or phantasmal Whiteboyism in *Knocknagow*. This scene also casts light on Kickham's unusual view of the land question in Irish nationalism (in his later years, he was an opponent of Davitt's Land League campaign).[35] In *Knocknagow*, the tenant farmer Tom Hogan embodies the narrow obsession with land that Kickham believed characterized this class. Kickham did not consider that such people would ever be in the vanguard of the struggle for political freedom; "[I]f ever a successful blow is to be struck for the poor old country," he declared, "it is the hand of the toiler that will strike it."[36] The novel gives a sympathetic diagnosis of the pathological servility of those "conceived and born under a notice-to-quit" that "taught them to cringe, and fawn, and lie" (302). Nevertheless, it is clear that the spiritedness of a landless laborer such as Mat (a member of that impoverished class regarded by Carleton and many others as so unsettled and dangerous) is preferable to Hogan's cowardice. The latter is ultimately humiliated by losing his wits as well as his farm. On one earlier occasion, Hogan's face is blackened in an accident. When the corrupt agent Isaac Pender catches sight of him, he is instantly paralyzed with terror, while the attorney Hanley jumps into a drain to escape being "guillotined" with a spade (340). But as Hogan proudly tells his oppressors: "I'm not that soart of a character, an' never was. I never fired a shot in my life, an' plase God I never will" (344). For Kickham, such emasculating passivity is even worse than the violent passion of Phil Morris or Mick Brien.

Comerford has argued that *Knocknagow* is the novel in which modern Irish society, "dominated by the ethos and mores of an agricultural community," could "presume to see an explanation of its own origins in a struggle against the vicissitude of insecurity of tenure."[37] But there are elements in the text, especially in the representation of Mat, that trouble the conventional associations between rootedness, moral stability, and national progress that are indeed so obvious elsewhere. Mat's mobility, as he travels to Dublin and America in pursuit of Bessy, is an indication of the difference between him and the scions of the more respectable, settled classes. Kickham also promotes the class of craftsmen and tradesman as key to the achievement of prosperity (see the discussion of the respective merits of manufacturing and farming [231–33]). The tailor Phil Lahy (after he has given up alcohol) and Hugh Kearney, the forward-looking son of one of the larger tenant farmers, who tellingly describes himself as "a manufacturer of arable land" (40), are characteristic examples of this practical, independent type thought to be predominant in the world of commerce. Unlike Griffin, Kickham can find a place for capitalism in his vision of Ireland's future: Mat combines folk-cultural charm with modernity in a way impossible for, for instance, Griffin's Myles-na-Copaleen in *The Collegians*. In Kickham's Tipperary, the ties that bind embrace all classes. Unlike Griffin, Kickham is not unduly worried about an inassimilable or recalcitrant native culture. Griffin's Dalton, in *Tracy's Ambition*, had feared that Moore's *Melodies* "have not enough of the *bog*, enough of a plain and vigorous nature, I mean, in their composition, to find a sympathy among people whose sentiment springs warm and unrectified . . . from the heart,"[38] but everyone in Knocknagow loves Moore. However thoroughly organic a community it may be, it should also be registered that Knocknagow is a *village*—much more reminiscent of the teeming countryside of pre-Famine Ireland than the dispersed pattern of Irish rural settlement after the goal of peasant proprietorship had been achieved. A good deal is made of the newly married couples at the end of the novel, but these new nuclear families are really the remaining fragments of a lovingly commemorated, richer communal life. Kickham's relative lack of interest in the rights of tenants can make him look conservative indeed (as with the quasi-feudal portrayal of the benevolent landlord taking part in his tenant's wedding festivities in chapter 31). But in all of these ways, the novel is somewhat at odds with what would later become De Valera's ideal of a "traditional" rural society of mostly small landowners.

In the best-known scene from *Knocknagow*, Kickham describes Mat the Thrasher's victory in the sledge-throwing competition. As Mat prepares to make his throw, "Some one struck the big drum a single blow, as if by accident, and, turning round quickly, the thatched roofs of the hamlet caught his eye." The sight of the mud walls and thatched cabins rouses Mat to utter the words, "'For the credit of the little village!' in a tone of deepest tenderness" before he releases the winning shot: "A shout of exultation burst from the excited throng; hands were convulsively grasped, and hats sent flying into the air; and in their wild joy they crushed round him and tried to lift him up on their shoulders" (461). It is in the popularity of such competitions and in the increasing importance of the rituals and rivalries of sport that the later success of the Gaelic Athletic Association was based. Part of the importance of this novel is that it reveals how the activities of this local community have the appeal of an innocent unselfconsciousness that the text itself, by the very act of representing them as innocent, is beginning to alter into a set of abstract values.

John Barrell argues that Oliver Goldsmith's pastoral vision of country life in *The Deserted Village* (1770) was much easier to appropriate for radical political aims than, for instance, George Crabbe's portrayal of rural misery. Whereas Goldsmith's poem depicts a rural idyll in which "the best part of life was spent in the alehouse and on the green," Crabbe tends to naturalize unremitting labor and suffering.[39] Like Kickham, Goldsmith may have failed to represent real history, but "only those who think that the past was different from the present are enabled to imagine that the future may be so too."[40] "But how long can it be said that Knocknagow is not gone?" (462) asks the priest toward the end of the novel, when so many of the clay-walled cabins have been pulled down and the pathetically few possessions of their inhabitants dumped on the roadside (see passage beginning "Half of Knocknagow is swept from the face of the earth" [523]).[41]

Knocknagow cannot be eliminated because it is not an image of the past as it was, but as it should have been. Kickham surrenders historical narrative for the anecdote, which means that he largely exchanges analysis for a loyally affectionate report on the foibles and eccentricities of the community. In this way, *Knocknagow* gives to the emerging nation a previously unavailable sense of its own interiority. This sense might earlier have been associated with music alone, but Kickham produces a *novelization* of Moore's sentimental project. He thus lends momentum to a developing ideology of national solidarity, which should not be judged merely in the light of later religious and political orthodoxies. To live the past as it never was is to live the future; in this, Kickham's pastoralism is based not just on a sanitized version of the past, but it retains a political and utopian dimension. This is what makes the novel's treatment of temporality—which is intimately related to its own historical timing—so unique.

4

The Pope's Green Island

Irish Fiction at the Fin de Siècle

Catholicism and the Land Question

The field of Irish fiction underwent considerable expansion during the final decades of the nineteenth century. Among the chief developments were the consolidation of an indigenous publishing industry, the creation of a comparatively large readership for fiction as well as political and religious works, and a great increase in the number of women novelists.[1] A variety of fictional genres flourished in this period. Although not set in Ireland, Bram Stoker's *Dracula* (1897) was the most successful and is by now the best-known work in the tradition of Anglo-Irish Gothic. Corresponding to some features of the old Anglo-Irish reforming literature that began with Edgeworth and Morgan, we have what James H. Murphy calls "Catholic Upper Middle Class Fiction," which like its earlier, Protestant counterpart, was dominated by women writers.[2] But perhaps most historically significant of all was the literature of liberal Catholic dissent, which was often autobiographical or confessional in form, and gave pre-eminence to individual subjectivity over group conformity.[3] Generally, it stressed sexuality as the crucial zone of freedom, and sometimes took as its model the harsh and candid documentary approach of French naturalism, pioneered in English by George Moore, the son of a Catholic landlord from Co. Mayo. Naturalism —sometimes uncritically taken as an index of political radicalism—was to dominate the Irish novel in twentieth century. But despite the range and diversity of Irish fiction in period of the fin de siècle, what we do not find (after Kickham) are Catholic novelists who undertake to interpret or sympathetically engage with key historical developments in the style of the Banims or Griffin.

125

Instead, a good deal of energy was absorbed by definitional disputes within Irish Catholic culture. At the very moment when the agrarian question in Ireland was reaching its final crisis and resolution, even nationalist writers like Gerard O'Donovan and Canon Sheehan became disillusioned with the political alliances that had been forged by the Church. They were profoundly concerned about the nature of the society that would emerge under middle-class Catholic leadership. In this regard, there is significant overlap between Catholic writers and English or Anglo-Irish novelists, including Anthony Trollope and Emily Lawless, for whom the notion of Catholic Emancipation would have been oxymoronic from the outset.

It is no coincidence that in novels such as Trollope's *The Landleaguers* (1883) and George Moore's *Drama in Muslin* (1886), agrarian themes and feminist protest are juxtaposed. These novelists anticipate a new emphasis that reveals itself in works of the following decade, such as Lawless's *Grania* (1892) and Moore's *The Lake* (1905). There is a decisive shift in the fictional treatment of the condition of women, from a concentration on elite society to a consideration of native or Irish Catholic culture as well. The celibate (whether male or female) becomes a key figure in the exploration of the deficiencies of the new Ireland. While this in part represents a liberalizing or feminist critique of conservative strains in nationalism, it also contributes to a depoliticization of the novel form. It is Joyce who both exemplifies and transcends many of these trends in fiction, reconnecting the fin de siècle modes of sexual dissidence or bohemian disengagement with the earlier political project of the nineteenth-century Catholic novel. But for most Irish novelists after Joyce—Seán O'Faoláin, John McGahern, and Edna O'Brien among others—the "truth" of the Irish revolution will continue to be understood primarily in terms of the "repression" disclosed by the realist or naturalist novel.[4]

Efforts had been made to reform the Catholic priesthood and to strengthen episcopal and papal authority in Ireland before the Famine. These efforts were greatly intensified after the first National Synod of Thurles in 1850. Under the stewardship of the formidable Paul Cardinal Cullen, popular spiritual practices, such as patterns, were discouraged, while attendance at Mass and at a range of devotions sponsored by the institutional Church came to be regarded as definitive of Irish Catholic identity.

Historians have disagreed over the extent to which the success of this "Devotional Revolution" can be attributed to the mere imposition of clerical authority on a cowed populace still traumatized by the Famine and its aftermath. Small and medium landholders were by now the "nation-making" majority class; clearly, there were both psychological and economic motives behind the readiness of farmers, in particular, to conform to the Church's demands for familial piety, frugality, and sexual abstinence.[5] Many political agitators, intellectuals, and writers were apprehensive about the conservative, materialistic character of this rural bourgeoisie in the later decades of the nineteenth century. Some looked to groups outside this emerging establishment—the Anglo-Irish or even the Catholic gentry, the lower middle-class individuals from the towns who had swelled the ranks of the Fenians, or the inhabitants of the Gaelic margins in the West—to challenge its orthodoxies. Such observers were increasingly influenced by the racial and ethnographic theories that eventually fed into the movements for Celtic Revival at the end of the century. In this context, they were ever more likely to celebrate the "primitive" or premodern, and to find moral and aesthetic value in the lifestyles linked to subsistence agriculture that most Irish people were so anxious to leave behind.

The increasingly confident and ultramontanist complexion of the Catholic Church after the Famine also brought into focus the question of its relationship to political and cultural nationalism.[6] Did adherence to a universal Church take primacy over all other cultural and historical affiliations? The long-suffering and patient endurance of Irish Catholics during the Penal Era had always been regarded as a sign of their natural spirituality and fidelity. But was this loyalty now to be mobilized for an international project, with the Irish rediscovering their true role in world history as missionaries and evangelists? This ambition was at the heart of Cardinal Newman's plan to establish a Catholic university in Dublin.[7] Throughout the nineteenth century, there were tensions between nationalist interpretations of Irish Catholic identity and the versions of Irish national character deemed to be desirable by an ascendant Catholic Church. These achieved perhaps their most poignant and famous literary expression in the Christmas dinner scene in Joyce's *A Portrait of the Artist as a Young Man* (1916), as the young Stephen Dedalus watches his family and his father's friend

Mr. Casey argue bitterly about the Irish rejection of Parnell in the wake of the O'Shea divorce scandal. In response to the taunts of Stephen's aunt, the loyal Parnellite Mr. Casey declares that he is "no renegade catholic,"[8] but the descendant of men who gave up their lives rather than betray their religion. Mr. Dedalus points to the portrait of his grandfather on the wall, "a good Irishman when there was no money in the job. He was condemned to death as a whiteboy" (Portrait, 37). But Casey is eventually provoked by the vengeful Dante into blasphemy: "No God for Ireland! he cried. We have had too much God in Ireland. Away with God!" (39). Such conflicts also left their mark on other Catholic authors, who present a largely disenchanted and critical account of the religious and social revolution that preceded Ireland's national revolution by some decades. Initially, this was a quarrel about authority and liberty that was internal to Irish Catholicism; in twentieth-century Irish fiction, this was to be superceded by a broader struggle between faith and the liberation of unbelief.

The fiction of ex-priest Gerald O'Donovan is typical of an earlier stage of development of the dissident Catholic novel. In theological terms, O'Donovan was a modernist, or liberal. However, so-called modernists tended to value local tradition more than the official Catholic Church in Ireland did at this time. For example, O'Donovan advocated the revival of the Irish language and was also active in Horace Plunkett's cooperative movement—which sought to develop the Irish agricultural economy on a collective, "self-help" basis, "mitigating the exploitative practices of naked capitalism associated with the gombeen class."[9] It is often noted that the realist novel was a poor enough vehicle for some of the literary ambitions of the Celtic Revival, such as the elaboration of new forms of poetic Hiberno-English or the exploitation of Gaelic myths and legends. Arguably, this helps to explain the weakness of Irish fiction (before Joyce), relative to achievements in poetry and drama, in this period. However, what we can find in O'Donovan is an exceptionally detailed analysis of how the emancipatory potential of nationalist movements was suppressed by specific political actors: the priests, the land-hungry farmers, and the gombeen shopkeepers and publicans. Many of these issues had already been brought into sharp focus by the controversy created by Plunkett's critique of the supposedly anti-industrial nature of Irish Catholicism in

Ireland in the New Century (1904). In this work, Plunkett blamed emigration on the deadening influence of the Church and criticized the diversion of the country's capital into extravagant projects of church building.[10]

O'Donovan's first novel, *Father Ralph* (1913), like Joyce's *Portrait* in some respects, tells the story of a precocious boy stranded between maternal piety and fierce priestly attention, on the one hand, and a good-natured but ineffectual father, on the other. Ralph O'Brien's father tries to calm the religious scruples of the anxious young boy by reminiscing about his own education:

> There was not as much talk then as now among Catholics of saints and sinners. . . . I think it's all the convents that have sprung up since that have worried the lives out of children. . . . My mother told us how our branch of the O'Briens had always been Catholic and had suffered bitter persecution in the penal times. It was in our blood to be Catholics, she said, and it would disgrace our name to give up the old faith.[11]

Ralph trains for the priesthood in the seminary at Maynooth, described by one of his friends as "a miasmic pest-hole enveloped by intellectual and moral fog" (*Father Ralph*, 182), before being sent to serve in a small country town "run by priests and gombeen men" (231). There he encounters a series of setbacks that eventually lead to his effective expulsion from the community and the priesthood. The bishop orders him to close his cooperative club; his mother sides with the Church hierarchy against her only child; and he is utterly dismayed by the papal decree *Lamentabili Sane* (a syllabus condemning the errors of the modernists, issued by Pope Pius X in 1907), which meant that "religion, as he understood and felt it, was condemned as heresy" (344). But unlike so many priests in Irish novels, he does not fall in love; there is no sexual motive for his final flight to England. The situation he leaves behind in small-town Ireland looks grim indeed, but no sustained attempt is made to redeem it by pointing to the possible redemption of the individual through exile.[12]

O'Donovan himself settled and married in England. His late, experimental novel, *The Holy Tree* (1922), demonstrates how he ultimately did come to link the liberation of Ireland to sexuality in a phantasmagoric combination of motifs from social critique, Celticism, and Catholicism. The chief protagonist is a peasant woman, Ann, who falls in love with an outsider to the community, a language activist called Brian Hogan. But Ann's family has already forced her into a marriage of convenience. O'Donovan emphasizes the spiritual nature of this adulterous love: "But it's the bells of heaven rang out for the birth of a new god when two straying souls, that in themselves were nothing, saw in the eyes of the other not only the answer of their flesh but the answer of their souls."[13]

But there is no appreciation among Ann's people for this conception of the religious life. There is little support in the text for O'Donovan's increasingly desperate assertion of the compatibility of Catholicism with folk belief and traditional energy and festivity. Only a dream vision of her grandfather brings such a vision to life. The old man tells of seeing a hillside rolled back, from which Oisin and Cuchulain issued forth as the Holy Ghost floated overhead. "Tir na n'Og [the Gaelic paradise of eternal youth] and heaven were rolled into one," says the grandfather, as he tells Ann that: "I give you my word that the Blessed Virgin herself footed a reel with the purtiest of them pagans. God looking down all the while, with a smile on him" (*Holy Tree*, 84–85). In the end, Ann's lover drowns in an accident and, chastened and subdued, she belatedly takes up her appointed social role: "Joe [her husband] says it was the proper woman of the house she was at last" (318).

The conflict between the Church and Fenianism (which Kickham attempted to mediate in his journalism) foreshadowed the catastrophic split between the Parnellites and anti-Parnellites in 1890. Joyce's Mr. Casey gives us a powerful account of nationalist grievances against the Church after the death of Parnell:

> Didn't the bishops of Ireland betray us in the time of the union when Bishop Lanigan presented an address of loyalty to the Marquess Cornwallis? Didn't the bishops and priests sell the aspirations of their country in 1829 in return for catholic emancipation? Didn't they denounce the fenian movement from the pulpit and in the confession box? And didn't they dishonor the ashes of Terence Bellew MacManus? (*Portrait*, 38)[14]

But even apart from such specific religious and political controversies, evidently there was something intrinsically uninspiring for writers in the movement for tenants' rights and land reform, spearheaded by Michael Davitt's Land League in alliance with Parnell's Irish Parliamentary Party, which dominated the political scene during the final two decades of the nineteenth century. The centrality of the land question to Irish politics in this period cannot be overemphasized. Yet leaving aside all those writers—from Anthony Trollope to Emily Lawless and even George Moore—who took a haughtily feudal view of the prospect of peasant proprietorship and Irish democracy, there is no prominent Catholic or nationalist Irish novelist who wholeheartedly welcomed the social changes brought about by the new legislation of the late nineteenth and early twentieth centuries. In this context, we might speculate about how different British Victorian fiction would have looked if a major figure such as George Eliot had been extremely doubtful about the wisdom of passing the great Reform Acts and had leaned toward a more radical or Chartist view of the national situation instead.

We have already seen that Kickham, whose *Knocknagow* is usually regarded as one of the chief sources of Eamon De Valera's rhetoric about a society based on "cosy rural homesteads" in the 1940s, was highly suspicious of many aspects of the Land League campaign and of late-nineteenth-century Irish nationalism. William O'Brien, himself a Nationalist MP and a novelist, also confronted the question of the unromantic nature of Land League politics in his preface to W. P. Ryan's novel, *The Heart of Tipperary: A Romance of the Land League* (1893). O'Brien evokes the crowded landscapes of O'Connell's Ireland, inhabited by high-spirited country people who lived without any thought of tomorrow. But those multitudes disappeared, and with them went what O'Brien refers to as the people's "craving for a national literature." Instead, Ireland now had politicians who concerned themselves "primarily with how people were to live rather than how they were to look in the eyes of the intelligent foreigner." This was "a dingier heroism [than that of armed rebellion] but it was more successful; and I am afraid it will be found that critics who find most fault with the prosaic methods of the Land League are those to whom its success is more objectionable than even its drab-colored realties."[15] But in his own very popular novel,

When We Were Boys (1890) (a book that Mr. Bloom of Eccles Street has on his shelf), O'Brien returns to the era of the Fenians to supply the heroism and romance. Although he welcomes the fact that, since that time, "Irishmen have discovered a saner resource than the wild weapons of boyish insurrection,"[16] it is clear that he is nonetheless nostalgic for the idealism of political "boyhood." For instance, at the climax of the novel, the Fenian hero, Ken Rohan, who has already been tried and condemned to death, discovers that he has been elected to Westminster by a courageous group of tenants:

> a constituency of close-fisted, closer-minded farmers; yet, by one of those electric impulses which now and again set the veins of a nation tingling with a fine frenzy, up those dumb, cautious, terrorized, crushed farmers rose, with their blood afire, and, oversetting all calculations and barriers, dashing aside the Monsignors' gold-knobbed sticks, and the agents' whips, and the Castle's bribes, and the hussars' sabers, shook the young rebel by the hand at the gallows' foot in the face of the world, and decided that his were the wild hopes which were whispered in sacred moments round their firesides—his the immortal longings which nestled in their heart of hearts![17]

In such passages O'Brien revisits the laudable acts of political self-assertion on the part of the peasantry in which the agitation for ownership of the land originated. But the anxiety in these lines arises from the belated recognition that, toward the end of the century, Irish peasants, far from being incapable of changing into a materialistic, selfish bourgeoisie, may in fact have been all too eager and well-equipped for that transformation.

Liberals such as Gerald O'Donovan and journalist and novelist W. P. Ryan (author of several works of trenchant social critique, including *The Plough and the Cross* [1910] and *The Pope's Green Island* [1912]) feared that the association between Catholicism and the native middle class would stymie real economic progress in Ireland. But Canon Patrick Sheehan, Catholic intellectual and revered popular novelist, also wrote scathing denunciations of this class and of its baleful alliance with the Irish Church. However, his chief concern was not that the Irish bourgeoisie would fail in its project of capitalist development, but rather that it would succeed too well—reproducing a version of England's dreary industrial civilization that would inevitably lead to an atheistic socialism. Especially in his final novel, *The Graves at Kilmorna* (1915), Sheehan (like O'Brien) contrasts Fenian idealism with Land League pragmatism. His hero, Myles Cogan, lives to behold "the old flag with its watchword 'Ireland for the Irish' pulled down, and the new standard with its more selfish motto: 'The land for the people' erected for the guidance of the nation."[18] The old patriot queries whether "the material benefit accruing to the farmers of Ireland [will] balance the moral deterioration that must follow, when you appeal only to selfish interests?" (*Graves*, 224). Sheehan who, along with Kickham, is usually read as presenting an entirely benign fictional portrayal of post-Famine rural life, also offers this comment on the superior culture of *urban* Ireland: "It will be found that the more comprehensive idea of Irish nationhood has always been cherished by the dwellers in the towns and cities of Ireland. To them Ireland has been a whole—a homogeneous entity to be welded more and more until it took on the consistency of the nation. The people of flocks and herds can only conceive of patriotism as it affects the land" (226–27).

Sheehan's novel tries to have it both ways, praising the material development and social advance of urban life while also espousing a version of patriotic martyrdom that has an essentially rural, heroic-pastoral basis. The spectacularly unfortunate Myles is ultimately stoned to death on a public platform by a vulgar mob and laid to rest with his old Fenian comrade and best friend in an obscure grave. In Sheehan's novel, a younger Myles had declared that the "political degradation of the people which we shall have preached with our gaping wounds will shame the nation into at least a paroxysm of patriotism once again!" (68). This certainly chimes with the ideology of martyrdom that inspired some of the rebels of 1916, a year after the novel's posthumous publication, although it would be going too far to say Sheehan actually ratifies the philosophy of blood sacrifice.[19]

In short, Sheehan asserts that the Fenians, who "went out in the open field, prepared to give a life for a life," were therefore more noble than the Land Leaguers who operated by means of "the breaking of contracts, the subversion of society, the possibility of crime" (223). The contrast between "constitutional" and "violent" methods of liberation is part of the standard rhetoric of much Irish history- writing—although Sheehan here reverses its usual form. Many agreed instead with William O'Brien, who welcomed the less violent methods of protest employed during the Land War.[20] For those more hostile commentators who derived their analyses of the historical situation from ready-made caricatures, all of these phases of agrarian and political struggle were simply various manifestations of an inherent Irish lawlessness or Whiteboyism (Trollope's villain Lax from *The Landleaguers* [1883], a masked assassin credited with supernatural powers by his gullible neighbors, might have come straight from a loyalist novel of the 1820s). But the whole idea of liberation into a bureaucratic, administered society is resisted by a range of Catholic authors in this period. There is no strong endorsement in any Irish fiction of the very successful popular protests of the 1880s and afterward. In place of the sponsorship of such campaigns, the Land War became, in some key novels of the period, the context for the exploration of rebellions of an apparently very different kind.

Land and Desire: Emily Lawless and George Moore

Both Anthony Trollope's *The Landleaguers* and George Moore's *Drama in Muslin* (1886), the two best-known novels about the Land War, are concerned with the travails of economically dependent middle- or upper-class women as well as the inequities of traditional marriage and the marriage market. Yet what makes these novels more than usually interesting is how they divide our attention between these increasingly inflamed social issues and the political repercussions of the agitation in Ireland. In *The Landleaguers*, for instance, Trollope devotes nearly as much of the narrative to Rachel O'Mahony, daughter of an Irish American radical politician and sweetheart of Frank Jones, the elder son and heir of an embattled Irish landlord, as he does to dramatic and violent events at Castle Morony, the Joneses' seat in the west of Ireland. Moore's *Drama in Muslin* concentrates mainly on the fate of young women from landed families at a time when "Irish money"[21] can no longer be counted on. Most of the story is told from the viewpoint of the young heroine Alice Barton, who is kind and intelligent but irredeemably plain.

Trollope's Rachel O'Mahony is a talented musician who attempts to make a career singing on the London stage. Her father, who embraces Irish republicanism and is eventually elected to Westminster, has no conscience about living off his daughter's earnings; Frank, however, will not agree to marry Rachel unless he can support her, and the young lovers seem destined to unhappiness as a consequence. The professional woman artist and the unruly tenants threaten the stability of the private and public spheres respectively. Both threats are eventually extinguished in the course of Trollope's story. Frank's anxieties about Rachel are ended when she is forbidden to sing again after an illness ("All that was now set to rights by the absolute destruction of Rachel's voice").[22] The tenants tire of the tyranny of the Land League and begin "to feel that there might be something worse in store for them than the old course of policemen, juries and judges" (401). Lax, the murderer of Frank's young brother, is hanged in Galway jail; the Joneses' old servants drift back to them, breaking the boycott that the household had endured. Trollope's depiction of the secrecy and criminality of the Land League agitators throughout this novel is relentlessly negative. Nonetheless, through his sympathetic portrayal of both Rachel and her father, "an alternative way of figuring the disruption of the status quo is offered."[23] In other words, women present a more radical challenge to the social order than the downtrodden tenants.

In 1880, George Moore's subsidized bohemian life as a painter in Paris was brought to a peremptory close by the tenants on his estate in Co. Mayo. His agent there wrote to inform his absentee Catholic landlord employer that the tenants were refusing to pay any more rent until they were granted a reduction. Moore could no longer count on the income from his lands. His subsequent decision to become a professional writer in London arose from this characteristic action of the Land War, which had its roots in Mayo. Irish peasant militancy made Moore more alert to the political realities that governed his work as a writer; he was inevitably more self-conscious than Trollope about the ironies of dwelling on the sufferings of relatively privileged women in fiction at a time of radical social upheaval in Ireland. In *Drama in Muslin* he gives the standard response of the novelist of domestic realism to the charge of historical irrelevance:

The history of a nation as often lies hidden in social wrongs and domestic griefs as in the story of revolution, and if it be for the historian to narrate the one, it is for the novelist to dissect and explain the other; and who would say which is of the most vital importance—the thunder of the people against the oppression of [Dublin] Castle, or the unnatural sterility, the cruel idleness of mind and body of the muslin martyrs who cover with their white skirts the shames of Cork Hill? (*Drama*, 203–4)[24]

Charlotte Brontë or George Eliot might have expressed the same sentiments. But while English women novelists were chiefly concerned with creating exemplars of what Gayatri Spivak has described as a revolutionary "female individualism,"[25] Moore's "muslin martyrs" are in contrast generally represented as helpless casualties of what he understood to be the imminent and inevitable fall of feudalism in Ireland. Alice Barton is a partial and telling exception to this. She repeats the journey undertaken by the heroine of *Middlemarch* (and both Alice and the humble doctor she eventually marries are devoted readers of George Eliot), from aristocratic idleness to suburban domesticity, but is never invested with either the vocational passion or the sexual charisma of Dorothea Brooke. Despite its disappointments, Dorothea's life contributes to the general good. In Eliot, realism retains its romantic individual residue; Moore's naturalism, parading itself as more scientific, declares the futility of trying to influence historical processes.

Moore's fictional manifesto in *Drama in Muslin* nonetheless identifies key themes that will evolve in significant ways both in his later work and in twentieth-century Irish fiction. He does not initially entertain the notion that the affective or sexual lives of the peasantry could provide material for the novelist; their revolution is the business of the historian only. The unnatural sterility he identifies seems to afflict only the decadent higher social classes (in his collection of short stories, *Celibates* [1900], he also explores the thwarted lives of such individuals, showing how a repressed sexuality and compensatory spirituality are intertwined). By contrast, as in *Drama in Muslin*, the peasants who stare out of their crowded cabins at the ladies and gentlemen inhabit a zone of natural instinct and fecundity; they embody the elemental forces that will soon create "an outburst of national energy" (325). Later, in the stories of *The Untilled Field* (1903), Moore sees the priests as the repressors of the instinctual life of the people; they try to prevent young people courting, and their venal matchmaking and charging of large fees for weddings reduce the possibilities of happy marriages. He initially presents this kind of clerical intervention as an externally imposed repression, but in his later work—as in much literature in succeeding decades—the repression is internalized. The figure of the celibate, who plays such a minatory role in *Drama in Muslin*, becomes the typical (eventually even the stereotypical) victim of post-Famine and postindependence Ireland. These are the lonely people who paid the price for the regime of late marriage and the depopulation of the countryside consequent on mass emigration, forcing them into modes of behavior endorsed by the Church as appropriately "Catholic" and chaste. (But as the Ulster Protestant Filson Young remarked of the supposedly high rates of mental illness in Catholic Ireland, "a hundred bastards would be a more gracious and healthy sign than a lunatic.")[26] As we shall see in *The Lake*, Moore interestingly reconfigures the role of the victim of Catholic orthodoxy through his account of a correspondence between a rural priest and a runaway fallen woman. He acknowledges, more subtly and sympathetically than some later Irish writers, that the theme of liberation from sexual repression involves complex and asymmetrical issues for modern women and men. Yet it is in this recurrent theme—the social phenomenon of celibacy obsessively represented in a literature that took it as the key to all political and ideological mythologies—that we see the aftermath of the Famine remain as a haunting presence in independent Ireland. Patrick Kavanagh's long poem *The Great Hunger* (1942) is the best-known example of an author recalling the great, tragic event of mid-nineteenth-century history to talk about "hunger" as an abiding condition that had been transmitted through the three or four generations that separated the Famine from the mid-twentieth century.

In their representations of upper-class Irish family life at the time of the Land War, Trollope and Moore register the impact of the late-nineteenth-century "Woman Question" on the late Victorian understanding of the contract of marriage and of the domestic sphere. While both novelists were responding primarily to developments in Britain, consciousness of feminist issues was also advancing in Ireland at this time. In 1881, Anna Parnell (sister of Charles Stewart) founded the Ladies Land League; this was the first Irish nationalist organization specifically for women (although the alliance between feminism and nationalism in Ireland remained uneasy). Irish women writers were extensively concerned with the question of women's social roles as well as with broader political issues.[27] Several of these, such as the extremely popular Rosa Mulholland, were associated with the *Irish Monthly*, which articulated a Catholic upper-middle-class, pro-Union perspective.[28] In Mulholland's *Marcella Grace* (1886) and M. E. Francis's *Miss Erin* (1898), female characters take on the role of (Catholic) landlords. These novels tend to uphold the colonial system of land tenure, while their heroines are shown to be capable of exercising their power in a benevolent and progressive way. The most innovative Irish woman writer of this era was Emily Lawless. Her father, Lord Cloncurry, was an Anglo-Irish aristocrat who was sympathetic to the Catholic cause, and her mother a member of the Kirwan family from Galway, where Lawless spent childhood holidays. She wrote one celebrated novel concerned mainly with agrarian violence, *Hurrish* (1886), before producing the work now often regarded as the seminal text of feminist protest in this period, *Grania* (1892). In this, she resembles Moore who, in his Irish fiction, also moved away from plots based on colonial and agrarian conflict toward an increasing preoccupation with private and especially sexual experience. Unlike Moore, however, Lawless experiments with new modes of representing subaltern, peasant consciousness from the outset. The divergent strategies of Moore and Lawless have their own distinctive strengths and weaknesses.

The eponymous heroine of Mulholland's *Marcella Grace* is the daughter of a weaver from the Liberties of Dublin and an aristocratic mother who married beneath her and died when her daughter was too young to remember her. Rediscovered by her maternal aunt, Marcella learns that she is the heiress to a large estate. She is a social conservative by instinct ("In her secret heart Marcella was on the side of the powers that be"),[29] but she also resists the idea of her tenants becoming the owners of their farms because that would deprive her of her recently acquired authority ("She felt a strong desire to try her own power of working good before throwing the reins out of her hands that had as yet hardly grasped them" [126]). Any potential tension between this desire for control and Marcella's benevolent, sweetly feminine nature is resolved when a former Fenian, Bryan Kilmartin, becomes her husband and co-manager of her estates. Such a marriage will ensure that Marcella avoids the fate of Bryan's intensely patriotic mother—a woman unsexed by too much political commitment. Mrs. Kilmartin was "six feet high, with a masculine voice, and had been implicated, while Bryan was still a child, in International outrages abroad, when she had escaped from pursuit disguised as a man" (182).

The conclusion of Francis's *Miss Erin* is more ambiguous in its political implications. Here, the central woman character is the daughter of a Young Ireland rebel who died in exile in America; Erin inherits land after the death of her much more conservative and politically conventional uncle. She is a fiery young woman and fancies that she may become an Irish Joan of Arc. On the one hand, Erin's identification with the cause of the poor people of Ireland is pathologized in the novel. She has no one to love her, so she loves Mother Ireland instead.[30] Later, her lover, a Tory Englishman, tells her that she is "making a kind of fetish of this imaginary personification of Ireland" (352). She is impressed by the placid, hard-working English countryfolk who are "undisturbed by revolutionary theories" (271), and concerned about how her English friends will respond to her own activism in Ireland: "All my sympathies are with the people. I feel at present all kinds of instincts asserting themselves within me. Do not be more angry than you can help, if you hear of my saying or doing things which seem to be unfeminine!" (314).

Her radicalism is subdued after she has to be rescued from the scene of a violent eviction, her green cloak soaked with blood. She confesses that "it was wrong to try and stir up the people" (340). Yet Erin is to some degree rewarded for her fidelity to the poor. Even though she refuses to marry her English sweetheart, his political ambitions are ruined and he comes to join her in Ireland instead. "One day," he promises her, "we may work out some of your projects—together!" (356). Only some of her childish dreams may come true, but at least she is no longer alone.

As these examples illustrate, late-nineteenth-century Irish women novelists used some of the familiar plots and resolutions of romantic fiction to unexpected ends. Emily Lawless, however, ignores such conventions altogether. The peasant women in her fiction have little chance of satisfying their desires for romantic love or domestic happiness in their own communities; to the more delicate among them, the life of a nun seems infinitely preferable to marriage in the squalid conditions of cabin life. Yet in her two key novels, Lawless counters her "realistic" account of domestic life with a romanticization of the hard physical labor that both her male and female protagonists must endure to survive in such remote and beautiful regions of Ireland as the Burren in Clare or the Aran Islands.

Hurrish O'Brien and Grania O'Malley, the eponymous heroes of Lawless's two most significant novels, are both profoundly attached to their native places. Through them, Lawless naturalizes the harsh subsistence economy of those geographical locations where "starvation [is] made visible, and embodied in a landscape": "Mother Earth, once young, buxom, frolicsome, is here a wrinkled old woman, sitting alone in the evening of her days, and looking with melancholy eyes at the sunset" (*Hurrish*, 3–4).[31]

Lawless is resolutely opposed to those historical forces that threaten to transform these wretchedly poor environments. She asserts that "No Irishman—no Irishman born of peasant parents at any rate—is ever genuinely and at heart a democrat. The whole theory is exotic—never has been, and never will be, otherwise" (*Hurrish*, 124). Despite his sentimental weakness for patriotic songs and stories, Hurrish is devoted to his landlord and namesake, Pierce O'Brien of Donore. Although Grania has never even met any of the "quality," as she approaches the only large, imposing house on Inishmann, now abandoned and in ruins, she too feels "a dim sensation of respect. . . . inherent, born in her race, and not therefore easily dissevered from it."[32] In *Hurrish*, Lawless sees Land League violence as the consequence of the alliance between "shmart fellars"—ambitious young men with socialist leanings and everything to gain from a state of "social ferment, of 'veiled' rebellion" (60)—and the old secret societies with which the whole of Ireland is "honeycombed," that "subsist upon murder, and upon murder only" (13). Maurice Brady is the representative of this young male type in *Hurrish*, set during the Land War. The loquacious, discontent Murdough Blake, the man apparently destined to marry the heroine in *Grania*, is a quarter-century too early for the "golden political era for promising young men of his class" (*Grania*, 61). He can only continue in the tracks of his father and grandfather, or emigrate to America.

But what is most distinctive and unusual in Lawless's peasant fiction is her insistence that the new Ireland will be no better than the old, mainly because the Irish—especially Irish men—are almost completely indifferent to sexual feeling. This is as true of a gentle, virtuous son of the soil such as Hurrish as it is of the upstart Murdough. She ventures that it is possibly just as well that such men are not much subject to romantic passion, for if it "were to exercize an equal ascendancy over such pieces of touch-paper as our friend Hurrish,—if he and such as he were to be as excitable in this direction as they are in some others—politics, to wit,—surely not all the rain that ever fell upon Ireland would keep that unlucky island from being in a state of perpetual conflagration!" (*Hurrish*, 153).

In *Grania*, Lawless states that declarations or demonstrations of physical attraction between the sexes are simply unknown in traditional Irish society. This extreme reserve does not have to be enforced by the priest; it is age-old and natural, the cause and the effect of generations of loveless marriages. Lawless's vision of folk culture in the west of Ireland is here totally at odds with that of later writers associated with the Irish Literary Revival, who celebrated the primitive, unspoiled life of the people. (J. M. Synge claimed that *Grania* lacked "the real Aran spirit.")[33] Lawless ceaselessly scans for grim evidence of Irish cultural and racial degeneration as exhibited by the common people but, unlike George Moore, shows little interest in the decadence of the Ascendancy.[34] The passionate Grania is exceptional, the product of a genuine love match between her father Con O'Malley and Delia Joyce from Connemara, "a tall, wild-eyed, magnificently handsome creature, with an unmistakable dash of Spanish blood in her veins" (23). In one scene, some visiting tourists stare at the girl through an eyeglass: "Grania stood doggedly waiting—her head a little thrown back; something of the stir and stress that filled her visible in her whole look and bearing; a wild, untamed vision of strength and savage beauty standing beside that crooked and stunted thornbush" (273).

Grania represents something older and more authentic than the respectable modernity of these shocked and curious ladies with their parasols and waterproof cloaks. But she can find no one among her own people to understand or love her. Her wild cry, "full of uncomprehended pain, and of still less comprehended dissatisfaction" (199), suggests a demand for an emancipation that would go well beyond anything in Murdough Blake's dreams of a social revolution. Yet how might we understand the nature of what Siobhán Kilfeather refers to as "Grania's social, sexual and spiritual frustrations"?[35] For Lawless appears to ratify the Aran woman's rebelliousness only by denying legitimacy to other forms of protest among the Irish peasantry.

Lawless's *Hurrish* certainly presents us with something extremely unusual in Anglo-Irish fiction: a positive portrayal of an Irish peasant who achieves virtue by choosing at key moments to defy the law of the land and to act instead in accordance with the "well-known if unwritten local laws" (7) of his community. Although Hurrish abhors the violence associated with the agrarian code ("Och . . . 'taint that way ould Oireland's to be freed anyhow" [25], as he tells his bloodthirsty mother), he abides by the community's notions of justice, not because of extreme suffering or vengeful madness, but out of conviviality and fellow feeling: "For what, it may be asked, *is* a good-natured and a naturally gregarious man to do, when all the sociability of his neighbourhood is concentrated around a single focus, and that focus a criminal one?" (14). When Hurrish kills his neighbor Matt Brady, who has transgressed against the communal rules by taking the land of an evicted tenant, he does so by accident. Even though the dead man's brother, Maurice, betrays Hurrish to the authorities (an act that renders Maurice anathema to the community) and then completes his vengeance by fatally wounding him, Hurrish refuses, even on his deathbed, to disclose the name of his murderer to the police. Here, a noble version of Christian charity and the agrarian secret society's oath of *omertà* appear to be in harmony with each other. But Lawless is certainly not endorsing resistance to the official law as a mode of moral definition or self-accomplishment. Hurrish is heroic, but he is no rebel. True to the conventions of the Victorian deathbed, the individual death affirms a wider solidarity; individual goodness manifests itself in loyalty to communal values. But this is largely accidental. One of the things that Hurrish seeks to achieve by protecting Maurice from the law is to salvage the long-standing engagement between that promising young patriot and Hurrish's niece. The alliance between the

ambitious Maurice and the gentle, maternal Alley would result in a very
different kind of family life to the one presided over by Hurrish's mother
(whose witchlike, wrinkled face might have been an "inevitable accompa-
niment to the gibbet or the guillotine" [26]). But Alley will never accept
the traitor Maurice and becomes a nun instead. The community venerates
the memory of Hurrish as a man who triumphed "over the law and the
'polis'" (195), but it is not at all enlightened or redeemed thereby.[36]

Grania O'Malley, who shares her name with a famous sixteenth-
century Gaelic pirate queen, is defiant by nature. She rebels against the
enslavement of women with spontaneous anger; as she tells her sister
Honor, she would strike any priest who treated her unfairly (*Grania*, 101).
When Honor tells her about a young girl, married off to a stranger, who
cried out for her mother as her new husband dragged her away, Grania
responds, "Did she kill him? 'Tis I would have killed him, no fear of me
but I would!" (130). The pious Honor tries to instruct Grania that such
suffering is all that women can expect, but she refuses to accept this lesson. As the girl matures, her "animal zest and intoxication of living" (106)
give way to a strange tune ringing incessantly in her ears and brain (197);
she fears that she is suffering from a terrible "disease . . . of which she had
never heard; which nobody else so far as she knew had ever had; a disease
which had no name, and therefore was the more mysterious and horrible"
(250). She thinks she must be going mad because she wants not a husband, but a lover; not the "unsatisfactory, conversational Murdough, the
Murdough who got tipsy and mocked at her . . . but the real Murdough,
the Murdough she had never ceased to believe in; . . . the Murdough who
loved her, even as she loved him" (298). But Grania has to recognize that
there is no real Murdough; he is a verbose and ineffectual drunkard, no
different from all the other men she sees around her. However, even this
insight deserts Grania in her final moments. As she loses consciousness,
drowning during a futile attempt to fetch a priest for her dying sister
during a storm, she imagines that she has at last achieved a real union
with Murdough: "Arrah, take me up, then, darling, take me up! Be quick,
dear, and gather me up out of this cold, creeping water! Augh, but 'tis the
strong arms you have, though you would always have it 'twas me was the
strongest, you rogue!" (354).

It could be argued that Grania is a radical heroine because her desire cannot issue in any domestic settlement that could be taken as an allegory of social or national renovation. For this reason alone, Lawless's novel is of enormous significance in the history of Irish fiction; here is a story of an attempt at individual renaissance that is not tied to a national currency to establish its value. But the limitations of *Grania* should also be registered. Of course, it is futile to look here for the combination of elements that gives a novel such as *Jane Eyre* its historical and innovative power—an alliance of realism and feminism that attacks both feudal and patriarchal privilege from the point of view of a woman of the rising class. Nevertheless, it is interesting to recall the powerful eloquence of the female protagonists in the Brontës or George Eliot.[37] Lawless's heroine by contrast can find no language that is at once both personal and social. Grania cannot read or write, and she speaks only Irish (unlike Synge, Lawless did not learn the language of the Aran Islands). She has moments when she cannot but cry out incoherently as a release for feelings she can neither understand nor express in any other way. This trope of incoherence is much used in Irish fiction and is often derived from the notion that those who speak Irish are incoherent because they cannot be understood by the speaker of English. But another danger here is that both author and reader understand what Grania wants rather too well, or reductively. It is hardly difficult for the contemporary critic to interpret such lines as these: "She stopped short, hot and panting. The words had rushed out with a fluency quite unlike her usual utterances. They were driven by that fierce current behind them. They came in this form because they were longing but forbidden to come in quite another one" (260).

Grania has only one ambition that distinguishes her: She wants to be loved. This seems to be at the heart of her rejection of Catholicism and its bloodless vision of the afterlife. Otherwise, in her attachments to the land and to agricultural labor, for instance, she is entirely conventional. She belongs to a population that is both overproductive and doomed to sterility (theorists of racial degeneration could never quite decide whether degenerates would breed like rabbits or die out). In an environment like that, or one so understood, authentic sexual passion and gratification are unavailable.

No doubt such desires were very severely repressed in late-nineteenth-century Irish rural society—although when we find Lawless suggesting that they were virtually unknown in traditional Irish culture, the absurdity of the claim reveals the author's anxiety for a racial explanation of a pathology. Desire is given an exclusive, emancipatory role, disarticulated from the novel's account of the actualities of Irish life. Lawless's understanding of Grania's condition inhibits any investigation of women's desire as a sphere of creative conflicts. She confines the spare, poetic narrative of *Grania* to the story of desire fighting only with *absolute* repression; it is in racial mythology alone that any reason for this can be found. This severely curtails the power of the novel as social critique.

As in his book *Parnell and His Island* (1887), George Moore uses his fiction about rural Ireland to launch a sustained attack on the crippled and suppressed society that ignorance, superstition, and the clergy have conspired to produce. In several of the stories from *The Untilled Field*, he describes how naïve but often well-meaning priests enforce a regime of extreme sexual discipline in rural communities, ostracizing lively young women for their sinfulness. Moore's later novel, *The Lake*, is about the relationship between one such priest and a woman whom he has denounced from the altar. "A Play-House in the Waste" and "Julia Cahill's Curse" focus on some of those individuals who suffer most as a result of the severe sanctions against extramarital liaisons.

Moore's Father MacTurnan would like to see his parishioners prosper, but even building a road across the bog or developing a harbor might only encourage them to escape to America. So he begins rehearsals for the performance of a miracle play, hoping that visitors might travel down from Dublin to see it. This project ends in disaster when Margaret, one of the actors, falls pregnant. The people believe that MacTurnan's playhouse is cursed, and it falls into ruin. They tell how "when the signs of [the girl's] wakeness began to show, the widow Sheridan took a halter off the cow and tied Margaret to the wall, and she was in the stable until the child was born. Then didn't the mother take a bit of string and tie it round the child's throat, and bury it near the play-house; and it was three nights after that the storm rose, and the child pulled the thatch out of the roof" (*Untilled Field*, 162–63).

The child's white form—the unholy ghost of "the only bastard that was every born in the parish" (163)—can be seen fluttering around the road by night until the priest dashes bog water over it to baptize it. Its mother is dispatched to America. Julia Cahill is thrown out her house by her father, after (or so it is reported) the priest threatens to turn him into a rabbit. Father Madden warns Julia: "You're the encouragement of the dancing and courting here; but I'm going to put a stop to it" (168). Her neighbors believe that Julia spends two years living with the fairies before she emigrates. Her parting curse on the parish is that "every year a roof must fall in and a family go to America" (165). Twenty years later, a departing emigrant from the district expects to find her at the other side of the Atlantic; he believes that she will be as young and beautiful as ever, thanks to the fairies' protection. In these stories, the victims of the Catholic clergy are popularly imagined to have acquired primitive, supernatural powers that enable them to take vengeance against the Church. The ascription of these archaic, magical gifts to women such as Julia indicates that even their victimizers may have some sympathy or admiration for these excluded individuals. But Rose Leicester (renamed Nora Glynn in the 1921 edition of the novel), the disgraced unwed mother in *The Lake*, who is of lower-middle-class rather than peasant provenance, ultimately makes sense of her expulsion from the parish of Garranard in quite a different way.

Father Oliver Gogarty rages against the schoolmistress Rose in his Sunday sermon, after a local gossip tells him that she is expecting a child. Rose slips out of the church while he is preaching and never returns to the parish. Only much later can the priest admit that he was jealous of the schoolmistress's lover and furious that she would not disclose the name of the man responsible for her pregnancy. Gogarty realizes that he tried to get Rose to come back from London simply because he wanted to see her again—and not because he believed that living in a Protestant country would be a moral danger for her. By the time he acknowledges his love for Rose, she has formed a relationship with a well-known scholar, Mr. Ellis, with whom she travels around Europe and the Middle East researching the historical origins of Christian scripture. Gogarty loses his faith in the sacraments and in his spiritual vocation. To avoid scandalizing his flock, he stages his own death by drowning and, following the stigmatized woman into exile, flees to New York, where he hopes to find work as a journalist. But while Rose's flight from Garranard was the beginning of a joyful process of self-discovery, which she tells Gogarty that she had been planning for some time, the priest's departure from his native place is lonely and furtive.

In this novel, we find many characteristic features of the naturalism that will dominate Irish literature during the twentieth century. The protagonists are defined against a community that is represented as mindlessly conformist, from which they must escape in order to survive. Rose writes affectionately of the "kind, sweet, docile animal life" of Garranard,[38] but Gogarty is convinced that "the people never change, only individuals change" (*Lake*, 25). Even if the priest had married a sensible local woman like Annie McGrath, instead of taking a vow of chastity, he would have had to resign himself to "a froglike acquiescence in the stagnant pool" (303). Only in the natural world can Gogarty find an inkling of the "phantom life" (39) that beckons him. The lake, with its beautiful woods and islands, remains animated by the life force that seems to have utterly deserted the people. (The priest is fascinated by the hermits of medieval Ireland, but his teachers at Maynooth inculcate only a "steadfast piety . . . more suited to modern requirements" [21].) In order to understand the "Irish melodies" (6) of the landscape, Gogarty must leave Garranard. Clearly, the true spirit of the place has nothing to do with the political unrest of the peasantry, which is completely ignored in this novel. There appears to be no possibility that this degraded culture could ever be revivified from within. Not even love can overcome its repressive force; Rose and Gogarty utterly fail to understand each other while they are still living in Garranard.

But the epistolary form of the bulk of *The Lake* enables Moore to play some interesting variations on themes that will reappear in the works of many later Irish writers. We encounter Rose as the author of her own life story, and in this way she exceeds what Eagleton describes as a "mysterious, elusive, instinctual" feminine stereotype.[39] She forces Gogarty to accept his own hypocrisy, but she never entirely forgives him. The correspondence is intensely combative—as well as extremely amusing for the reader, who follows the attempt of each partner in turn to dominate the relationship. In this charged exchange, details such as the length of time it takes either (but especially Rose) to respond to a letter, or whether Gogarty adds the "P.P."

(standing for "Parish Priest") to the end of his name, become highly significant. Nor does the woman always come out best in these letters. Gogarty is right to accuse Rose of patronizing and satirizing him at times, and he legitimately questions her motives in inviting him to visit Rome with her and Mr. Ellis. She merely wants Gogarty to feel his intellectual inferiority by comparison with her new friend; as he writes, nothing would have been accomplished by such an encounter, "except the astonishment of a poor Connaught priest, the proving to him that you are making great progress towards a cultured comprehension of the Renaissance" (181). Gogarty also points out the complete dependence of the now-supposedly emancipated Rose on the guidance and wisdom of Ellis, even to the point of falling back on his very words (180). Yet we might ask that if her relationship with Ellis is so absorbing, why does she maintain such close contact with her former persecutor?

As a woman with intellectual as well as romantic aspirations, who expresses no desire to regularize her union with Ellis, Rose Leicester is a quite unusual figure in Irish fiction of this time. *The Lake* makes it clear that modern, more equal relationships between men and women are complicated and exhausting. In the novel, Garranard is compared to Bayreuth and Rome. Of course, the Irish village is found wanting; of course, the parish priest abandons his people to escape to a big city. But the novel does not depend on a straightforward contrast between the benign cosmopolitan world and the malign local world, and the struggle between the local and the cosmopolitan has not been completely uneven.

Moore understands the nature of the historical change that is slowly evolving in Ireland, and he rejects any romanticization of traditional Irish ways. He offers instead a subtle view of an emancipatory process governed by a woman who is the senior figure in the intricate, contested series of exchanges recorded in this correspondence. Rose Leicester's letters may be inconsistent and sometimes unfair, but they still offer an alternative model of Irish modernist "feminine writing" to, for instance, the voice of Joyce's Molly Bloom, the eroticized but domestic heroine in *Ulysses*. Joyce apparently loathed Moore's novel, which he read in Rome in 1906. He poured scorn on Moore's "'lithery' man Ellis, and all the talk about pictures and music" in *The Lake*.[40] In letters to his brother, Joyce makes no objection to

Moore's depiction of rural Ireland but mercilessly mocks the novel's European pretensions—especially Rose's long letters about the delights of Ger-
many and Italy.[41] Although himself an emigré, Joyce debunks the notion of
a flight from Ireland to a more "advanced" culture, signaling his rejection
of a key trope of Irish naturalistic fiction. Moore seems doomed to his role
as a John the Baptist figure in Irish fiction; it is with Joyce that the great
sea change takes place. But nevertheless, at least in relation to questions of
gender, Moore's analytic subtlety in this novel may exceed that of even the
most radical of his successors.

5

James Joyce and the History of the Future

"Moromelodious"[1] Joyce

On one page of *Finnegans Wake*, in the midst of numerous other references to famous Irish books such as John Mitchel's *Jail Journal* and Oscar Wilde's *De Profundis*, Joyce alludes to at least eight nineteenth-century Irish novels.[2] The titles of the novels appear during an account of how the character Shem (associated with Joyce himself) wrote *Ulysses*—"a most miraculous jeeremyhead sindbook for all the peoples" (*Wake*, 229)—while in exile in Europe. So Joyce mentions "knockonacow and a chow collegions" (228) (Kickham's *Knocknagow* and Griffin's *The Collegians*), or "Croppy Crowhore" (220) (Michael Banim's *The Croppy* and *Crohoore of the Billhook*), presumably as examples of the Irish "scribenery" (220) that his books incorporate but supercede.

No one would dispute Joyce's own estimate of his historical significance in comparison to earlier Irish writers. But while in recent years Joyce's work has been extensively reread in relation to the aesthetics and politics of the mostly Anglo-Irish figures associated with the Irish Literary Revival, it is generally presumed that he has little or nothing in common with earlier Irish Catholic writers in English.[3] Nevertheless, Joyce's transformation of the genre of the novel can be illuminated by returning to Thomas Moore, the first major Irish Catholic author of the nineteenth century, and to the line of Irish writers who were inspired by Moore's example.

It would be absurd to claim that Moore is the father of any Irish novelistic tradition in the way that, for instance, Defoe and Richardson have been regarded as the originators of the English novel. Rather, his *Melodies* (which arguably had a greater influence on Joyce than any purely literary text by an Irish author) inaugurated a particular mode of aestheticizing Irish history that had an enormous impact on much of the prose fiction as well as on the poetry of nineteenth-century Ireland.[4] In the *Melodies*, Moore generally assumes the role of the archetypal romantic poet, affiliated to his community by his rendering of its longings for self-realization and his acknowledgement of the trauma it has undergone. For example, in "Silent, O Moyle" (which Joyce loved to sing), fidelity, endurance, and sincerity of feeling are silhouetted against a tragic nightscape that nevertheless holds the promise of a new dawn in which old glories can be reborn. In Joyce's "Two Gallants," from *Dubliners*, this song is played on a Irish harp, which is "heedless that her coverings had fallen about her knees . . . weary alike of the eyes of strangers and of her master's hands."[5] At the very end of Anna Livia Plurabelle's terminal monologue in *Finnegans Wake*, the embodiment of Dublin's River Liffey tells us that she can see before her the "moyles and moyles" of her "cold father" (628), the sea. In both cases, images of vulnerable femininity are associated with Fionnuala, the heroine of the legend of the Children of Lir on which Moore draws. She was turned into a swan by her wicked stepmother and condemned to wander the seas of Ireland, until she should hear the bell announcing the arrival of Christianity. In Moore's song, a passively suffering Ireland awaits the sunrise that will bring her liberation. This is not to say that what the narrator of the "Cyclops" episode in *Ulysses* calls "the Tommy Moore touch about Sara Curran and she's far from the land"[6] is not often mocked and exploited by Joyce, but he always takes it seriously enough to explore and diagnose its appeal.

It is often proposed that Joyce revels in the adulterated or hybridized condition of Irish urban culture that nationalist ideologues regarded as corrupt.[7] Yet he does not dismiss the preoccupations of the nineteenth-century national novelists that we have considered here. After all, they too had frequently been charged by Gaelic purists and Irish Revivalists with dealing only with the debased culture of English-speaking Ireland. Joyce may have little enough to say directly about the major events of the nineteenth century in Ireland, but the traces of this history can be read everywhere in his fiction. Gibbons, for instance, suggests that the characters from *Dubliners* exhibit the "pathology of post-Famine Ireland" in their paralysis and emotional sterility, but even the Halloween rituals in the story "Clay" show how vestiges of the communal past survive in petit-bourgeois Dublin.[8] Joyce understands how even a supposedly low culture addresses and assuages real grief and longing. In one typical example, Stephen Dedalus, as he dwells on his mother's recent death, recalls the poignant mementos of the nights she spent at dances or laughing with her friends at the pantomime: "Phantasmal mirth, folded away: musk-perfumed" (*Ulysses*, 8–9). Indeed, Joyce's contemporary Wyndham Lewis protested against the inclusion of so much of the cultural ephemera of Edwardian Dublin in *Ulysses*, complaining that the novel "lands the reader inside an Aladdin's cave of incredible bric-à-brac."[9] Although *Ulysses* itself resists commodification in its linguistic and formal difficulty, Joyce offers a largely sympathetic depiction of commodity culture in the book. Jennifer Wicke, for example, contends that *Ulysses* is "indisputably allied" to mass cultural narratives such as those of modern advertising, and she suggests that the "unabashed sentimentality" of the work also demonstrates its "mass-cultural aspect."[10] So to some degree, Joyce shares the tendency toward a sentimental blurring of a violent history that lends a kitschy, low-cultural feel to such Irish national novels as *The Collegians* and *Knocknagow*. As Deane puts it, Moore's lyrics (and other popular songs, poems, and stories) have become "as integral a part of the Irish culture as the airs and songs that they replaced or displaced"; the past is recuperable now only in melody and sentiment.[11]

The lavishness of Joyce's allusions to the *Melodies*, and to dozens of other Irish songs in *Ulysses* and the *Wake*, does not of course mean that we can use the songs to interpret his works in any straightforward way. Nevertheless, the evocative appeal of popular music clearly plays a major part in Joyce's representation of history and collective memory.[12] One celebrated example is the use of the ballad "The Lass of Aughrim" in "The Dead," in which the private memory of Gretta Conroy is interfused with historical memory, bringing these realms into conjuncture with each other. (The imagery at the end of the story is also inspired in part by Moore's lyric "O, Ye Dead.") Joyce's particular mode of mobilizing, through music, a collective memory that may also stir up a tragic individual memory is anticipated by the scenes of musical performance and by the protagonists' various emotional responses to song in *Knocknagow*. In Kickham, too, the inclusion of music as a mode of shared feeling makes formal demands on the novelist. He uses repetition and close verbal patterning to reinforce the politically crucial representation of the absorption of the experience of a suffering individual into that of a larger group consciousness. In addition, Kickham's project of mapping the shared space of a community that has undergone enormous historical disturbance anticipates Joyce's great experiment. But a good deal changes between *Knocknagow* and *Ulysses*. The village has given way to the city, although some of the close-knit features of the village remain and resist the atomization of city life. The acoustic environment is immensely more diverse. Irish music competes with opera and operetta (although the nationalist appeal of Italian opera makes the fusion of, for instance, Moore and Verdi less anomalous than it might at first appear). Then there are the music hall numbers and advertising jingles. The music of consumerism spreads to colonize consciousness and, with its refrains and rhymes, along with the fading memories of the more prestigious music or national airs, creates a cacophony unknown to the world of *Knocknagow*. Thus, fragments of traditional culture, and of nationalist rhetoric and art, take their place within an emergent mass culture, much of it British or American in origin.

So Joyce appears to embrace the multiplicity and excess of modern capitalist culture (incipient rather than actual in the Dublin of 1904). He explores this culture in relation to Irish historical experience and Irish culture in its English-language forms. But Joyce himself has by now become an emblem of the commodification of the once professionally solitary artist of the modernist period. Despite the esoteric aspects of his writings, he is regarded as a rather uncontroversial Irish literary icon; in Ireland, quotations from Joyce's texts have been used to sell all kinds of commodities, from lemon soap to sausages. The official celebrations of the centenary of Bloomsday in 2004 confirmed that the Irish state now wants to lay belated claim to the "cultural capital" associated with the most famous literary personality of the twentieth century.[13] But could Joyce only have been accepted in his own country after the demise of "de Valera's Ireland"? Certainly, we can point to specific reasons why Joyce should only now be coming into his own as an interpreter of the complexities of Irish modernity. But instead, Joyce is often taken to represent an Irishness that is merely "reassuringly modern."[14]

Ireland passed through a period of revolutionary upheaval between the Rebellion of 1916 and the Anglo-Irish Treaty of 1922. But it was only during three much later periods—from the 1960s to the oil crisis of 1973; even more emphatically in the 1990s from 1993 to 2001; and again from 2002 to the present—that economic transformations on a par with the political transformations of 1922 were achieved. Independent Ireland did not participate in the general postwar economic development of Western Europe and the USA. In addition, the late 1960s saw the renewed outbreak of violence in Northern Ireland, dormant since that statelet's foundation. Even Ireland's accession to the Common Market (later the European Union) in 1973 did not bring about many immediate benefits; the economic recession of the 1980s was severe and protracted. But all of this changed in the mid-1990s with the beginning of the economic boom referred to as the "Celtic Tiger"—the European equivalent of the economic "miracles" experienced by several Asian countries in the postwar period.[15] In addition, the Northern Irish Peace Process seemed to promise an eventual resolution of the Northern conflict.

Joyce has long been read as the prophet of a transnational or cosmopolitan modernity.[16] Contemporary Ireland, therefore, may seem to represent the fulfillment of all his dreams for the country. Immigration now far outstrips emigration, creating the conditions for the emergence of a new multicultural nation; the Belfast Agreement, ratified by a popular vote north and south of the Irish border in 1998, may yet lead to the peaceful coexistence of nationalists and unionists. This situation seems to correspond to the multivocal modernism of *Ulysses*; even *Finnegans Wake* seems newly relevant in its amalgamation of Ireland with "the polyglot atopia of the information age."[17] There are a number of ways in which Joyce's work seems peculiarly well attuned to the specificities of the Irish experience of late capitalism. Just as there appears to be a correlation between the disjunctures and traumas of Irish history and the various abrupt interventions and crosscuts of *Ulysses* and *Finnegans Wake*, so Joyce also registers the belief (or the moment of belief) in the fact that traumas of this kind are being overcome, subsumed into the euphoric excitements of advanced consumer society, with all its goods and pleasures; "Pray for us" is replaced by "Buy from us" (*Ulysses*, 309).

Contemporary Ireland is often understood to have bypassed the economic stages of industrialism (most of its initial expansion was reliant on the new electronic and pharmaceutical industries, and current growth is based mainly on a massive services sector, including financial services). This has not been a history of slow advances or gradual evolution. In Joyce's fiction, too, we witness a series of abrupt transitions between one phase of development and the next. The pleasures available to consumers may have been extraordinarily limited in the Dublin of 1904 (we might recall Maria's painful hesitation over her purchase of a plumcake in "Clay," or the young boy's bitter disappointment when he finally arrives at the Oriental bazaar in "Araby"), but many of the city-dwellers in his later work appear to have acquired the habits of a leisure class without its income. For in *Ulysses,* Joyce breaks with the grim naturalism of *Dubliners* and transcends the material restrictions of the city through an unprecedented rendition of the speech, politics, and the conscious and unconscious fantasies of those who live there, including his antihero Leopold Bloom. These Dubliners are preoccupied with the political project of recreating a purportedly once lively and commercial Irish nation, but also with the pleasures of drink, food, conversation, gossip, and sex. But in Joyce these are the pursuits of the masses, not the more rarefied avocations of the European elite, which had supposedly disappeared in the catastrophe of the Great War, and whose great memorialist is Proust. The Soviet critic Karl Radek condemned Joyce for depicting "these Blooms and Dedaluses, whom the author relentlessly pursues into the lavatory, the brothel and the pothouse," at the very moment when the Irish petit bourgeois were preparing for the insurrection of 1916.[18] But in this, Joyce successfully forecasts one of the eventual results of that revolution—not the Free State repression that followed shortly afterward, but the regime of modern consumerism of which Bloom is the avatar.[19]

Joyce's great counterpart in the exploration of the culture of the modern metropolis is Walter Benjamin. For both of them, the aesthetic always has a political character; consumerism is never merely reducible to privatized self-indulgence—although Joyce certainly admits that element with the Blooms. Joyce, like Benjamin, shows us how at a particular stage in the evolution of the commodity form, its products are imbued with the power of a collective memory of better times and with utopian desire for the future.[20] These objects are laden with memory and with the longing of the possessor to express an identity in and through them. On the cusp between a social order dominated by religion and one dominated by commerce, Joyce shows us how the two systems overlap in key areas. Many of the rituals of Catholicism, with their endlessly repetitive features and their fetishization of artifacts such as medals, statues, and the like, are transposed into commercial forms with astonishing ease. As Bloom remarks of the prayers in the church in Sandymount: "Good idea the repetition. Same thing with ads" (309). Joyce provides what we might call (after Weber) the epic of Catholicism and the spirit of capitalism.

So we gain from Joyce an important insight into how the nightmares of history are converted into what Benjamin would call the dreamworlds of nationalism and consumerism. Joyce does not mock the Irish for their fantasies about their approaching "liberation," nor for the fact that they are so much in thrall to advertising, popular culture, and the allure of the modern commodity. Rather, he too stands between a tragic history and the deformations of the marketplace. Most nineteenth-century Irish authors, like the Moore of the *Melodies*, can be accused of having capitulated too readily to the latter. One great difference between Joyce and his Irish predecessors is that he discovered the means by which this endless translation of historical nightmare into modern consumerist phantasmagoria could be represented; moreover, he found the range of voice, the registers, in which both the tragic and the comic reverberations of this process could be heard. Joyce encouraged and even participated in his own transformation into a celebrity. The current commodification of his works was anticipated by his display of the first copy of *Ulysses* in the window of Shakespeare and Company in Paris, in February 1922, for onlookers to gaze at and admire. More generally, Lawrence Rainey has analyzed how many modern artists refuse the economics of the marketplace, only to remain complicit with its operation at a higher level: They abjure the mass audience for popular art, only to turn their works into *objets d'art*, saleable commodities of a different kind.[21] Yet Joyce survived his own cult status and—unlike most of his nineteenth-century Irish predecessors, but especially Mangan and Oscar Wilde—did not become a symbol of a wretched collective fate.[22]

There are traces in Joyce, too, of the other Moore—the Moore of *Captain Rock*. They both investigate stereotypes of Irishness with glee as well as understanding. Unlike the fiction of the fin de siècle or a later postindependence naturalism, Joyce does not merely dwell on the individualized victims of large historical forces and systems. Like Moore, Joyce has his oscillations: between the sardonic critique of "Grace" and the lyricism of "The Dead" in *Dubliners*, between the savagery of "Cyclops" and the rapture of "Penelope" in *Ulysses*, and between the raucous ballad of Tim Finnegan and the lonely song of Fionnuala in *Finnegans Wake*.[23] What is referred to in "Cyclops" as "Doing the rapparee" (*Ulysses*, 243) sometimes involves an encounter with what Joyce called the "intransigent" or "physical force"[24] elements in Irish popular resistance. But as well as this, Joyce shows that while all that is solid in Dublin or Irish culture might melt into a national air, it can also be condensed or rematerialized for the purposes of historical understanding.

Simony: The Sin of the Century

Joyce initially planned to begin and end *Dubliners* with two notably anticlerical stories: "The Sisters" and "Grace." (The addition of the final story, "The Dead," was intended to soften his harsh portrayal of Dublin in the book.)[25] In the first story, the young protégé of Father Flynn broods on the mysterious word *simony* in his catechism, which he associates with the paralysis that afflicts the disgraced priest (*Dubliners*, 1). But it is Father Purdon in "Grace" ("Purdon" was also the name of a street in Dublin's red-light district) who might more appropriately be accused of being a simoniac—guilty of selling spiritual favors for material gain, or at least of subordinating religion to the pursuit of Mammon. "Jesus Christ was not a hard taskmaster" (174), he assures his congregation of down-at-heel "business men and professional men" in the Jesuit church in Gardiner Street. Father Purdon's God understands the temptations that beset those who have to make their own way in the world, and merely demands from them what the priest describes as a little "spiritual accountancy" (173).

In this story, we find Joyce in effect repeating one of the most familiar charges made by Irish Catholic novelists of the later nineteenth century:

that the Church had betrayed the faith in order to court the native bourgeoisie. In their turn, the majority of Irish people had submitted to the centralizing, authoritarian tendencies of the ultramontane Church. This is allegorized in "Grace" through the ludicrous conversation at the bedside of the ailing Tom Kernan, a tea-merchant who has bitten off part of his tongue after a fall down a flight of stairs in a pub. Kernan's friends want to encourage him (and themselves) to more virtuous ways, so they prepare Kernan (a convert from what Joyce refers to in "The Dead" as "the other persuasion" [195]) for attendance at Father Purdon's retreat. They do this by regaling him with a hilariously inaccurate account of nineteenth-century Church history and particularly of the Vatican Council at which the doctrine of papal infallibility was promulgated in 1870.

Martin Cunnigham tells the men that John MacHale, the Irish-speaking, nationalist archbishop of Tuam and opponent of the ultramontanist Cardinal Paul Cullen, had vigorously resisted this doctrine. But when it was declared a dogma by the pope, "On the very moment John MacHale, who had been arguing and arguing against it, stood up and shouted out with the voice of a lion: Credo!" (169).[26] His companions are thrilled by the word of "belief and submission" (170). Throughout this scene, the high register of the language that the men imitate and mutilate is at the heart of the comic effect. Yet it is not simply that they are bad or ignorant Catholics. Their mild interest in the history of the papacy seems almost idealistic when set against the ingratiating venality of Father Purdon's sermon. The priest's worldliness is matched by the bland servility of Father Conmee in Ulysses—although Conmee's exchange of pleasantries with Mrs. David Sheehy MP in the opening of the "Wandering Rocks" episode demonstrates that he moves in rather more elevated social circles. Just as the military-commercial British empire claimed to be spreading civilization, regularly described as a spiritual, not just material, boon to places such as Ireland, so the Roman Catholic empire inverted this ideology by trading its spiritual dominion for material gain. The latter tyranny was even worse because it occupied the soul of the Irish.[27] As Leopold Bloom thinks to himself: "Squareheaded chaps they must be in Rome: they work the whole show. And don't they rake in the money too? . . . The doctors of the church: they mapped out the whole theology of it" (68).

Catholic ritual and belief are repeatedly demystified in *Ulysses* through the secular consciousness of Bloom, advertising canvasser and thrice-baptized Jew. Nevertheless, several later Irish Catholic writers debated whether Joyce should still be regarded as a Catholic artist, and recent historicist critics have emphasized Joyce's lifelong identification with Irish Catholic culture.[28] For it seems obvious that Joyce can only be described as a religious writer if we accept that his late interest in cyclicalism and recurrence (like that of his modernist contemporary W. B. Yeats) extended beyond the realm of the aesthetic into that of the metaphysical. Joyce's Wakean religion (if it can be so called) is based on the imagined reawakening of HCE—the universal principle of paternity and creativity. Thus it is therefore intimately associated in the book with the traditional Irish funerary practice of the merry wake, which had long been a prime target of a reforming and modernizing Catholic Church in nineteenth-century Ireland. The resurrection of the waked corpse was also a staple of Irish popular culture and of nineteenth-century Irish stage melodrama, as in Dion Boucicault's *The Shaughran* (1874).

But rather than pursue the chimera of Joyce's own specific religious affiliation, it is more promising to investigate how those aspects of institutional Catholicism that most fascinate Stephen and Bloom are carried over into Joyce's larger project of representing modern Irish culture. Among these is the connection between Catholicism and arcane or esoteric knowledge; in Joyce's work it stretches from Father Flynn's rather sinister theological lessons in "The Sisters" to "Ithaca," the "scientific" chapter of *Ulysses*, where the question-and-answer format of the Catholic catechism is used to parody both religion and science. "Ithaca" provides the reader with a comic excess of data, much of it to do with astronomy, engineering, or mathematics; yet all these facts relating to Bloom's final conversation with Stephen are summoned up by the narrator in the dogmatic spirit of a priest or teacher. But there is an important distinction between Stephen's and Bloom's views of Catholicism as a system that works according to discernible principles and for particular purposes. Both see it as a system of power. But while Stephen is preoccupied with the intellectual-aesthetic appeal of Catholicism (as when he broods on "the slow growth and change of rite and dogma like his own rare thoughts" in the first episode of *Ulysses*

[17]),²⁹ Bloom is much more impressed by the commercial-cultural power of the Church. It is through him that we gain an insight into the popular or demotic side of post-Famine Irish Catholicism.

In "Lotus Eaters" and "Hades," Bloom reflects on the Church's reliance on holy objects; these musings anticipate his later ruminations about the modern marketplace and the quasimagical power with which it invests commodities. (We are reminded here of the hapless Kernan in "Grace," obliged to submit to Catholicism, but begging to be spared at least the candles and the "magic-lantern business" [*Dubliners*, 171].)³⁰ Yet Bloom's interventions cut deep into the obsessional preoccupations of Stephen and allow us to see how recognizably Catholic these are. Stream of consciousness as a mode of narration reminds us that the interior life is a kind of secret conversation; secrecy fascinates Bloom, especially when he sees how the Church can gain access to the private thoughts of the faithful. He recognizes the erotic nature of the desires that priests manipulate, particularly through the confessional: "Great weapon in their hands. More than doctor or solicitor. Woman dying to. And I schschschschsch. And did you chachachachacah?" (*Ulysses*, 68). Like Michel Foucault, Joyce acknowledges the Catholic sacrament of confession as a forerunner of modern discourses about the sexual experiences and proclivities of individuals, such as sexology or Freudian psychoanalysis.³¹ It could even be argued that the religious objects that surround the scene of penitence and confession—"Flowers, incense, candles melting" (*Ulysses*, 68)—prefigure the fetishes that are such a prominent element in Joyce's theatrical portrayal of Bloom's masochistic sexuality in "Circe."³² Certainly, Joyce was never one to underestimate the sexual arousal provoked by guilt and punishment: "Lovely shame. Pray at an altar. Hail Mary and Holy Mary. . . . Hide her blushes" (*Ulysses*, 68).

Lawrence Birken describes how modern sexual science emerged during the transition from a culture of industrial production to one of mass consumption. This new science closely associated desire with spending, assuming that individuals had "an innate tendency to spend or discharge energy."³³ With his characteristic vices of masochism, voyeurism, and onanism, Bloom is an icon of a consumerist sexual economy in which men and women (as Birken argues) are increasingly defined in relation to their specialized erotic preferences. Joyce is positioned at the historical juncture between a newly repressive Irish Catholicism and twentieth-century liberal challenges to that regime, which would mainly be based on the claim that every individual has the right to free sexual self-expression. In *Ulysses*, he discloses how much the repressive authority shares with its "liberating" alternative by showing how the "desire" freed by the loss of religious faith is instead invested in the capitalist marketplace. His continuing explorations of what Freud called the "polymorphous perversity" of modern sexuality, which to some degree his work has been taken to celebrate, is indicated by the fact that *Ulysses* concludes with the memory of the embrace of Leopold and Molly on Howth Head sixteen years earlier. This final image is of a love that is both marital and reproductive, as the courtship was followed quickly by their marriage and the birth of their only surviving child, Milly.

Finally, Bloom is also sensitive to the collective needs that Catholicism promises to satisfy: the longing for community, and the protection against the meaninglessness of death (as he puts it in "Lotus Eaters," "Not so lonely. In our confraternity" [66]). The reassurance of religion (according to Bloom) depends on the believer's capacity for self-delusion and the acceptance of superstition and its accompanying commercialized kitsch: "Lourdes cure, waters of oblivion, and the Knock apparition, statues bleeding. Old fellow asleep near that confessionbox. Hence those snores. Blind faith. Safe in the arms of kingdom come" (66). As a religious and ethnic outsider, Bloom is well placed to see the limitations of both religion and nationalism, although he is also on that account sympathetic to the longings that each satisfies. Nationalism may be, as Benedict Anderson has claimed, to some degree a secular substitute for the imagined community of traditional religion; but Bloom, while not affecting, like Stephen, to be allergic to the communal appeal of either, puts his trust instead in the capacity of technology and economic development to bring about a mass utopia (see *Ulysses*, 399).[34] For Bloom, all human aspiration to community has a poignancy that is enhanced by his own isolation, although Joyce exploits its simoniac dimension—its trafficking in relics, trinkets or such "massproducts" (553) as Bloom's Epp's cocoa. Stephen regards the transition from the religious to the commercial as a degradation of the sacred, whereas Bloom thinks of it as historically inevitable and accepts it in a mat-ter-of-fact manner. As Bloom sees it, the fundamental desire for a paradisal happiness is retained in this transition and the chances of its realization may even be advanced.

In this context, we can appreciate what Dedalus might have made of the efforts of Kernan and his cronies in "Grace" to "wash the pot" (*Dublin-ers*, 162) at Father Purdon's retreat. For him, the event could only have appeared as a monstrous parody of penitence or spiritual renewal. In Dub-lin, even Church doctrine has been reduced to half-remembered gossip or rumor, and the priest is obviously more concerned with congratulat-ing than instructing his flock. The characters are cruelly exposed in that bleakly naturalistic light cast by Joyce's famously lean and scrupulous style; we are spared no detail, from the "personal odor" (155) that impregnates the air in Kernan's bedroom, to Martin Cunningham's problems with his "incurable drunkard" of a wife (156). Yet this not all that is at stake in Joyce's most intimate examination of early-twentieth-century Irish Cathol-icism in *Dubliners*.

The inner lives of Kernan and company remain unknown to us. These are not fully realized individuals in the style of Bloom, Stephen, or even Gabriel Conroy. But they still are to be distinguished from such pathetic, isolated victims of historical and social circumstance as Eve-line, Maria, or Farrington, who feature in some of the other stories from *Dubliners*. These men have not evolved into the atomized individuals of the modern metropolis. As such, they are the precursors of the alcohol-soaked and verbose crowd that dominates most of the public space in *Ulysses*. But the most remarkable feature of the story is Joyce's contemp-tuous but amused portrayal of these characters as they go through the ritual of renewing their Catholicism, even though the Church to which they pledge themselves seems to have entirely lost its grandeur. In this way, they resemble the characters from the earlier story, "Ivy Day in the Committee Room," who briefly become Parnellites again as they listen to Joe Hynes's dreadful poem.

We could say that Joyce attacks the servility and hypocrisy of these groups as they submit to inadequate or surrogate leaders (Edward VII instead of Parnell, Father Purdon instead of John MacHale). But it could also be argued that the little band in "Grace" resists political and religious authority, if only in its convivial habits and venomous humor. These groups still have the language of combination; as canvassers for an election or as attendants at a religious retreat, they have the network of vocabularies and of gossip, of pretended personal acquaintance with the great (Parnell, McHale), which is the substitute for acquaintance with political agency or power. Their invective is gloriously cynical. Mr. Power, for example, asserts that "None of the Grays was any good" (*Dubliners*, 170), a remark which, in view of the contribution of this well-known Ascendancy family to civic and national life, Terence Brown describes as "especially ungracious, crudely sectarian in its implications and sadly ignorant" (304). They are outraged by "these ignorant bostoons . . . the thundering big country fellows" (160) that swell the ranks of the Dublin Metropolitan Police. Even Archbishop MacHale, the champion of the Irish peasant, does not escape Kernan's unflattering personal description ("crabbed-looking old chap" with bushy eyebrows [170]). There are dark suggestions about some of the "priesthoods on the continent" (162); Kernan even ventures that some of the "Old Popes" might not have been "not exactly . . . you know . . . up to the knocker" (168). While they profess to be proud to belong to "*the religion, the old, original faith*" (165), they are not unduly troubled by the stirrings of private conscience (the men meet in a pub before the retreat, even though excessive drinking was clearly the cause of Mr. Kernan's accident). Although obedience is a key theme of the story—epitomized by MacHale's ultimate surrender to the doctrine of papal infallibility—it seems extremely unlikely that these penitents will embrace even the extremely gentle form of self-discipline recommended by Father Purdon. This seems to bear out the lesson that Catholicism allows people to obtain spiritual benefits while remaining ethically inconsistent.[35]

Joyce does not then here reproduce the familiar tropes of an earlier Irish fiction of Catholic dissent, with its concentration on a cowed populace, a pitiless clergy, and the thwarted victims of the new sexual orthodoxy. Rather than focusing on either a general capitulation to an authoritarian Church or on individual protest against it, Joyce intimates that all of Dublin will submit to the new regime of commercialism and consumerism. Although demoralizing in its effects, this regime is powerfully attractive and even addictive in the pleasures it promises. There is also the suggestion here that the leaders of the people, who have betrayed them or whom they have betrayed, have already yielded to sexual or alcoholic pleasures (as the little red light in Father Purdon's church hints at his connection with the world of prostitution). The critique of early twentieth-century Catholicism in the penultimate story of *Dubliners* may well appear misplaced in its own historical context, as many Irish historians have agreed that a powerful institutional Church with strong political influence significantly inhibited the capitalist development of independent Ireland for much of the twentieth century.[36] But in its suggestion that this economic system will ultimately dominate over all else, "Grace" offers a grimly realistic alternative to the Christian and nationalist symbolism with which Joyce concludes the last story of *Dubliners*.

The Country and the City in *Ulysses*

Joyce's literary treatment of urban consciousness in *Ulysses* is generally free from the disenchantment or despair that often accompanies the recognition of the incoherence of city life. For this reason the usual modernist terms—alienation, shattering of an idyllic wholeness—do not seem to apply to Joyce's Dublin. Joyce (who was perhaps anticipated in this by Baudelaire) discovered an appeal or fascination in the stream of consciousness of city dwellers that needed no preceding experience of stable continuities as a foil.

But any assumption that Joyce makes an absolute break with earlier Irish fiction set in the country merits some reconsideration. Even within the so-called pastoral tradition in the early nineteenth century (as in Griffin), we discover a melodramatic sensibility that is more usually seen as modern and urban.[37] Yet the crowd, a recurrent image of degradation, threatening destruction and horror in political and fictional writings in France and England since the French Revolution, makes no comparably ominous appearance in Irish fiction. At the same time, the representation of the rural masses, especially of those stimulated to political activity by the O'Connellite and later campaigns, is almost a requirement in those Irish novels that sought in the masses a validation of the demand for emancipation and greater democratic inclusion. For members of the Catholic intelligentsia, the mass society of Ireland was the source of a social and ethical vigor that the Anglo-Irish elite plainly lacked. Thus, in Ireland, the masses played a role almost exactly the reverse of that conventionally assigned to them in accounts of the French Revolution and the onset of modernity, from Edmund Burke's *Reflections on the Revolution in France* (1790) to Charles Dickens's *A Tale of Two Cities* (1859). In the Irish novel, the crowd is the preserver of the traditional, not its enemy. But it is also the harbinger of the future.

The Banims frequently experiment with ways of representing large groups and crowds; the rural masses become an important agency in their own right in several of their novels. Even the ancient race of the fairies appears to be thriving and numerous in a novel such as Michael Banim's *Crohoore of the Billhook*, in which the *sidhe* inhabit a vast, underground city of their own. In the Banims, such crowds become gatherings, and their behavior is more often associated with exotic display and energy rather than with any surly threat. The marketplace and the fair are typical locales, commercial yet traditional. In *Crohoore*, Banim confesses to being distracted from his own plot by "the ever-changing varieties" of the fair in Killkenny: "We regret that now, when we have not rehearsed the hundredth part of its novelties, pleasures, and incidents, we are no longer free to indulge our teeming garrulity: but the story to which we have yoked ourselves requires immediate attention" (327).

Of the novelists in this line, only Kickham explicitly asserts that the intimate, face-to-face community of the village is morally preferable to life in the city. But there is nothing natural or organic about the recently created community of small, independent homesteads in *Knocknagow*; Kickham describes in great detail how starvation and emigration have cleared the land of its surplus population. Yet he does at times appear to suggest that it is necessary to narcotize the survivors of this history. The inhabitants of Knocknagow should be encouraged to adhere to their supposedly immemorial habits and customs, rather than to recall the cataclysmic events of the recent past. It is this image of the comatose, self-enclosed country town that is taken at face value by some later writers of the Revival period, who go on to advocate that such communities should open themselves up to the shocks and pleasures of the modern—heedless of the particular experience of modernization that this population had already endured.

Thus nineteenth-century Irish fiction complicates our conventional understanding of the advent of urban modernity in Ireland. But standard views of the opposition between the country and the city are also called into question by *Ulysses* itself. The text lacks many of the familiar *topoi* of the novel about the metropolis. For instance, Dublin is not the worldly place in which a self-formation that would have been impossible in the provinces takes place: Stephen is not one of those generic young men who come up from the provinces to enter into the world of the modern and of adulthood, such as Julien Sorel or Pip—or even the narrator of Proust's *À la recherche*. This is not a *bildungsroman*.[38] Neither are we are offered any panoramic vision of the imposing metropolis in all its potential or threat. Instead, as Enda Duffy points out, Joyce's Dublin remains in many ways a community of insiders. Joyce offers a rather uncanny "hyperrealization" of a few urban spaces in *Ulysses*, within what Duffy calls a more general "derealization" of the material city of Dublin. In this way, the reader feels constantly excluded from a local knowledge that is never explicitly shared—about the street network, for instance. Duffy goes on to suggest that to be a *flâneur* in Dublin has nothing to do with becoming a blasé cosmopolitan, equally at home in any European city, but rather it is "to display one's almost secret knowledge of the urban labyrinth which is exclusive to those who inhabit it."[39] Indeed, rather than exploiting the cultural distinction between rural and urban space, *Ulysses* does not really concede its importance at all.[40] Throughout the text, Joyce is drawn to images of the crowd-filled Irish past that emphasize its dynamic variety. In many ways, it appears that the city itself offers the best possible image of the complicated genealogies of all of Irish colonial history.

In an essay of 1912, Joyce quoted a sixteenth-century travel narrative about Ireland "in which the writer says that, although he had travelled throughout the world, he never saw in one glance what he saw in Galway: a priest raising the host, a pack chasing a deer, a vessel entering the harbor under full sail and a salmon killed with a spear."[41] These details illustrate the visual pleasures afforded by what Joyce calls the "unsettling modernity" of this western Irish city (Joyce was much more interested in Galway, the birthplace of his wife Nora Barnacle, than in the wilder and more sparsely populated regions of the West, which attracted Yeats and other Revivalists).[42] In a similar style, the citizen in the "Cyclops" episode of *Ulysses* insists that all the regions of Ireland were once bustling and European: "We had our trade with Spain and the French and with the Flemings before those mongrels [the British] were pupped, Spanish ale in Galway, the winebark on the winedark waterway" (269). The citizen is often taken to represent an insular Irish nationalism, yet in his verbal exuberance, and in his lists and catalogues, he too reflects the excitement and energy of a distinctly modern view of the past, which is also his blueprint for the Irish economic future: "Our harbours that are empty will be full again, Queenstown, Kinsale, Galway, Blacksod Bay, Ventry in the kingdom of Kerry, Killybegs, the third largest harbour in the wide world with a fleet of masts of the Galway Lynches and Cavan O'Reillys and the O'Kennedys of Dublin when the earl of Desmond could make a treaty with the emperor Charles the Fifth himself" (269).

Walter Benjamin illustrates how at a particular point in the development of capitalism, images of a commercial paradise combine in popular consciousness with suggestions of a mythical land of plenty. He quotes one song from 1832, which tells how Parisians are looking forward to a Golden Age during which "sheep roasted whole will frisk on the plain" and "sautéed pike will swim in the Seine."[43] Similar fantasies seem to have overtaken the narrator of one of the first interpolations in "Cyclops." In the course of a description of the markets area of Dublin, we are told of the wondrous "foison of the fields," and of the many varieties of farm animal that arrive in the city from all over Ireland with "their udders distended with superabundance of milk and butts of butter and rennets of cheese" (242).[44] These good things to eat will taste all the better because it seems that no one will labor to produce them. In such lines, *Ulysses* may again appear to reflect the historical experience of late-twentieth-century Ireland which, bypassing the classic modes of industrial production, greatly increased its agricultural output and became a model case of consumer capitalism. Such passages also represent another instance of Joyce's intermingling of the rural or so-called pastoral with metropolitan modernity.

It is lamentably inadequate to conclude that Joyce merely satirizes such modernist-nationalist discourses in "Cyclops" or in *Ulysses* as a whole; rather, his own stylistic dynamism also mimics and experiments with the diverse discourses of modern capitalism.[45] The note of celebration, derived from the idea of national autonomy's causal link with economic wealth, is not merely mocked in the novel. It could hardly be the case that an author so concerned with the question of personal autonomy in colonial Ireland (dramatized through Stephen in particular) would regard the project of national autonomy or independence with the jejune dismissiveness so often ascribed to him.

From the "horde of jerkined dwarfs, my people, with flayers' knives" (*Ulysses*, 38), which Stephen pictures hacking at a school of whales washed up on Sandymount strand (this is based on an incident that occurred during a famine in the fourteenth century)[46] or the "hundredheaded rabble" (33) that confronted Swift in the close of St. Patrick's cathedral, to the more recent crowds that listened to O'Connell ("A people sheltered within his voice" [118]) or that shouted support for the Boers (133), Joyce represents the Irish past as a communal history. The collective nature of historical experience reduces the pain of its apparently random cruelty. In this, Joyce conveys a sense of what Stanley Cavell calls "knowing as first person plural," or the "knowledge a culture has of itself."[47] In *Ulysses*, we hear the Irish ruminating on "The Irish." This is a people half-conscious of how it has been formed by important and catastrophic happenings.

Of course, Dublin's history was not exactly the same as that of the rest of Ireland; in the nineteenth century, for example, neither the Famine nor the Land War had the same impact on the city as they had on the rest of the country. Nevertheless, Joyce's treatment both of the theme of hunger, and of such occasional "outrages" as the Phoenix Park murders, sheds light on the way in which collective memories are reawakened by walkers and talkers in the streets and pubs of Dublin.[48] As Benjamin puts it, every city street is precipitous; it leads downward, conducting the *flâneur* "into a vanished time. . . . into a past that can be all the more spellbinding because it is not his own, not private."[49] Joyce's familiarity and empathy with the historical memory of the urban crowd means that mass society is a much less melancholy spectacle for him than it is for other modernists such as Ezra

Pound or T. S. Eliot. Here again, Joyce is in line with the experimentations of the earlier Irish novelists.

After Emmet's rebellion of 1803, political violence in Dublin was for the most part rare. But the sensational case of the Phoenix Park murders in the year of Joyce's birth became a kind of urban legend. This event has a strange scatter effect in the city of *Ulysses*, with its reality dispersed into rumor and its protagonists becoming characters remembered by their nicknames ("Skin-the-Goat"). The demotic element creates both a familiarizing and distancing effect (the incident now belongs to the genre of the significant but long-ago event).[50] But this also serves as a model of how Joyce depicts the traces of more remote historical experience in *Ulysses*, often through gossip or anecdote. The particular details are often vague enough (see Bloom's allusions to the coffins with sliding panels used during the Famine [90], or to Soyer's soup kitchen, which operated in Dublin during the 1840s [140]), but the status of some of them is attested by their having entered the popular imagination. The issue is not really that of vagueness versus precision. It is of the depth to which a specific event has been absorbed by the community, so that it is constantly recast as a form of generalized reflection by the community on itself.[51] And memories of suffering and violence are insistently associated with intense deprivation in the present. In *Ulysses*, even the dead in Glasnevin cemetery are clamoring for food and love (89), while the living seek gratification in churches, pubs, or from cheap publications like *Titbits*. This is in part what makes the citizens of Dublin so vulnerable to occasionally extravagant fantasies of liberation. Joyce's own text is in many ways a larger scale reproduction of such fantasies, as he recreates provincial Dublin as an image of a modern cosmopolis.

It is true that both Stephen and Bloom are at times alienated and even revolted by the appetitive restlessness of the city crowd in *Ulysses*, and that after the central episodes dealing with the public life of the city, the final three episodes of the text ("Nostos") return to these characters and ultimately to the domestic space of No. 7, Eccles Street. There, the sound of Molly's jingling bedsprings evokes an apparently simpler kind of desire than that which drives the needy crowd. But the crowd or group from which the two male protagonists are separated has to be understood differently as a social phenomenon in each case.

In Stephen, Joyce highlights the degree of moral heroism needed by an individual in order to make the great refusal of family and nation in the name of freedom. Dedalus wants to re-create himself as radically autonomous; he wishes to be something more than the child of his parents ("the man with my voice and my eyes and a ghostwoman with ashes on her breath" or the product of "the coupler's will" (32). In some of the earlier Irish novels, the individual achieves definition insofar as he or she embodies the values of a community; a nickname ("Mat the Thrasher") exhausts all subjective possibility for the sake of an iconic communal status. To some degree, the novels of the Irish fin de siècle period merely invert this community/individual hierarchy. In his complex treatment of mass society and of popular values and conventions, Joyce goes far beyond this relatively simple inversion. Stephen's desire for autonomy is certainly even fiercer. But his fears about the dangers of mass conformity seems excessive or even ridiculous when set against the more humane or genial qualities of Leopold Bloom or even of Dubliners more generally. Dedalus is also acutely conscious of the catastrophic nature of Irish historical experience, which throws his project of aestheticist self-creation into crisis.[52] This consciousness is much more muted in Bloom. He holds out for an ideal of modern development that will eventually lead to a peaceful world of private consumption ("A revolution must come on the due instalments plan" [Ulysses, 525]). With his own family history of migration and his experience of racism, he is well placed to bear witness to the historical transitions and dramas unfolding around him in the colonial city, but as a cultural outsider he is not the ideal interpreter of their tonalities and significance. But in neither case is Dublin figured as the site of the some straightforward battle between the etiolated elites and the deadened masses of T. S. Eliot's Waste Land, or between what Thomas Hardy called "nerves and primitive feelings." The intimacies of village or traditional life still remain; the metropolitan life absorbs them but is not disengaged from them. It is not by any means a city that has lost all animating rhythms or rituals; it has its cuts and splices, but is not completely chaotic. In his intricate representation of Dublin's colonial urbanism, Joyce suggests how the community attempts to process and counter the historical upheavals both of colonialism and of late capitalism, as the one segues into the other.

"Oh Kosmos! Ah Ireland!" (*Wake*, 456):
Modalites of the Modern in Late Joyce

As the public world of *Ulysses* recedes during the last three episodes of
the novel, Joyce concludes with his most extensive explorations of two
key modern discourses in particular: the idiom of scientific rationality in
"Ithaca," and the erotic language of subjective desire in "Penelope." It is
usual to contrast the "Penelope" section with the two immediately preceding it and to assign to Molly's feminine consciousness the restorative
vitality that the men have lost. But this is itself highly problematic. Joyce
does not merely counterpose the world of impersonal system and that of
individual desire; it is the connection, not just the opposition, between
them that is disquieting.

By midnight on Bloomsday many of the sources of energy that have
contributed to the textual experiments of *Ulysses* are depleted. The streets
are almost deserted. In "Eumaeus," Stephen's heroic project is in abeyance,
and Bloom's exhaustion is reflected in the clichéd banality of the narration.
The catechetical style of "Ithaca" proves woefully inadequate to the task of
rendering the human significance of the exchanges between Stephen and
Bloom. Instead we are offered—among many other details—the precise
dates of their previous meetings and a mathematical account of the relation between their respective ages (555–56). But is this merely a question
of style? Perhaps the attempt at social interaction has been a complete
failure, leaving Bloom to the dubious comforts of his conjugal bed. Viewed
in the light of this reading, the status of Molly's discourse as emancipatory
is all the more ambiguous. After our immersion in what Jameson has aptly
described as "the radical contingency and meaninglessness of our object
world"[53] in "Ithaca," what is the meaning of Molly's sexual warmth?

At the simplest level, Molly's intentions are left unclear. Does she plan
to continue her adulterous career (and did it begin with Boylan, or much
earlier)? We do not really know whether Molly's memories of Bloom's kiss
sixteen years ago will move her to re-dedicate herself to him. What we
do not expect to hear in Eccles Street is the slamming of any doors—the
sound that signaled the departure of Nora in Ibsen's *A Doll's House* (1879)
from her wifely role (a play greatly admired by the young Joyce, and part

of the inspiration for Dedalus's defiance of conventional morals). But the enigma of "Penelope" goes deeper than this. In her uninhibited enthusiasm for, as examples, fashion and sex, Molly may appear to be much more contemporary than most of her fellow citizens. The fact that she is virtually confined to her bed and her house is no longer, it would seem, a tragic or even a sordid condition—as such restriction might seem to be in *Dubliners*. Molly is almost entirely consumed by her sexual role; in her world of fetishized commodities, all desire is reduced to or replaced by appetite. It is in this regard that her contrast with Stephen and even Bloom is most telling. Both of them have longings or ambitions that cannot be satisfied by mere appetite. At the conclusion of *Ulysses*, is there any place for desire that might still be collective and political? It is as if Gibraltar and Howth Head are the new Pillars of Hercules that mark the limits of the knowable world. For this is a discourse that seems to transgress convention, but it does so in order to confine itself to private, fleshly remembrance.

Ulysses was published in 1922, just as the Irish Free State and the statelet of Northern Ireland were instituted under the terms of the Anglo-Irish treaty. After a bitter civil war, the independent Irish state settled down to several decades of economic stagnation and an extremely illiberal social regime. Literary naturalism, of a kind very close to that pioneered in Ireland by George Moore and the young Joyce, enjoyed a new lease of life as writers responded to the squalid and repressive aspects of social life in the new state. That is to say, *Dubliners* had more influence as a literary model than *Ulysses*. For both skeptics and admirers, it seemed that the sexual frankness or obscenity of Joyce's later work was its key feature, which they interpreted as an indicator of his antinationalist cosmopolitanism. Some writers may also have seen in his experience of censorship an anticipation of their own battles with state repression.[54] But neither the bleakness of, for instance, "A Painful Case" nor the semipornographic candor of "Penelope" adequately represents Joyce's entire experimental range. The conclusion of *Ulysses* may seem to conform to some of the standard features of novelistic realism, sponsoring the reestablishment of the family as the solution to social distress and anomie. This is of course complicated (and perhaps even undermined) by the fact that much of the sexual excess promised by Dublin's emerging consumer society is also associated with Molly. Will she nevertheless prove to be a loving wife, a true Penelope? But Joyce does not stop here. The "Nostos" section of *Ulysses* may seem to ratify the separation of public and private spheres on which the conventional realist novel depends. In *Finnegans Wake*, the secret or scandalous family story of HCE and ALP is offered, in a series of ingenious ways, as the story of Ireland itself.

Gibson argues that although the concept of setting has a limited application to *Finnegans Wake*, "the range of reference to Irish materials in the book—Irish topography, geography, mythology, Irish lore and literature . . . —vastly exceeds other kinds of reference. If there are characters, events, scenes, landscapes and cityscapes in the *Wake*, they are consistently Irish at root . . . . no one has ever claimed that it is set in Paris or Trieste."[55] The *Wake*, according to Deane, is "Joyce's Irish answer to an Irish problem. It is written in a ghost language about phantasmal figures; history is haunted by them and embodies them over and over again in specific people, places and tongues."[56] Chief among these specific places is the Irish Free State, as Joyce records his responses to the developments of the 1920s and 30s in Ireland. In particular, this phase of Irish history is personified by Eamon de Valera, the dominant political figure of his time, especially between 1932 (when he became president of the Free State) and 1959 (when after several terms as Taoiseach [prime minister], he left government for the presidency of the Irish Republic, the state having been declared a republic in 1949). De Valera remained in public office as president of Ireland into the early 1970s.

Joyce aligns the character of Shaun in *Finnegans Wake* with de Valera, and opposes this figure to his brother or twin, Shem the Penman, Joyce's own alter ego (de Valera and Joyce were both born in 1882). This contributes to Joyce's elaboration of the key theme of fraternal conflict in the text (and in this way, the *Wake* also testifies to the bitter divisions of the Irish Civil War). Shaun has been taken as the embodiment of a repressive, institutionalized state nationalism in the *Wake*. Against this, Joyce celebrates the creative and libidinal freedom that has been seized by the exiled Shem. But it is significant that Shem is also nostalgic and solipsistic; as his brother charges, "anarch, egoarch, hiresiarch, you have reared your disunited kingdom on the vacuum of your own intensely doubtful soul" (188).

While the artist Shem is in Europe, he is never entirely disengaged from Ireland. At one point, the sound of music recalls him to the ongoing story of its people: "And lo (whish, O whish!) mesaw mestreamed, as the green to the gred was flew, was flown, through deafths of durkness greengrown deeper I heard a voice, the voce of Shaun, the vote of the Irish, voise from afar (and cert no purer puer palestrine e'er chanted pangelical mid the clouds of Tu es Petrus . . .)" (407).

At this time, Joyce was an avid listener to the new state radio station, Radio Athlone (later Radio Éireann);[57] in the *Wake*, the messages that reach Shem from Ireland are also aural. There is an allusion in these lines to the legend of St. Patrick, who heard the voice of the Irish calling to him in a dream, inspiring him to return to the island in 432 to convert its people to Christianity. Joyce also refers to the famous Irish tenor, John McCormack, with whom the young Joyce had once shared a platform. McCormack sang "Panis Angelicus" at Mass in the Phoenix Park during the Eucharistic Congress of 1932, which commemorated fifteen hundred years of Christianity in Ireland.

The Phoenix Park had witnessed great events before. In 1929, half a million people had attended a Mass there to celebrate the centenary of Catholic Emancipation. But the congregation of over double that number at the Eucharistic Congress was unprecedented. The successful hosting of the Congress was a memorable triumph for the fledgling state, as well as an indication that—as Flann O'Brien once quipped—independent Ireland was set to become a "Roman Capitalist country."[58] The success of the event was also a personal victory for de Valera, who had only just taken his new party into the parliament of the Free State and become president of its executive council. During the Civil War in the previous decade, many of de Valera's fellow republicans had been excommunicated by the Catholic Church during the Civil War. The Phoenix Park was also the venue for what will presumably come to be thought of as the last great popular gathering of Catholic Ireland. In 1979, John Paul II became the first pope to arrive on Irish soil, with the declaration also that he, like St. Patrick, had heard the voice of the Irish calling to him. He celebrated Mass for over a million people in the Phoenix Park, as well as for huge crowds in other parts of the country. What may then have looked like a resurgence of Irish Catholicism turned out to be something of a swan song, as the Church leaders supported bitterly contested referenda on divorce and abortion during the 1980s, and then endured a series of sexual scandals and a huge loss of moral authority in the decade that followed.

In *Finnegans Wake,* the Phoenix Park is also represented and commemorated as the site of the assassinations of 1882, and of a mysterious sexual transgression that determines the entire subsequent history of the Wakean family. The fall in the garden (or park) is the traumatic source of Ireland's and civilization's history. That history is so varied that it seems to be endlessly creative, but also it is so monotonous that it is inescapably the same. Thus, the mutilated island is like anywhere else. Indeed it is now (as Joyce puts it, in a parody of one of Moore's *Melodies,* "at the split hour of blight when bars are keeping so sly" [*Wake,* 519])[59] that Ireland—far more unambiguously than in *Ulysses*—provides the most detailed allegory of world history. Just as the Eucharistic Congress had harnessed modern technology to celebrate Irish Catholic tradition—the congregation had the benefit of a PA system that, to their astonishment, even allowed them to hear a live address from Pope Leo XIII in Rome—so the experimental, avant-garde language of *Finnegans Wake* represents Joyce's deepest excavation of the oldest layers of Irish historical experience. In the *Wake,* Finn MacCool and the Four Masters (the annalists of Gaelic Ireland) are contemporary presences, and present-day events are transformed and estranged by the technological miracle of broadcasting. (In a speech marking the opening of the Athlone Broadcasting Station in 1933, de Valera spoke of how the station would "enable the world to hear the voice of one of the oldest and, in many respects, one of the greatest of the nations.")[60] Although *Finnegans Wake* portrays the mind-set of Shaun as limited and oppressive, it does not present an image of postcolonial Ireland as fixed or paralyzed in its 1930s incarnation. Rather, partitioned Ireland and the Free State are particular historical instances of human effort and failure and so take their place within Joyce's overarching vision of comic and redemptive recurrence. Its exuberant literary experimentalism is linked to the same irrepressible, popular energies that Moore had celebrated in *Memoirs of Captain Rock.* But *Finnegans Wake* also represents Joyce's solution to the problem of allegory in the national novel that had preoccupied Irish writers since Moore's day.

In the standard reading of the rise of the English novel, characters such as Robinson Crusoe or Clarissa Harlowe represent the triumph of the newly dominant bourgeoisie. But as we have seen, the situation of Irish middle-class novelists was seriously complicated by Ireland's colonial conditions. The native bourgeoisie faced formidable obstacles in its bid for national leadership. While it won significant victories with Catholic Emancipation in 1829 and the Disestablishment of the Church of Ireland in 1869, representing the Catholic masses as potentially "civilized" individuals proved difficult. What kind of "modern" culture should native artists and writers promote? While the realist novel was obviously an important and prestigious literary genre, might not a truthful depiction of the life-world of the typical Irish peasant family or community do as much harm as good for the Irish Catholic cause? In Ireland, was allegory a realistic proposition?

We have reviewed how some of the most successful Catholic authors responded to these aesthetic and political challenges. Moore's *Captain Rock* is an unprecedented attempt to narrate a history of collective consciousness in Ireland. Moore uses Rock to explore the history that has produced Irish national character in both its romantic and its "criminal" forms. His achievement is reflected in the work of the earliest and most prolific of Ireland's self-consciously national novelists, John and Michael Banim. But many of the protagonists and indeed the storylines of their novels may also seem strongly to suggest the unfeasibility of allegory in Irish fiction. The opacity of the bizarre Crohoore, or even of the young priest John Nowlan, is an indication of the strain involved in rendering such characters as developed individuals and as positive cultural exemplars at the same time. But this is not the whole story with the Banims. In their historical fiction, enigmatic modes of subjectivity become the basis of alternative allegorical narratives; in turn, these occasionally subvert the Banims' ostensible commitment to the modernizing mission of Catholic intellectuals. And while Catholic novelists such as Gerald Griffin wanted native vivacity to be subdued, they regarded it as essential that something of the national spirit be preserved in the transition to modern rationality—otherwise, traditional Irish culture would lose its claim to distinctiveness and integrity. Yet in *The Collegians*, the paradigmatic Catholic novel of the 1820s, there is no place for even a lovely Irish colleen like Eily O'Connor; instead we are left with the tedious Kyrle Daly and his bride, lip-synching the music of modernity.

Griffin seems to conceive of modern discipline as a threat to natural spontaneity and desire (as in the seemingly passionless marriage that concludes *The Collegians*). He believes that the otherworldly mentality of the Irish peasantry is a safeguard against the evils of modern materialism and self-indulgence—even when popular belief appears to be notably unorthodox (for example, see Davy Lanigan's extraordinary vision of heaven in *The Rivals*, in which the dead can use only the clothing and goods that they have given away in charity during their lifetimes [chap. 14]). But the ideal of the frugal rural homestead (more developed in Kickham than in Griffin) was an attempt to counter both of these negative faces of modernity. Kickham hoped that Irish peasants could be hard-working and provident, and still dance at the crossroads.

It was in the period dominated by Eamon de Valera (or in Catholic dates, between the Eucharistic Congress and the Marian Year), that this image flared before a decisive fading. Just on the verge of becoming an open, modernized economy, independent Ireland manifested in this period the terms of its resistance—those of an idyllic Catholic pastoral. This landscape had been most effectively realized in the Irish imagination by a central group of popular nineteenth-century novelists, although it endured even after their individual works had been forgotten. Some of the appeal of Griffin, and even more of Kickham, lies in their promise to distill the essence of this distinctively Irish mode of modern life, supposedly rooted in a specific attitude toward material possessions and especially toward ownership of the land.[61] Kickham is often accused of seeing Ireland in misty soft-focus. However, unlike the Revivalists a generation later, he does not elide the recent history of Ireland to take shelter in any archaicizing myth. His version of national allegory is determined by the class privilege of most of the Famine survivors who live on in Knocknagow. Kickham readily admits that these country people are simply the inhabitants of an idyll; they are, after all, living in a ruined economy and landscape. In such conditions, they are liable to all kinds of internal disturbance and vulnerable to any consolations on offer. They are shown, for instance, to be tempted to self-destruction, violent revenge, and hedonism (women in particular being much drawn to cities and their dangerous pleasures). Only the village community can subdue and regulate desire in the interests of all. In such circumstances, communal action and belief is redemptive. So Kickham hopes that shared memories (including the memory of trauma) will prevent the collective from becoming an undifferentiated, atomized mass.

Perhaps this version of Ireland was never more than an ideological projection. For many commentators the distinguishing feature of the Irish in the first half of the nineteenth century was their total disregard and unfitness for modern discipline of any kind. They were no more than slaves to their immediate desires. This was epitomized by their attachment to the potato, so easy to cultivate and cook; even the dependence of the poor of England on bread represented a more advanced level of culture. Then, after the Famine, the Irish seemed to undergo a complete reversal. Their slack squalor was transmuted into tight-lipped respectability; so subservient did they become to the authority of the Church, then at the height of its Vaticanist antimodernism crusade, that all desire in them seemed to be extinguished. Having been notorious for violence, fecklessness, and a carnivalesque popular culture, the Irish became notorious instead as the most repressed and sexless population in Western Europe. This national character now seems to be in the midst of a further makeover, as the Irish take with gusto to the accelerated consumption of the post-boom economy. But this is not some exceptional social set-up. These are recognizable stages of the process of becoming fully incorporated into the system of global capitalism—despite the southern Irish state's several decades of unavailing resistance to this system. We cannot look to Joyce for some sketch of a more liberating alternative to the course Ireland took during his lifetime or since. We can find in him a glimpse of that late capitalist future. But he does not assume that this would be either the climax or the termination of Irish history.

Joyce understood the Irish crowd as one of the most important agents of political change in the nineteenth century, even when it menaced revolutionary or violent change in its earlier O'Connellite or later Fenian guise (publicly manifested at rallies, funerals, and the like). He remained attracted to the idea of the great leader (Parnell) who would lead his people to the Promised Land. His literary career began with a repudiation of the mob that had almost been transformed into a people but, at the final moment, had reverted to its insensate stupidity by the betrayal or rejection of that leader at the behest of the priests. Indeed, the position of the hero was a little crowded in Joyce's imagination. Parnell was there, but so too was Ibsen and most of all was James Joyce, the artist for whom solitude was a mark of integrity. But the hero could only be aestheticized so far: He was archaic in a mass society. The heroic position does not become so rooted in Joyce as to be a governing idea.

The project of challenging the opposition between Protestant culture and Catholic anarchy in Ireland had been inaugurated in the eighteenth century by antiquarian scholars such as Charles O'Conor and Sylvester O'Halloran (on whom Thomas Moore drew extensively for his *Memoirs of Captain Rock*), but it was Joyce who most decisively altered its terms. The whole conception of an aristocratic or cultural elite that could somehow control the surge of the masses toward political power was endlessly debated in nineteenth-century Europe and in the European novel. In Ireland, however, the Arnoldian concept of "Culture and Anarchy" had kept its sectarian tinge well into the twentieth century, largely due to Yeats's laments for a lost Anglo-Irish prestige and his assaults on the *arriviste* Catholic middle class. Yet heroic, individual subjectivity becomes an appealing but abortive project in the village society that was becoming mass society in *Ulysses*. In *Finnegans Wake* the masses achieve consciousness. The representative figure of that consciousness is the archetype, and with the archetype's replacement of the hero or character the idea of allegory returns—and returns. Allegorical correspondences flit about as possibilities and phantoms in *Dubliners* and *Ulysses*. But when they occasionally emerge fully, such as in the apparent references to Dante in "Grace" or in some of the Homeric parallels in *Ulysses*, they are taken to be mock-heroic parody; allegorical correspondence becomes a kind of joke. Yet in *Finnegans Wake*, with the island divided, Ireland becomes the site of a lost unity, a unity only apprehensible in the aftermath of partition. The island becomes the setting for an all-encompassing allegory that promises to redeem the chaotic fragmentation of history, or at least show how, through Ireland's first fall, and the many subsequent to that, the world fell. Indeed, the nation appears now to be the most complete and fertile exemplar of the relationships between the individual and the system, the local and the global. This is a view of the country's historical significance that few would have shared in 1930s Ireland, although Joyce's fellow modernist W. B. Yeats had his own reactionary version of it.[62] In the *Wake*, the Irish national project has become the most powerful and poignant local instance of a universal recurrence, as all the rivers of the world debouch finally into a specific and generic Irish Sea.

NOTES

BIBLIOGRAPHY

INDEX

Notes

Preface

1. W. J. McCormack, *Ascendancy and Tradition in Anglo-Irish Literary History from 1789–1939* (Oxford: Clarendon Press, 1985), 241.

2. Thomas Flanagan, *The Irish Novelists, 1800–1850* (New York: Columbia Univ. Press, 1959), 334. Flanagan's pioneering study of Irish fiction in the early nineteenth century delivers a notably negative critical judgment on the authors (Anglo-Irish as well as Catholic) that it surveys.

3. See Flanagan, *Irish Novelists*, 333–40, and especially Terry Eagleton, *Heathcliff and the Great Hunger: Studies in Irish Culture* (London: Verso, 1995), 145–225. Eagleton comments on both the Anglo-Irish and the Irish Catholic resistance to realism between the eighteenth and twentieth centuries.

4. For example, Jacqueline Belanger argues that the insistent focus on the Irish novel's relationship to British literary and generic forms has reinforced a regrettable critical perception of nineteenth-century Irish fiction as "generally problematic." Jacqueline Belanger, ed., *The Irish Novel in the Nineteenth Century: Facts and Fictions* (Dublin: Four Courts Press, 2005), 17 (hereafter referred to as *Irish Novel*). David Lloyd counters that the question of realism was never merely a "retrospective difficulty," but one regularly raised by Irish novelists themselves. He adds that the sense of the inadequacy of the Irish novel is not limited to a peculiar shame in relation to *English* examples only ("It is not only that Ireland produced no *Middlemarch*, . . . it also produced no *Père Goriot*, . . . no *Moby Dick*, . . . no *War and Peace*"). See David Lloyd, "Afterword: Hardress Cregan's Dream—for Another History of the Irish Novel," in *Irish Novel*, 230.

5. See Lloyd, "Afterword," 232.

6. Daniel Corkery, *Synge and Anglo-Irish Literature* (1931; reprint, Cork: Mercier Press, 1966), 10, 24–25.

7. Ibid., 25–26.

8. As noted by R. V. Comerford, *Ireland* (London: Hodder Arnold, 2003), 178.

9. Albert Sonnenfeld defines the Catholic novel as "a novel written by a Catholic, using Catholicism as his informing mythopoeic structure or generative symbolic system, and where the principal and decisive issue is the salvation or damnation of the

hero or heroine." Quoted by Malcolm Scott, *The Struggle for the Soul of the French Novel: French Catholic and Realist Novelists, 1850–1970* (Houndmills: Macmillan, 1989), 5.

10. For example, Norman Vance suggests that the specificity of the nineteenth-century Irish novel as a Catholic art form lies in its relationship to Irish popular culture, as well as in its general generic fluidity. Norman Vance, "Protestant Form and Catholic Fiction?" in *Irish Novel*, 143. One of Vance's own examples, however, Canon Sheehan's *The Triumph of Failure* (1895), may represent a different kind of Irish Catholic fiction, portraying the protagonist's visionary experiences and offering what Vance aptly describes as a "satire on the materialist-realist novel" (147).

11. See Joe Cleary, *Outrageous Fortune: Capital and Culture in Modern Ireland* (Dublin: Field Day Publications, 2007), 64–66.

12. Eamon de Valera, "The Undeserted Village Ireland," in *The Field Day Anthology of Irish Writing*, ed. Seamus Deane (Derry: Field Day, 1991), 3:748.

13. See Cleary, *Outrageous Fortune*, 111–79.

14. James S. Atherton comments on Joyce's numerous allusions to Moore and to other Irish writers in *The Books at the Wake: A Study of Literary Allusions in Joyce's* Finnegans Wake (New York: Viking Press, 1959).

15. So described by Ernest Boyd (one of Joyce's most perceptive early Irish readers), *Ireland's Literary Renaissance* (London: Grant Richards, 1923), 382.

16. On the phantasmagoric dreamworld of capitalism, see Walter Benjamin, *The Arcades Project*, trans. Howard Eiland and Kevin McLaughlin (Cambridge, Mass.: Harvard Univ. Press, 1999).

1. Thomas Moore: *Irish Melodies* and Discordant Politics

1. Quoted by Harry White, *The Keeper's Recital: Music and Cultural History in Ireland, 1770–1970* (Cork: Cork Univ. Press, 1998), 43. See also White's discussion of Moore and traditional Irish music (36–52).

2. The view that the United Irishmen were uninterested in indigenous Irish culture has been refuted by Luke Gibbons, "Republicanism and Radical Memory: The O'Conors, O'Carolan and the United Irishmen," in *Revolution, Counter-Revolution and Union*, ed. Jim Smyth (Cambridge: Cambridge Univ. Press, 2000), 211–37.

3. Letter to the Marchioness Dowager of Donegal, prefixed to the third number of the *Melodies*. *The Poetical Works of Thomas Moore* (New York, 1887), 290.

4. Liam de Paor, *Tom Moore and Contemporary Ireland*, Ó Riada Memorial Lecture (Cork: Univ. College, Cork, 1989), 7. Hoover H. Jordan, among Moore's biographers, offers the most comprehensive account of the author as a fearless political radical. Jordan, *Bolt Upright: The Life of Thomas Moore*, vols. 1–2 (Salzburg: Universität Salzburg, 1975).

5. On the modular nature of modern nationalism, see Benedict Anderson: "In effect, by the second decade of the nineteenth century, if not earlier, a 'model' of 'the'

independent national state was available for pirating." Anderson, *Imagined Communities: Reflections on the Origin and Spread of Nationalism*, rev. ed. (London: Verso, 1991), 81. Moore himself more or less consciously exploited this. After the success of the *Melodies*, he went on to compose a series of "National Airs," using French, German, Russian, and many other airs. Some of these are remarkably similar in tone and imagery to the *Irish Melodies*, and the best known of them, "Oft in the stilly night," is often mistakenly regarded as one of the *Melodies*.

6. See Marjorie Howes, *Colonial Crossings: Figures in Irish Literary History* (Dublin: Field Day Publications, 2006), 10.

7. This is especially true of the illustrations that accompany "One bumper at parting," "Wreath the bowl," and "And doth not a meeting like this."

8. Thomas Moore, appendix to "Corruption and Intolerance," *Poetical Works*, 209.

9. Clare O'Halloran points out that English and Irish antiquarians tended to have divergent "primitivist paradigms," involving a positive conception of the modern in the English case and a negative one in the Irish case. See O'Halloran, "Irish Re-creations of the Gaelic Past: The Challenge of Macpherson's Ossian," *Past and Present* 124 (1989): 72–73. In the *Melodies*, Moore is unable wholeheartedly to endorse either conception of the modern.

10. William Hazlitt, *The Spirit of the Age: or, Contemporary Portraits* (London, 1825), 397.

11. Luke Gibbons, "Republicanism and Radical Memory," 226.

12. The first two songs are apparently about Robert Emmet and Sarah Curran respectively, and the third about Fitzgerald. However, some critics presume that "When he, who adores thee" is written in the voice of Emmet, not Fitzgerald. Moore's evocation of '98 in these songs is shadowy indeed.

13. "The Prince's Day."

14. Moore, appendix to "Corruption and Intolerance," 208.

15. As suggested by Mary Helen Thuente, *The Harp Re-strung: The United Irishmen and the Rise of Irish Literary Nationalism* (Syracuse: Syracuse Univ. Press, 1994), 181.

16. *The Journal of Thomas Moore*, ed. Wilfrid Dowden (Newark: Univ. of Delaware Press, 1984), 2:848.

17. See Jordan, *Bolt Upright*, 30–33.

18. Thomas Moore, *The Life and Death of Lord Edward Fitzgerald*, 2 vols. (London, 1831), 1:301.

19. Ibid.

20. Ibid., 260.

21. Ibid., 98–99.

22. Ibid., 2:7. The Defenders were the most highly politicized of the agrarian secret societies at this time.

23. Ibid., 1:305.

24. Ibid., 254–55.

25. Ibid., 306.

26. Ibid., 2:185–86.

27. Moore wrote to his friend Lady Donegal, who had advised him against consorting with "Irish Democrats": "[I]f there is anything in the world that I have been detesting and despising more than another for this long time past, it has been those very Dublin politicians who you so fear I should associate with. I do not think a good cause was ever ruined by a more bigoted, brawling and disgusting set of demagogues." *The Letters of Thomas Moore*, ed. Wilfrid S. Dowden, 2 vols. (Oxford: Clarendon Press, 1964), 1:359.

28. In addition, for an innovative reading of Moore's treatment of non-European culture in such works as *Lallah Rookh*, see Joseph Lennon, *Irish Orientalism: A Literary and Intellectual History* (Syracuse: Syracuse Univ. Press, 2004), 156–60.

29. See in particular Tom Dunne, "Haunted by History: Irish Romantic Writing, 1800–1850," in *Romanticism in National Context*, ed. R. Porter and M. Teich (Cambridge: Cambridge Univ. Press, 1988), 86. See also Seamus Deane, *Strange Country: Modernity and Nationhood in Irish Writing since 1790* (Oxford: Clarendon Press, 1997), 67; Joep Leerssen, *Remembrance and Imagination: Patterns in the Historical and Literary Representation of Ireland in the Nineteenth Century* (Cork: Cork Univ. Press, 1996), 79; and Terry Eagleton, *Crazy John and the Bishop and Other Essays on Irish Culture* (Cork: Cork Univ. Press, 1998), 156.

30. Thomas Moore, *Memoirs of Captain Rock, the Celebrated Irish Chieftain, with some Account of his Ancestors. Written By Himself* (London, 1824), 354. This work, hereafter *Captain Rock* in text, was published in two books, so references to chapters are distinguished by book number as well. There has been no modern critical edition of Moore's text to date, but see Thomas Moore, *Memoirs of Captain Rock*, ed. Emer Nolan (Dublin: Field Day Publications, forthcoming).

31. Scullabogue was the site of an infamous massacre of Protestants during the 1798 rebellion in Co. Wexford.

32. "Works on Ireland," *Blackwood's Edinburgh Magazine* 15 (May 1824): 545–46.

33. Ibid., 544.

34. *Westminister Review*, 1 April 1824, 494.

35. Ibid., 492–93.

36. Leerssen, *Remembrance and Imagination*, 83–84. Thus, as Luke Gibbons remarks: "Moore's Captain Rock has run together in his own name three of the forces designed to strike fear in the heart of the Protestant Ascendancy: the Catholic cause in its most sectarian and millenarian forms; republicanism, of the maverick variety associated with the eccentric Roger O'Connor. . . . and finally, at a more recondite level, the Gaelic tradition in its distinctively anti-colonial Phoenician variant." "Between Captain Rock and a Hard Place: Art and Agrarian Insurgency," in *Ideology and Ireland in the Nineteenth Century*, ed. Tadgh Foley and Sean Ryder (Dublin: Four Courts Press, 1998), 26–27.

37. [Roger O'Connor], *Letters to His Majesty, King George the Fourth, by Captain Rock* (Dublin, 1828), 3, 7–8.

38. *Journal of Thomas Moore*, 2:659.

39. Luke Gibbons, "Between Captain Rock and a Hard Place," 28.

40. [Mortimer O'Sullivan], *Captain Rock detected: or, the Origin and Character of the Recent Disturbances, and the Causes, both Moral and Political, of the Present Alarming Condition of the South and West of Ireland, fully and fairly considered and exposed: by a Munster Farmer* (London, 1824), 196.

41. Patrick O'Sullivan, "A Literary Difficulty in Explaining Ireland: Tom Moore and Captain Rock," in *The Irish in Britain: 1815–1939*, ed. Sheridan Gilley and Roger Swift (Dublin: Gill and Macmillan, 1989), 268.

42. [O'Connor], *Letters to His Majesty*, 3.

43. [Mortimer O'Sullivan], 1.

44. Ibid., 214.

45. Sir Jonah Barrington, *Personal Sketches of his Own Times* (London, 1869), 1:350.

46. See Oliver MacDonagh, *O'Connell: The Life of Daniel O'Connell* (London: Weidenfeld and Nicolson, 1991), 299. In fact, O'Connell died before *Uncle Tom's Cabin* was published.

47. Tadgh O'Sullivan, "'The Violence of a Servile War': Three Narratives of Irish Rural Insurgency Post-1798," in *Rebellion and Remembrance in Modern Ireland*, ed. Laurence M. Geary (Dublin: Four Courts Press, 2001), 74.

48. Tadgh O'Sullivan, "Captain Rock in Print: Literary Representation and Irish Agrarian Unrest, 1824–1833" (M.Phil. thesis, University College Cork, 1998), 96.

49. Michael Davitt, *The Fall of Feudalism in Ireland* (London: Harpers, 1904), 48.

50. [O'Connor], *Letters to His Majesty*, 339–40.

51. See Michael Beames, *Peasants and Power: The Whiteboy Movements and Their Control in Pre-Famine Ireland* (Brighton: Harvester Press, 1983), 89–101, and Luke Gibbons, "Between Captain Rock and a Hard Place," 41. See also Heather Laird's reinterpretation of various forms of peasant resistance in Ireland. Laird, *Subversive Law in Ireland, 1879–1920: From "Unwritten Law" to the Dáil Courts* (Dublin: Four Courts Press, 2005).

52. But see Patrick O'Sullivan, "Literary Difficulty," 239–74; Leerssen, *Remembrance and Imagination*, 77–89; Deane, *Strange Country*, 67–68; Luke Gibbons, "Between Captain Rock and a Hard Place," 23–44; and Tadgh O'Sullivan, "'Violence of a Servile War,'" 73–92, and "Captain Rock in Print," 70–105.

53. See, for example, the Irish novels of Lady Morgan and Maria Edgeworth, and in particular, the glossary and commentary to Edgeworth's *Castle Rackrent* (1800). We may also note the revealing and programmatic titles of such works as Thomas Crofton Croker's *Researches in the South of Ireland. Illustrative of the Scenery, Architectural Remains and the Manners and Superstitions of the Peasantry with an Appendix containing a Private Narrative of the Rebellion of 1798* (London, 1824).

54. See Irene Whelan, *The Bible War in Ireland: The "Second Reformation" and the Polarization of Protestant-Catholic Relations, 1800–1840* (Dublin: Lilliput, 2005).

55. Deane sums up the prevailing view of Irish "blarney": "Verbose, inaccurate, melodramatic, unreliable, in sad need of some form of sobriety, Irish speech and the Irish political condition required a rational articulation that was beyond the capacity of the national character to produce." Deane, *Strange Country*, 55.

56. Quoted by Patrick O'Sullivan, "Literary Difficulty," 268.

57. [Maurice O'Sullivan], 235.

58. "Works on Ireland," 545.

59. See, in particular, Deane, *Strange Country*; David Lloyd, *Nationalism and Minor Literature: James Clarence Mangan and the Emergence of Irish Cultural Nationalism* (Berkeley: Univ. of California Press, 1988), and *Anomalous States: Irish Writing and the Post-Colonial Moment* (Dublin: Lilliput Press, 1993); and Leerssen, *Remembrance and Imagination*.

60. Tadgh O'Sullivan emphasizes that the Rockite disturbances were the most serious outbreak of violence since 1798, and seemed to some observers to represent a "continuing echo" of the rebellion. Tadgh O'Sullivan, "'Violence of a Servile War,'" 76. See also James S. Donnelly, Jr., "Pastorini and Captain Rock: Millenarianism and Sectarianism in the Rockite Movements of 1821–4," in *Irish Peasants: Violence and Political Unrest 1780–1914*, ed. Samuel Clark and James S. Donnelly, Jr. (Dublin: Gill and Macmillan, 1983), 102–39.

61. Gerald Griffin, "Conclusion," in *The Rivals; Tracy's Ambition* (1829; reprint, with an introduction by Robert Lee Wolff, New York: Garland, 1979), 3:295. This edition includes two novels, *The Rivals* and *Tracy's Ambition*, and is hereafter *Rivals; Tracy* in text.

62. So described in George Cornewall Lewis's *On the Local Disturbances in Ireland* (London, 1836), 189.

63. Donnelly describes how resentment over tithes, hostility to Protestant proselytizers and to the yeomanry, and the campaign for Catholic Emancipation all helped to stoke the sectarian fires, and so contributed to the Rockite unrest. See Donnelly, "Pastorini and Captain Rock," 27.

64. S. J. Connolly, quoted by Tadgh O'Sullivan, "'Violence of a Servile War,'" 82.

65. See Donnelly, "Pastorini and Captain Rock," 134–35.

66. Ibid.

67. Pastorini was the pseudonym of an English Benedictine, Charles Walmesley, author of *The General History of the Christian Church* (1771), which had predicted the destruction of Protestantism in 1825.

68. Donnelly, "Pastorini and Captain Rock," 114. Stephen Gibbons provides the texts of many Rockite letters in his useful collection, *Captain Rock, Night Errant: The Threatening Letters of Pre-Famine Ireland, 1801–1845* (Dublin: Four Courts Press, 2004).

69. See E. P. Thompson, "The Crime of Anonymity," in *Albion's Fatal Tree: Crime and Society in Eighteenth-Century England*, ed. Douglas Hay et al. (London: Allen Lane, 1975),

for a suggestive analysis of anonymous threatening letters in eighteenth- and nineteenth-century England. Resemblances between English and Irish letters are noted by Patrick O'Sullivan, "Literary Difficulty," 68.

70. Kevin Whelan, *The Tree of Liberty: Radicalism, Catholicism and the Construction of Irish Identity 1760–1830* (Cork: Cork Univ. Press, 1996), 93.

71. Beames, *Peasants and Power*, 64.

72. Donnelly, "Pastorini and Captain Rock," 18.

73. Kevin Whelan, *Tree of Liberty*, 93.

74. Daniel O'Connell, quoted by Donnelly, "Pastorini and Captain Rock," 110.

75. See Patrick O'Sullivan on the trope of "the man in the gig," which surfaces in both English and Irish accounts of agrarian protest. "Literary Difficulty," 255.

76. [Mortimer O'Sullivan], *Captain Rock detected*, 53, 67.

77. Charlotte Elizabeth [Tonna], *The Rockite* (London, 1829), 252, 254. Tonna was also a prolific producer of fiction for the Religious Tract and Book Society for Ireland, an extremely active organization during the Second Reformation of the 1820s.

78. See E. P. Thompson, *Customs in Common* (London: The Merlin Press, 1991), 9–10. Thompson describes eighteenth-century England in these terms: "Hence the plebian culture is rebellious, but rebellious in defence of custom. The customs defended are the people's own, and some of them are in fact based upon rather recent assertions in practice. But when people search for legitimations for protest, they often turn back to the paternalist regulation of a more authoritarian society, and select from among these the parts most calculated to serve their present interests."

79. Karl Marx, "The Eighteenth Brumaire of Louis Bonaparte," in *Selected Writings*, ed. David McLellan (Oxford: Oxford Univ. Press, 1977), 317.

80. David Lloyd, "Violence and the Constitution of the Novel," in *Anomalous States*, 140.

81. Ranajit Guha, "The Prose of Counter-Insurgency," in *Selected Subaltern Studies*, ed. Ranajit Guha and Gayatri Spivak (Oxford: Oxford Univ. Press, 1988), 46–47.

82. See Tadgh O'Sullivan, *Captain Rock in Print*, 37, regarding the continued insistence on "the knee-jerk nature of these waves of protest" in many accounts of Whiteboyism.

83. E. J. Hobsbawm, *Bandits* (Harmondsworth: Pelican, 1972), 10.

84. See, for example, Partha Chatterjee, *The Nation and Its Fragments: Colonial and Postcolonial Histories* (Princeton: Princeton Univ. Press, 1993). For Luke Gibbons's adaptation of such ideas to Ireland, see *Transformations in Irish Culture* (Cork: Cork Univ. Press, 1996), 134–47. See also David Lloyd, *Ireland After History* (Cork: Cork Univ. Press, 2000).

85. See Vinayak Chaturvedi, ed., *Mapping Subaltern Studies and the Postcolonial* (London: Verso, 2000).

86. Guha, "The Prose of Counter-Insurgency," 46, 78.

87. *Journal of Thomas Moore* 2:660–61.

88. Barry Sloan, *The Pioneers of Anglo-Irish Fiction, 1800–50* (Gerrards Cross: Colin Smythe, 1986), 41–42. See Leerssen, *Remembrance and Imagination,* 36.

89. Leerssen, *Remembrance and Imagination,* 36.

90. See Lady Morgan, *The Wild Irish Girl,* ed. Claire Connolly and Stephen Copley (London: Pickering and Chatto, 2000), 241–43; Robert Tracy, "Maria Edgeworth and Lady Morgan: Legality versus Legitimacy," *The Unappeasable Host: Studies in Irish Identity* (Dublin: Univ. College Dublin Press, 1998), 31. The politics of Morgan's national marriage have also been debated by Katie Trumpener, who argues against "the deceptive appearance of allegorical—and therefore political—transparency" in the text; *Bardic Nationalism: The Romantic Novel and the British Empire* (Princeton: Univ. of Princeton Press, 1997), 137.

91. As noted by Leerssen, *Remembrance and Imagination,* 37.

92. Mortimer O'Sullivan draws on the popular image of Moore himself as a rather effete creature of the drawing room. He complains that the missionary remains safely secluded in England, sipping tea with spinsters, while those in Ireland have to deal the real consequences of Captain Rock's literary mischief: "He has written a book, which, he may be sure, will be read and remembered; he has collected, within a portable compass, all the topics that can stir the blood of the uninstructed Irish; and this, in a new spirit of missionary heroism, *with perfect safety to himself.* It was a desideratum in the rebellion of 1798, to procure 'a gun which could shoot round a corner'" (*Captain Rock detected,* 199).

93. Napper Tandy was one of the founders of the United Irishmen; "Humanity" Dick Martin was a famously benevolent landlord from Galway. Moore's emphasis on Rock's clothing is not entirely fanciful. Paul E. Roberts reports that contrasting modes of attire were a key feature of the long-running feud between two rival gangs in Munster in the early 1800s: the Caravats (named in honor of their leader's flamboyant cravat), and the Shanavests (whose name means "old waistcoats"). In this case, it was the poorer faction who affected the more colorful dress, while the more middle-class group advertised their frugality through their plain clothing. See "Caravats and Shanavests: Whiteboyism and Faction Fighting in East Munster, 1802–11," in Clark and Donnelly, eds., *Irish Peasants.*

94. In 1824, Richard Wellesley (brother of the Duke of Wellington) was the lord-lieutenant of Ireland; Henry Goulburn (a staunch opponent of Catholic Emancipation) was chief secretary.

95. [Mortimer O'Sullivan], 37–51.

96. Charlotte Elizabeth [Tonna], *The Rockite,* 181–89.

97. Luke Gibbons, "Between Captain Rock and a Hard Place," 39.

98. See Michael J. Whitty, ed., *Captain Rock in London; or, the Chieftain's Gazette* (London: Robins, 1825–26), 35. Whitty's journal was another of the many publications

inspired by the success of *Captain Rock,* as detailed by Tadgh O'Sullivan, *Captain Rock in Print,* chap. 4.

99. Moore refers here to *Pacata Hibernia. Ireland appeased and reduced, or, an historie of the late wars in Ireland, especially within the province of Munster, under the government of Sir George Carew, Knight* (London, 1633), which was written by Sir Thomas Stafford (Carew's illegitimate son). The work is, in part, a record of the exploits and campaigns of Carew, brutal pacifier of Munster in the years after 1601 and adviser on the Ulster plantation.

100. See Michael Beames on Cosgrave's *The Lives and Actions of the Most Notorious Irish Highwaymen, Tories and Rapparees* (which Crofton Croker claims was one of the most popular books among the Irish peasantry in the 1820s), and on the career of James Freney in *Peasants and Power,* 22–24. See also Niall Ò Ciosáin, *Print and Popular Culture in Ireland, 1750–1850* (London: Macmillan, 1997), chap. 5.

101. Beames, *Peasants and Power,* 21, 23–24.

102. Quoted in ibid., 22.

103. For comments on Hall and Carleton, see Sloan, *Pioneers of Anglo-Irish Fiction,* 138–39, 166–67.

104. Cornewall Lewis, *Local Disturbances,* 90, 95–96.

105. Luke Gibbons, *Transformations,* 142.

106. Hobsbawm, *Bandits,* 40, 51. Patrick O'Sullivan comments that "the narrator of the *Memoirs* emerges as a literary creation of great charm" and compares him to the folk heroes described by Hobsbawm ("Literary Difficulty," 248–49).

107. Hobsbawm, *Bandits,* 58.

108. Barrington, *Personal Sketches,* 351.

109. Lloyd, *Anomalous States,* 140, 145–46.

110. See Christopher Morash, *Writing the Irish Famine* (Oxford: Clarendon Press, 1995), 74–75.

111. Leerssen, *Remembrance and Imagination,* 85.

112. Deane, *Strange Country,* 68.

113. Moore's text then bears out Anderson's argument that the "immediate genealogy" of nationalism "should be traced to the imaginings of the colonial state," and particularly to that state's development of such institutions of power as the census, the map, and the museum. Moore comments on the first two of these in *Captain Rock*—perhaps an instance of anticolonial nationalism's appropriation of such institutions. See Anderson, *Imagined Communities,* 163.

114. Quoted by Donnelly, "Pastorini and Captain Rock," 122.

115. See E. P. Thompson, "Crime of Anonymity," 303.

116. "Works on Ireland," *Blackwood's Magazine,* 557.

117. [Caesar Otway], *Sketches in Ireland: Description of Interesing and Hitherto Unnoticed Districts, in the North and South* (London, 1827), 275.

118. "Ireland," *Edinburgh Review* 41 (Jan. 1825), 356, 401. See Joel Mokyr, *Why Ireland Starved: A Quantative and Analytical History of the Irish Economy, 1800–1845*, rev. ed. (London, 1985) for a revision of the once-orthodox view that the Great Famine was the ultimate Malthusian catastrophe.

119. Morash, *Writing the Irish Famine*, 32.

120. As E. P. Thompson reports, "'Rough music' is the term which has been generally used in England since the end of the seventeenth century to denote a rude cacophony, with or without more elaborate ritual, which usually directed mockery or hostility against individuals who offended against certain community norms" (*Customs in Common*, 467).

121. Carlo Ginzburg, "Checking the Evidence: The Judge and the Historian," *Critical Inquiry* 18 (1991): 85–86.

122. See Mikhail Bakhtin, *Rabelais and His World*, trans. H. Iswolsky (Cambridge, Mass.: M.I.T. Press, 1968).

123. Daniel O'Connell, quoted by Beames, *Peasants and Power*, 62; Special Commission judge quoted in ibid., 72.

124. *Letters of Thomas Moore*, 1:369.

125. John Banim, *The Peep O'Day, or John Doe; Crohoore of the Billhook* (1825; reprint, by the O'Hara family, with introduction and notes by Michael Banim, Dublin, 1865), 25. This volume contains two novels, *The Peep O'Day, or John Doe* and *Crohoore of the Billhook*, and is hereafter *Peep O'Day; Crohoore* in text.

126. John Keegan, "Tales of the Rockites," *Legends and Poems*, ed. J. Canon O'Hanlon with a memoir by D. J. O'Donoghue (Dublin, 1907), 9.

127. Ibid., 56.

128. Peter Stallybrass and Allon White, *The Politics and Poetics of Transgression* (London: Methuen, 1986), 176–77.

129. Ibid., 78, 180.

130. See Deane, *Strange Country*, esp. chap. 2.

131. Quoted by Lady Wilde, *Notes on Men, Women, and Books* (London, 1891), 200.

132. J. K. L. [James Warren Doyle], *A Vindication of the Religious and Civil Principles of the Irish Catholics* (Dublin, 1823), 43–44.

133. See Davitt, *Fall of Feudalism*, 47.

134. "As the bourgeoisie produced new forms of regulation and prohibition governing their own bodies, they wrote ever more loquaciously of the body of the Other." Stallybrass and White, *Politics and Poetics*, 126.

135. See Gerald Griffin, *The Collegians* (1829; reprint, with an introduction by John Cronin, Belfast: Appletree Press, 1992), 272. Hereafter *Collegians* in text.

136. See Cronin, introduction to *Collegians*, vii.

137. The speaker is Danny Mann. Griffin, *Collegians*, 148.

138. "Ireland," *Edinburgh Review*, 387.

139. For a number of lurid counterparts to this vignette of the "grotesque body" in the (putatively) nonfictional literature about the Irish peasantry, see Caesar Otway, *Sketches in Ireland*, 270, 261–62, 326. In a more explicitly sectarian spirit, Otway distinguishes between the lazy Irish Catholic and his Protestant neighbor who "cannot bear to feed on an equality with his hog." He relates a communication from a doctor in Cork in 1823, who reported on the case of a woman who was constantly vomiting up beetles in all stages of development. Upon investigation, these beetles turned out to be of the "Bleps Mortisaga" species, usually found in graveyards. It emerged that this woman had long had the daily habit of eating clay from the graves of priests. Otway also tells how Catholics who had eaten meat in Lent were obliged to undergo the penance of going about on all fours with bones in their mouth, imitating dogs.

140. See Stallybrass and White, *Politics and Poetics*, 145, on how "the axis of the body is transcoded through the axis of the city." This transcoding is perhaps not confined to the modern *urban* setting. Interestingly, in James Connery's *The Reformer, or, an infallible remedy to prevent pauperism and the periodical returns of famine* (London, 1836), 54, we find a combination of a volcanic image of Whiteboyism (derived perhaps from Moore) with a quasi-excremental one: "And it is as impossible to suppress those ebullitions of public indignation as to extinguish the flames at the crater of Mount Ætna or Vesuvius, which, if subdued for any time, like these *Furnaces of Nature*, will create an inward burning in the bowels of the body politic, and end in an earthquake, such as Captain Right, White Boys, Hearts of Oak, John Doe, Caravats, Shanavests, Captain Rock, Terry Alt, &c. swallowing thousands of the human race in the *chasm*, until brought to a level surface by the *musket, sword, spear,* and *gibbet.*"

141. *Journal of Thomas Moore* 2:659.

142. See Dunne, "Murder as Metaphor: Griffin's Portrayal of Ireland in the year of Catholic Emancipation," in *Ireland and Irish Australia: Studies in Cultural and Political History*, ed. Oliver MacDonagh and W. F. Mandle (London: Croom Helm, 1986), 71.

143. As noted by Stephen Greenblatt, quoted by Stallybrass and White, *Politics and Poetics*, 108.

144. Samuel Burdy's description of Whiteboy outrages in his *The History of Ireland* (Edinburgh: Stevenson, 1817), 403.

145. Morash, *Writing the Irish Famine*, 37–38.

146. Ibid., 162–78.

2. The Irish National Novel

1. Ina Ferris, *The Romantic National Tale and the Question of Ireland* (Cambridge: Cambridge Univ. Press, 2002), 130. The Irish publishing industry had been devastated

by the extension of the Copyright Act of 1709 to Ireland after the Act of Union, and virtually all early-nineteenth-century Irish novels of note were first published in London.

2. However, Irish Protestant novelists continued to far outnumber Catholic novelists until the 1890s. See Rolf Loeber and Magda Loeber, with Anne Mullin Burnham, *A Guide to Irish Fiction, 1650–1900* (Dublin: Four Courts, 2006), lxxxv.

3. Flanagan, *Irish Novelists*, 178. Flanagan's account of the inadequacy of the early-nineteenth-century Irish novel has been extremely influential. As Lyn Pykett argues, however, the notion of the English "classic realist text" in the nineteenth century may itself merit some revision. See Lyn Pykett, "Sensation and the Fantastic in the Victorian Novel," in *The Cambridge Companion to the Victorian Novel*, ed. Deirdre David (Cambridge: Cambridge Univ. Press, 2001), 192–221. The work of every major English Victorian novelist (with the possible exception of George Eliot) had some melodramatic or sensationalist elements.

4. However, Tom Dunne's essays on Griffin and the Banims strongly underline the historical significance of these authors. See "The Insecure Voice: A Catholic Novelist in Support of Emancipation," in *Culture et pratiques politiques en France et en Irlande, XVIe–XVIIIe siècle*, ed. P. Bergson and L. Cullen (Paris: Centre De Recherches Historiques, 1988), 213–33, and "Murder as Metaphor: Griffin's Portrayal of Ireland in the Year of Catholic Emancipation," in *Ireland and Irish Australia*, 64–80. For other relevant critical accounts see Deane on *The Collegians* in *Strange Country*, 54–63; on the Banims, see Ferris, *Romantic National Tale*, chap. 5.

5. Eagleton, *Heathcliff*, 203.

6. Only recently has it been tentatively suggested that it is in these very sensationalist or melodramatic features that the abiding interest of these texts may lie. See Siobhán Kilfeather's interpretation of melodrama in the nineteenth-century Irish novel as a way of juxtaposing conflicting narratives without attempting to reconcile them, especially in relation to themes of repressed sexuality. Kilfeather, "Sex and Sensation in the Nineteenth-Century Novel," *Gender Perspectives in Nineteenth-Century Ireland*, ed. Margaret Kelleher and James Murphy (Dublin: Irish Academic Press, 1997), 86.

7. See Lloyd, *Anomalous States*, esp. p. 128.

8. The image is Franco Moretti's. Moretti, *Modern Epic*, trans. Quintin Hoare (London: Verso, 1996), 236.

9. For a suggestive account of the politics of mimicry, see Homi K. Bhabha, "Of Mimicry and Man: The Ambivalence of Colonial Discourse," *The Location of Culture* (London: Routledge, 1994), 85–92.

10. Flanagan, *Irish Novelists*, 240.

11. Ibid., 243.

12. Franco Moretti, *Atlas of the European Novel, 1800–1900* (London: Verso, 1998), 45.

13. Flanagan, *Irish Novelists*, 243.

14. William Carleton, "The late John Banim," *The Nation* 1, no. 50 (23 Sept. 1843): 796.

15. See Franco Moretti, *The Way of the World: The Bildungsroman in European Culture* (London: Verso, 1987) on how the novel of formation attempted to reconcile the conflicting demands of individuality and socialization in the nineteenth century.

16. Dunne, "Insecure Voice," 225.

17. See Nancy Armstrong's classic study, *Desire and Domestic Fiction* (Oxford: Oxford Univ. Press, 1987), which suggests that the rise of the realist novel in eighteenth- and nineteenth-century England is associated with the emergence of the domestic woman as a figure of considerable moral and political importance.

18. John Nowlan is initially given an elder brother; however, this character disappears from the novel at an early stage.

19. John Cronin argues that "The powerful realism of the first volume gives way to lurid melodrama. The realities of Irish life are once again forced into the unsuitable form of nineteenth-century sensational fiction." Cronin, *The Nineteenth Century*, vol. 1 of *The Anglo-Irish Novel* (Belfast: Appletree Press, 1980), 56.

20. Ibid.

21. John Banim, *The Nowlans* (1826; reprint, with an introduction by Kevin Casey, Belfast: Appletree Press, 1992), 11. Hereafter *Nowlans* in text.

22. In this regard, see remarks quoted by Christine Gledhill on the political implications of the melodramatic mode. In particular, Martha Vicinus comments that melodrama "always sides with the powerless," while David Grimstead argues that melodrama is an "echo of the historically voiceless." See Gledhill, "The Melodramatic Field: An Investigation," in *Home is Where the Heart Is: Studies in Melodrama and the Woman's Film* (London: British Film Institute, 2002), 14.

23. Sir William Wilde, *Irish Popular Superstitions* (Dublin, 1852), 81.

24. Willa Murphy, "Secrecy and Solidarity in the Fiction of John and Michael Banim," in *Was Ireland a Colony? Economics, Politics and Culture in Nineteenth-Century Ireland*, ed. Terrence McDonough (Dublin: Irish Academic Press, 2005), 287.

25. As noted by Mark D. Hawthorne, *John and Michael Banim (The "O'Hara Brothers"): A Study in the Early Development of the Anglo-Irish Novel* (Salzburg: Universität Salzburg, 1975), 79–80.

26. See Carlo Ginzburg's vivid account of early modern popular culture in *The Cheese and the Worms: The Cosmos of a Sixteenth-Century Miller*, trans. J. and A. Tedeschi (London: Penguin, 1992).

27. Penny Fielding, *Writing and Orality: Nationality, Culture and Nineteenth-Century Scottish Fiction* (Oxford: Clarendon Press, 1996), 23.

28. John Banim, *The Anglo-Irish of the Nineteenth Century* (1828; reprint, with an introduction by Robert Lee Wolff, New York: Garland, 1978), 3:2. Hereafter *Anglo-Irish* in text.

29. See Dunne, "Insecure Voice," 215.

30. Ferris, *Romantic National Tale*, 152.

31. Charles Townshend, *Political Violence in Ireland: Government and Resistance since 1848* (Oxford: Clarendon Press, 1983), 10–12.

32. [Thomas Moore], "Irish Novels," *Edinburgh Review* 43 (Feb. 1826): 357.

33. See James M. Cahalan, *Great Hatred, Little Room: The Irish Historical Novel* (Dublin: Gill and Macmillan, 1983), 1.

34. Georg Lukács, *The Historical Novel*, trans. H. and S. Mitchell (1937; reprint, London: Merlin Press, 1962), 53.

35. Dunne, "Insecure Voice," 221.

36. William Carelton, "The Late John Banim," *The Nation* 1, no. 50 (23 Sept. 1843): 795; Robert Lee Wolff, introduction to *The Boyne Water* (New York: Garland, 1978), vol. 1, xiii; Flanagan, *Irish Novelists*, 194.

37. Kevin Whelan, foreword to *The Wild Irish Girl* by Lady Morgan, ed. C. Connolly and S. Copley, xi; Trumpener, *Bardic Nationalism*, 141.

38. Leerssen, *Remembrance and Imagination*, 57–60.

39. Banim, *The Boyne Water* (1826; reprint, New York, 1885), 187.

40. See Cahalan, *Great Hatred*, 50–51.

41. Moretti, *Atlas*, 37–38.

42. See Armstrong, *Desire and Domestic Fiction*.

43. [Mortimer O'Sullivan], *Captain Rock detected*, 222.

44. See Eamon Ó Ciardha, *Ireland and the Jacobite Cause, 1685–1766: A Fatal Attachment* (Dublin: Four Courts Press, 2002), 23. In a telling omission, Banim makes no reference at all to eighteenth-century Jacobitism in *The Boyne Water*.

45. George Story, quoted by J. G. Simms, *Jacobite Ireland, 1685–91* (London: Routledge and Kegan Paul, 1969), 198–99.

46. Moretti, *Atlas*, 43.

47. The phrase is borrowed from Homi Bhabha, *Location of Culture*, 97.

48. Niall Ó Ciosáin comments on the appearance of the Rapparees in Banim's novel as the beginning of the elite nationalist appropriation of the motif of the dispossessed outlaw, away from its associations with popular narratives of banditry and criminality. However, I would argue that Banim's Rapparees lie somewhere between such texts as the notorious Cosgrave's *Irish Rogues* (which first appeared in the 1740s) and later nationalist ones (such as the Rapparee poetry of Charles Gavan Duffy), and are by no means as Victorianized as his account may suggest. See Ó Ciosáin, "The Irish Rogues," in *Irish Popular Culture, 1650–1850*, ed. J. S. Donnelly, Jr. and Kerby A. Miller (Dublin: Irish Academic Press, 1998), 92.

49. Carole Pateman, *The Sexual Contract* (Cambridge: Polity, 1988), 164.

50. [Thomas Moore], "Irish Novels," 365.

51. Moretti argues that "in cultures that belong to the periphery of the literary system (which means: almost all cultures, inside and outside Europe), the modern novel first arises not as an autonomous development but as a compromise between a western formal influence (usually French or English) and local materials." Franco Moretti, "Conjectures on World Literature," *New Left Review* 1 (Jan.–Feb. 2000): 58.

52. See Moretti, *Atlas*, 40.

53. Daniel O'Connell, *A Memoir on Ireland Native and Saxon*, vol. 1 (Dublin, 1843), 385.

54. See Tom Dunne, "Representations of Rebellion: 1798 in Literature," in *Ireland, England and Australia: Essays in Honour of Oliver MacDonagh*, ed. F. B. Smith (Canberra: Australian National University, 1990), 15.

55. Michael Banim, *The Croppy* (1828; reprint, with an introduction by Robert Lee Wolff, New York: Garland, 1978), vol. 1.

56. John Banim, *The Denounced; or, the last Baron of Crana* (1830; reprint, by the O'Hara family with introduction and notes by Michael Banim, Dublin, 1866), 295 (hereafter *Last Baron* in text). This volume also contains "The Conformists."

57. Ibid., 93.

58. W. B. Yeats, "William Carleton" (1896), *Uncollected Prose*, vol. 1, ed. John P. Frayne (London: Macmillan, 1970), 394.

59. Yeats, "Irish National Literature I: From Callanan to Carleton" (1895), in ibid. 1:359–64.

60. Yeats, introduction to *Representative Irish Tales*, ed. Helen Mary Theunte (Gerrards Cross: Smythe, 1979), 30–31.

61. Declan Kiberd, *Irish Classics* (London: Granta, 2000). Carleton was the earliest nineteenth-century Irish writer whose works were first published in Dublin, as the Irish publishing industry began to recover from its post-Union collapse after around 1830. See Margaret Kelleher, "Prose and Drama in English, 1830–1890," in *The Cambridge History of Irish Literature*, 2 vols. (Cambridge: Cambridge Univ. Press, 2006), ed. Margaret Kelleher and Philip O'Leary, 1:451.

62. See Morash, *Writing the Irish Famine*, 160. Helen O'Connell argues that Carleton's fiction is less a "realistic document of life in Ireland the early nineteenth century" than a literary counterpart to the didactic tracts of writers such as Hannah More, "The Fiction of Improvement," in *Irish Novel*, 118.

63. Kiberd, *Irish Classics*, 285–86.

64. See Morash, *Writing the Irish Famine*, 160, 178–80.

65. To borrow the terms used by Thomas Bartlett, *The Fall and Rise of the Irish Nation: The Catholic Question, 1690–1830* (Dublin: Gill and Macmillan, 1992), 347.

66. William Carleton, "General Introduction," *Traits and Stories of the Irish Peasantry* (1830–33; reprint, with a foreword by Barbara Haley, Gerrards Cross: Smythe, 1990), 1:xv. Hereafter *Traits* in text.

67. Idem, *The Autobiography of William Carleton*, rev. ed. (London: McGibbon and Kee, 1968), 77.

68. Eagleton, *Heathcliff*, 209. See Eagleton's comments on the "linguistic dissonance" of Carleton's tale.

69. William Carleton, *The Emigrants of Ahadarra* (London, 1848). Hereafter *Emigrants* in text.

70. See also Jason King's account of this theme in the works of William Carleton, "Emigration and the Anglo-Irish Novel: William Carleton, 'Home Sickness', and the Coherence of Gothic Conventions," in *Canadian Journal of Irish Studies* 26, no. 2 (fall 2000); 27, no. 1 (spring 2001): 105–18. This double issue of the journal is in fact one volume numbered continuously throughout.

71. However, the question of Carleton's religious affiliation has remained controversial. Many later Irish commentators—including Yeats—preferred to think that Catholicism was part of Carleton's essential identity and denied the significance of his conversion. But R. F. Foster has emphasized that much of this is "special pleading." In a letter written shortly before his death, Carleton declared that he "had not belonged to the Roman Catholic religion for half a century or more." R. F. Foster, "Yeats, Carleton and the Irish Nineteenth Century," in *The Irish Story: Telling Tales and Making it up in Ireland* (London: Allen Lane, 2001), 116.

72. For an example of such an appropriation of Carleton, see Patrick Murray, "Traits of the Irish Peasantry," *Edinburgh Review* 96, no. 196 (Oct. 1852): 384–403.

73. Yeats, introduction to *Representative Irish Tales*, 31. R. F. Foster remarks that Yeats's early championing of Carleton later gave way to a preference for Anglo-Irish writers such as Swift and Burke. But Yeats was always torn between a desire for popular authenticity and a longing for a cultured elite, especially when the folk turn out to be pious Catholics. Therefore it is logical for Yeats to have turned elsewhere when he decided that for Carleton (as for himself), "[Y]our background, and what has made you, survives repudiation and can return to claim you in strange ways at the end." Foster, "Yeats, Carleton," 125, 116.

74. Margaret O'Callaghan suggests that Carleton's descriptions of the savagery of the attackers in "Wildgoose Lodge" may be derived from such loyalist histories as John Foxe's *Book of Martyrs* (1583) and Richard Musgrave's history of 1798, *Memoirs of the different rebellions in Ireland.* O'Callaghan, "New ways of looking at the state apparatus and the state archive in nineteenth-century Ireland: 'Curiosities from that phonetic museum'—Royal Irish Constabulary reports and their political uses, 1879–91," *Proceedings of the Royal Irish Academy*, vol. 104C, no. 2 (2004): 42. This again underlines the difficulty of ascribing "authenticity" to Carleton's descriptions of peasant violence.

75. Carleton describes seeing the pitched sacks that contained the decomposing bodies of Devann and the other Ribbonmen, with "long ropes of slime" trailing from them, during the unusually hot autumn of 1818. Carleton, *Autobiography*, 114–17.

3. Irish Pastoral

1. Seamus Deane, "Poetry and Song, 1800–1890," *Field Day Anthology* 2:8.

2. Doris Sommer, *Foundational Fictions: the National Romances of Latin America* (Berkeley: Univ. of California Press, 1991). *Knocknagow* was first written for publication in serial form in the New York weekly, *Emerald* (with publication of the installments following a week later in Dublin), but the journal folded while the novel was still in its early stages. R. V. Comerford details the numerous editions of *Knocknagow* (whose success began with its second edition, produced in Dublin by the Catholic publisher James Duffy in 1879), as well as of Kickham's other fictional works and his poetry, produced in both Ireland and the United States between the 1880s and the 1940s. Comerford estimates that at least one hundred thousand copies of *Knocknagow* were published in Ireland alone. Comerford, *Charles J. Kickham: A Study in Irish Nationalism and Literature* (Dublin: Wolfhound Press, 1979), 209–10.

3. James M. Cahalan, *The Irish Novel: A Critical History* (Dublin: Gill and Macmillan, 1988).

4. See Griffin's conclusion in *The Rivals; Tracy*, 297, 301.

5. Moretti, *The Way of the World*, 185.

6. Nancy Armstrong, "Gender and the Victorian Novel," in *Cambridge Companion to the Victorian Novel*, 106.

7. Deane, *Strange Country*, 62.

8. Kiberd, *Irish Classics*, 271.

9. See Max Weber, *The Protestant Ethic and the Spirit of Capitalism*, trans. Talcott Parsons (1904–5; reprint, with an introduction by Anthony Giddens, London: Routledge, 1992). Anthony Giddens summarizes the most important criticisms that have been advanced of Weber's account of the connections between religion and the rise of capitalism in his introduction to this edition, xxiii–xxiv.

10. Ian Watt, *The Rise of the Novel: Studies in Defoe, Richardson and Fielding* (Berkeley: Univ. of California Press, 1957). On some of the continuing debates and controversies generated by Watt's book, see John Richetti, "The Legacy of Ian Watt's *The Rise of the Novel*," in *The Profession of Eighteenth-Century Literature: Reflections on an Institution*, ed. Leo Damrosch (Madison: Univ. of Wisconsin Press, 1992), 95–112.

11. Flanagan, *Irish Novelists*, 35.

12. Luke Gibbons comments of Boucicault that "Victorian melodrama lent itself particularly to the type of pictorial aesthetic which was to dominate romantic representations of Ireland." Gibbons et al., *Cinema and Ireland* (London: Routledge, 1988), 210.

13. Eagleton, *Heathcliff*, 204.

14. Kilfeather develops this insight in her analysis of *The Collegians* and nineteenth-century Irish fiction more generally in relation to the broader category of "sensation fiction." See "Sex and Sensation," especially 87–89.

15. See Pierre Joannon's account of the address of the French-liberal Catholics to O'Connell in Paris two months before his death. Joannon, "O'Connell, Montalembert and the Birth of Christian Democracy in France," in *Daniel O'Connell: Political Pioneer*, ed. Maurice O'Connell (Dublin: Institute of Public Adminstration, 1991), 98–99. See also Fergus O'Ferrall, "Liberty and Catholic Politics, 1790–1990," in ibid., 35–56.

16. On the question of accents and brogue in the novel, see Deane, *Strange Country*, 63.

17. Charles J. Kickham, *Knocknagow or, The Homes of Tipperary* (1879; reprint, with an introduction by John Kelly (Otley and Washington DC: Woodstock Books, 2002), 379. Hereafter *Knocknagow* in text.

18. This is a variation of the typical romance plot described by Sommer, in which the regional or racial differences that separate the "national father" from the "national mother" can only be overcome through a new project of national reconciliation. Sommer, *Foundational Fictions*, 49.

19. Fredric Jameson, "Third World Literature in the Era of Multinational Capital," *Social Text* 15 (fall 1986): 85–86.

20. Comerford, *Kickham*, 184.

21. Although in this, Kickham's novel bears out Partha Chatterjee's argument that anticolonial nationalist movements stake their claim for a separate state on the "spiritual" sphere of the dominated culture while admitting that the colonizing power may be superior on a material level. See Chatterjee, *The Nation and its Fragments* (Princeton: Princeton Univ. Press, 1993). See also Eagleton, *Heathcliff*, 208, for comments on the anecdotal or soap-opera qualities of much Irish fiction. But we should add that the significance of such nonprogressive narrative form varies from case to case. It is obvious that Kickham embraces the notion of dynamic, progressive, and popular forces at work in Irish history while not dramatizing these in any obvious realist way in *Knocknagow*.

22. See Comerford, *Kickham*, esp. pp. 9, 210. See also James H. Murphy, who argues that the novel offered its lower-middle-class readers a thoroughly flattering reflection of themselves as "noble victims," enabling them "to avoid seeing themselves as members of a new establishment that might be responsible for causing pain to others." Murphy, *Catholic Fiction and Social Reality in Ireland, 1873–1922* (Westport, Conn.: Greenwood Press, 1997), 82–83.

23. For Kickham's support for militarism but condemnation of terrorism, see Comerford, *Kickham*, 184.

24. Jane Tompkins, *Sensational Designs: The Cultural Work of American Fiction, 1790–1860* (Oxford: Oxford Univ. Press, 1985), 200.

25. Murphy, *Catholic Fiction*, 84–86. See Murphy's analysis of Mrs. Kearney's dream and of music in general in *Knocknagow*..

26. Charles Kickham, *Sally Cavanagh or, the untenanted graves: a tale of Tipperary* (Dublin, 1869), 209. Hereafter *Sally* in text.

27. John Kelly, introduction to *Knocknagow*, 27–28. Kelly notes, however, that the conditions depicted in the novel more closely resemble those of the 1840s than the 1870s.

28. Kai Erikson, "Notes on Trauma and Community," in *Trauma: Explorations in Memory*, ed. Cathy Caruth (Baltimore: Johns Hopkins Univ. Press, 1995), 185.

29. See Wyndham Lewis's account of Joyce as a member of the school of "Bergson-Einstein, Stein-Proust." Lewis, "An Analysis of the Mind of James Joyce," in *Time and Western Man*, ed. Paul Edwards (1927; reprint, Santa Rosa: Black Sparrow Press, 1993), 87.

30. See Erikson, "Notes on Trauma," 186–89.

31. For an investigation of the social transmission of non-inscribed, collective memories, see Paul Connerton, *How Societies Remember* (Cambridge: Cambridge Univ. Press, 1989).

32. See Kelly, introduction, 7. Kickham deployed his characteristically anecdotal style even in his nonfictional writing. See his description of how the Mullinahone blacksmith fashioned the "first pike made in that part of Tipperary since '98," in preparation for the doomed uprising of 1848. Cited by Gavan Duffy, *Four Years of Irish History* (New York, 1882), 659.

33. See Angela Bourke, *The Burning of Bridget Cleary: A True Story* (London: Pimlico, 1999), 114–15. Bridget Cleary, who was killed during an attempt to banish the changeling that her family believed the fairies had left in her place, lived and died just a few miles from the village of Mullinahone, the model for Knocknagow.

34. This also qualifies the critical view that there is no significant representation of meaningful conflict *within* the beleaguered society of *Knocknagow* (see, for example, Eagleton's description of Kickham's "self-identical community" [*Crazy John and the Bishop*, 215]). Any such view of Kickham is also contradicted by what Murphy refers to as the "cynical realism" of Kickham's last novel, *For the Old Land* (1886), which presents a final, bitter critique of native Irish greed and corruption. See Murphy, *Catholic Fiction*, 83.

35. But see Davitt's respectful account of Kickham's view: "He convinced himself, however, that any co-operation between extreme and moderate nationalists, in any line of public action, would work injury to the revolutionary cause without winning any substantial advantage to the country, and this stand, honestly taken by a man of singular earnestness and sincerity, determined the policy of other revolutionary leaders, and secured the rejection by them of the proposed new departure." Davitt, *Fall of Feudalism*, 134.

36. Kickham recalled from his own youth in Tipperary that "the better class of unmarried day-laborers were more manly and intelligent and far more full of fun and humor than the sons of the small and middling farmers." See Comerford, *Kickham*, 49–50.

37. Ibid., 210.

38. Griffin, *The Rivals; Tracy's Ambition* 2:94.

39. John Barrell, *The Dark Side of the Landscape: The Rural Poor in English Painting, 1730–1840* (Cambridge: Cambridge Univ. Press, 1980), 87. Crabbe's *Parish Register* (1807) was a riposte to Goldsmith's nostalgic pastoralism; Goldsmith's imaginary village of Auburn in *The Deserted Village* is a composite of English and Irish elements.

40. Barrell, *Dark Side*, 88. For parallels between Goldsmith and Griffin, see Dominick Tracy, "Squatting the Deserted Village: Idyllic Resistance in Griffin's *The Collegians*," in *Irish Novel*, esp. pp. 97–99. On Goldsmith and Kickham, see Comerford, *Kickham*, 198.

41. Presumably it is episodes like these in *Knocknagow* that Norman Vance describes as "preposterously melodramatic." Vance, *Irish Literature since 1800* (London: Longman, 2002).

4. The Pope's Green Island: Irish Fiction at the *Fin de Siècle*

1. For his remarks about Irish literacy and reading practices, see John Pope-Hennessy, "What do the Irish read?" *The Nineteenth Century* 15 (June 1884): 920–32. On the popularity of works that I consider in this book, see Loeber and Loeber, *A Guide to Irish Fiction*, lxx, lxxi. Comerford comments on the "profuse and lively (if largely undistinguished) tradition of Catholic-nationalist literature which flourished from the 1850s onwards," noting that Catholic publishers such as James Duffy and M. H. Gill published many novels as well as works of history and Catholic apologetics (Comerford, *Kickham*, 197). On developments in the publishing industry and in literary markets at this time, see Murphy, *Catholic Fiction*, 1–11, and idem, *Ireland: A Social, Cultural and Literary History, 1791–1891* (Dublin: Four Courts Press, 2003), 160–65. See also Margaret Kelleher, "Prose Writing and Drama in English, 1830–1890," in *Cambridge History of Irish Literature*, ed. Kelleher and O'Leary, 2:451–54. On women's writing, see Margaret Kelleher, "Women's Fiction, 1845–1900," in *The Field Day Anthology of Irish Writing*, vol. 5, ed. Angela Bourke et al. (Cork: Cork Univ. Press, 2002), 924–75.

2. See Murphy, *Catholic Fiction*, esp. chap. 2, and "'Things Which Seem to You Unfeminine': Gender and Nationalism in the Fiction of some Upper Middle Class Catholic Women Novelists, 1880–1910," in *Border Crossings: Irish Women Novelists and National Identities*, ed. Kathryn Kirkpatrick (Dublin: Wolfhound, 2000), 58–78.

3. This forms a large proportion of what Murphy categorizes as "Intelligentsia Fiction," in *Catholic Fiction*, 8.

4. On Irish naturalism after independence as an aesthetic of diminished expectations, see Cleary, *Outrageous Fortune,* 97.

5. See Emmet Larkin's seminal essay, "The Devotional Revolution in Ireland, 1850–1875," in *The Historical Dimensions of Irish Catholicism* (1976; reprint, Washington, DC, and Dublin: The Catholic Univ. of America Press and Four Courts Press, 1984). Larkin surveys subsequent treatments of these topics in his introduction to this volume (1–11).

6. For example, in George Moore's story "A letter to Rome," Father MacTurnan declares that "It was Cardinal Cullen who denationalized religion in Ireland." Moore, *The Untilled Field* (1903; reprint, with a foreword by T. R. Henn, Gerrards Cross: Colin Smythe, 1976), 135.

7. See Seamus Deane, *Foreign Affections: Essays on Edmund Burke* (Cork: Cork Univ. Press, 2005), 147–67.

8. James Joyce, *A Portrait of the Artist as a Young Man,* ed. Seamus Deane (1916; reprint, London: Penguin, 1992), 34. Hereafter *Portrait* in text.

9. P. J. Mathews, *Revival: The Abbey Theatre, Sinn Fein, The Gaelic League and the Co-operative Movement* (Cork: Cork Univ. Press, 2003), 33.

10. See Horace Plunkett, *Ireland in the New Century* (1904; reprint, foreword by Trevor West, Dublin: Irish Academic Press, 1983). The most notable response to Plunkett is Monsignor Michael Riordan's monumental *Catholicity and Progress in Ireland* (London: Kegan Paul, Trench, Trübner and Co, 1906), which ascribes Ireland's underdevelopment to British rule rather than to the influence of the Catholic Church. As Deane comments of this exchange: "Plunkett's linking of progress with material prosperity allows O'Riordan to take the higher moral ground, claiming for catholicism all those virtues that are not 'material' and relegating protestantism to the role of maidservant to imperial rapacity." Deane, ed., *Field Day Anthology* 3:696.

11. Gerald O'Donovan, *Father Ralph* (1913; reprint, with an introduction by John F. Ryan, Dingle: Brandon Press, 1993), 40–41.

12. Murphy discusses the transition between the struggle for reform and the hope for "the gradual freeing of individuals" in O'Donovan and some of his contemporaries. Murphy, *Catholic Fiction,* esp. p. 129. See also James Cahalan on the possible influence of *Father Ralph* on James Joyce. Cahalan, *Irish Novel,* 111.

13. Gerald O'Donovan, *The Holy Tree* (London: Heinemann, 1922), 164–65.

14. MacManus's case was particularly notorious. He was a Young Irelander whose huge funeral at Glasnevin in 1861 (which had been opposed by Cardinal Cullen) represented a major show of strength on the part of the Fenians.

15. William O'Brien, introduction to *The Heart of Tipperary: A Romance of the Land League* by W. P. Ryan (London: 1893), xii.

16. William O'Brien, *When We Were Boys* (1890; reprint, with an introduction by Robert Lee Wolff, New York and London: Garland Press, 1979), 550.

17. Ibid., 545.

18. Canon Patrick Sheehan, *The Graves at Kilmorna* (New York, 1915), 221. Hereafter *Graves* in text.

19. For example, Terence Brown suggests that we should not take the declarations of the Fenian Cogan at face value, asserting that Sheehan believes that "Education must inform the majority's nationalism so that the fatal dialectic between nobility and pragmatism can be transcended in a new social order." Brown, *Ireland's Literature: Selected Essays* (Mullingar: Lilliput Press, 1980), 75.

20. See Laird's detailed analysis of the cultural politics of boycotting and other forms of popular protest during the Land War. Laird, *Subversive Law,* esp. chap. 1.

21. George Moore, *A Drama in Muslin* (1886; reprint, Gerrards Cross: Colin Smythe, 1981), 126. Hereafter *Drama* in text.

22. Anthony Trollope, *The Landleaguers* (1883; reprint, with an introduction by Mary Hamer, Oxford: Oxford Univ. Press, 1993), 408.

23. Hamer, introduction to *Landleaguers,* xix.

24. Cork Hill was one of the entrances to Dublin Castle.

25. See Gayatri Spivak's discussion of *Jane Eyre,* "Three Women's Texts and the Critique of Imperialism," *Feminist Reader,* ed. Catherine Belsey and Jane Moore (London: Macmillan, 1989), 175–95.

26. Filson Young, quoted by O'Riordan in *Catholicity and Progress,* 271. O'Riordan retorts that "those who decry and disregard chastity qualify better for a lunatic asylum than those who practise it" (272).

27. Kelleher comments on the large number of novels about the Land War authored by women, including works by Letitia McClintock, Elizabeth Owens Blackburne, and Fannie Gallaher. Kelleher, "Prose and Drama in English, 1830–1890," 479; see also idem, "'Factual Fictions': Representations of the Land Agitation in Nineteenth-Century Women's Fiction" (forthcoming).

28. See James H. Murphy on Mulholland, "'Insouciant Rivals of Mrs Barton,'" in *Gender Perspectives,* 221–28. The *Irish Monthly* was founded in 1873 by Matthew Russell. Murphy quotes from a 1894 article in the *New Ireland Review,* which claimed that Mulholland was gaining Irish readers at the expense of Griffin, Carleton, and the Banims, but that *Knocknagow* remained the best-loved Irish novel. Murphy, "Things Which Seem to You Unfeminine': Gender and Nationalism in the Fiction of some Upper Middle Class Catholic Women Novelists," in *Border Crossings,* 59.

29. Rosa Mulholland, *Marcella Grace* (London, 1886), 23. Hereafter *Marcella* in text.

30. M. E. Francis [Francis Blundell], *Miss Erin* (New York, 1898), 110.

31. Emily Lawless, *Hurrish: A Study* (1886; reprint, with an introduction by Val Mulkerns, Belfast: Appletree Press, 1992), 3–4.

32. Emily Lawless, *Grania: The Story of an Island* (London, 1892), 300.

33. Quoted by Gerardine Meaney, "Decadence, Degeneration and Revolting Aesthetics: The Fiction of Emily Lawless and Katherine Cecil Thurston," *Colby Quarterly* 36, no. 2 (June 2000): 161.

34. For a discussion of degenerationist motifs in *Grania*, see ibid., 162–66. The best general treatment of the cultural and historical significance of degeneration theory is Daniel Pick, *Faces of Degeneration: A European Disorder, ca. 1848–1918* (Cambridge: Cambridge Univ. Press, 1989).

35. Kilfeather, "Sex and Sensation," 83.

36. For an alternative analysis of Lawless's portrayal of late-nineteenth-century Ireland in this novel, see Laird, *Subversive Law,* 43–59. Laird argues that Lawless represents feudal authority as benign yet hopelessly archaic, and that *Hurrish* points to the limits of the official legal system as well as of the peasants' own code of justice. It is true that Lawless distrusts both the modernizing, colonial state and the Land League campaign. However, I would suggest that the supposed historical impasse that Lawless depicts in *Hurrish* is best understood, not as radical refusal of "bourgeois socialization" in a colonial context, but as the inevitable consequence of Lawless's implacable hostility to popular politics.

37. Nancy Armstrong argues that partly on the basis of these fictions, feminist criticism established "a specific verbal performance as the precondition for achieving authority." Armstrong, *How Novels Think* (New York: Columbia Univ. Press, 2006), 139.

38. George Moore, *The Lake* (1905; reprint, New York: Carroll and Graff, 1986), 96.

39. Eagleton, *Heathcliff,* 218. Therefore, I disagree with his conclusion that *The Lake* "thus ends up endorsing a stereotypically priestly view of women, but merely reverses its value from negative to positive" (218). On similar grounds, I would also take issue with Adrian Frazier's remark that there is "something odd and anticlimactic about the fact that in the end Moore's hero . . . goes off to America in order to become a journalist." Frazier, *George Moore, 1852–1933* (New Haven: Yale Univ. Press, 2000), 348. Of course, Gogarty's fate is determined by Rose's rejection of him.

40. Joyce to Stanislaus Joyce, *Selected Letters,* ed. Richard Ellmann (Oxford: Oxford Univ. Press, 1975), 106.

41. Ibid., 99. Joyce also complained that he was so poor he wished someone would send him the underpants that Father Gogarty left in the bulrushes before his final swim across the lake (101).

5. James Joyce and the History of the Future

1. James Joyce, *Finnegans Wake* (1939; reprint, London: Faber and Faber, 1975), 184. Hereafter *Wake* in text. For further allusions to Thomas Moore in *Finnegans Wake*, see Atherton, *Books at the Wake,* 269.

2. See Atherton, *Books at the Wake*, 94–95.

3. On Joyce in relation to the revival, see Andrew Gibson, *Joyce's Revenge: History, Politics and Aesthetics in* Ulysses (Oxford: Oxford Univ. Press, 2002). But Len Platt, for example, comments that the "extraordinary volubility of *Ulysses* responds to the *relative silence* of Catholic Ireland in nineteenth and early twentieth-century literary culture" (my emphasis). Platt, *Joyce and the Anglo-Irish: A Study of Joyce and the Literary Revival* (Amsterdam: Rodopi, 1998), 23.

4. Pope-Hennessy, "What do the Irish read?" 920–32. Pope-Hennessy reported in 1884 that although the most popular collection for ordinary readers, *Penny Readings for the Irish People,* included stories by Banim, Griffin, and Carleton, it seems that *all* the songbooks sold at fairs or read in Land League Reading Rooms included large selections from the *Melodies*. In these volumes, Moore took his place alongside a popular literature that included selections from Swift and Burke as well as Irish histories by (for example) D'Arcy McGee and John Mitchel. This is just one indication of Moore's immense popularity.

5. James Joyce, *Dubliners* (1914; reprint, with an introduction and notes by Terence Brown, London: Penguin, 1992), 48.

6. James Joyce, *Ulysses*, ed. Hans Walter Gabler (1922; reprint, London: The Bodley Head, 1986), 251.

7. For example, see Joseph Valente, "Joyce's Politics: Race, Nation, and Transnationalism," in *Palgrave Advances in James Joyce Studies*, ed. Jean-Michel Rabaté (Basingstoke: Palgrave Macmillan, 2004), 73–96.

8. Luke Gibbons, "'Have you no homes to go to?': James Joyce and the Politics of Paralysis," *Semicolonial Joyce*, ed. Derek Attridge and Marjorie Howes (Cambridge: Cambridge Univ. Press, 2000), 162–63. More speculatively, David Lloyd traces Irish drinking practices as represented in *Dubliners* to "the sublimation and survival of the nonnucleated settlements of pre-Famine Ireland." Lloyd, "Counterparts: *Dubliners*, Masculinity and Temperance Nationalism," *Semicolonial Joyce*, 142. Christine van Boheemen-Saaf argues that all of Joyce's works testify to a traumatic, "unspeakable" history. van Boheemen-Saaf, *Joyce, Derrida, Lacan, and the Trauma of History: Reading, Narrative, and Postcolonialism* (Cambridge: Cambridge Univ. Press, 1999).

9. Wyndham Lewis, "An Analysis of the Mind of James Joyce," *Time and Western Man*, 89.

10. Jennifer Wicke, *Advertising Fictions: Literature, Advertisement, and Social Reading* (New York: Columbia Univ. Press, 1988), 125, 168. See also Franco Moretti's analysis of how advertising and stream of consciousness "pursue and implicate each other throughout *Ulysses*." Moretti, *Modern Epic: The World-System from Goethe to García Márquez* (London: Verso, 1996), 135.

11. Deane, "Thomas Moore," *Field Day Anthology* 1:1053.

12. For musical references in Joyce, see Mathew Hodgart and Mabel P. Worthington, *Song in the Work of James Joyce* (New York: Columbia Univ. Press, 1959). For Joyce's use of the *Melodies*, see 9–12.

13. See Joseph Brooker on Joyce as heritage in contemporary Ireland. Brooker, *Joyce's Critics: Transitions in Reading and Culture* (Madison: Univ. of Wisconsin Press, 2004), 203–18.

14. Ibid., 208.

15. For an account of this crucial period, see Ray MacSharry and Padraic White, *The Making of the Celtic Tiger: The Inside Story of Ireland's Boom Economy* (Dublin: Mercier Press, 2000). For a more skeptical account of the social effects of the boom, see Colin Coulter and Steve Coleman, eds., *The End of Irish History? Critical Reflections on the Celtic Tiger* (Manchester: Manchester Univ. Press, 2003).

16. I have challenged the critical construction of Joyce as a cosmopolitan anti-nationalist in *Joyce and Nationalism* (London: Routledge, 1995).

17. Brooker, *Joyce's Critics*, 205.

18. Karl Radek, "James Joyce or Socialist Realism?" (1934) in *James Joyce: The Critical Heritage*, ed. Robert H. Deming (London: Routledge and Kegan Paul, 1970), 2:625.

19. Declan Kiberd also finds in Joyce an anticipation of the economic boom of late-twentieth-century Ireland, when in his view the Irish middle class finally overcomes its disdain of and aversion to commerce. Kiberd, "The Celtic Tiger: A Cultural History," *The Irish Writer and the World* (Cambridge: Cambridge Univ. Press, 2005), 287. However, I am here at odds with Kiberd's construction of Bloom as a heroic entrepreneur, rather than primarily as a consumer, in *Ulysses*.

20. Benjamin describes the wish images that arise in the collective mind at certain transitional moments when the old and the new interpenetrate: "In the dream in which each epoch entertains images of its successor, the latter appears wedded to elements of primal history . . . that is, to elements of a classless society. And the experiences of such a society—as stored in the unconscious of the collective—engender, through interpenetration with what is new, the utopia that has left its trace in a thousand configurations of life, from enduring edifices to passing fashions." Benjamin, *Arcades Project*, 4–5.

21. See in particular Rainey's account of the fate of the deluxe first edition of *Ulysses*, which was mostly bought up by dealers and speculators in the rare book trade. Lawrence Rainey, *Institutions of Modernism: Literary Elites and Public Culture* (New Haven: Yale Univ. Press, 1998), 44.

22. See Joyce's two essays on James Clarence Mangan in *Occasional, Critical, and Political Writings*, ed. Kevin Barry (Oxford: Oxford Univ. Press, 2000). There are numerous allusions to the trial and disgrace of Oscar Wilde in *Finnegans Wake*.

23. See Deane's account of the "aestheticisation of critique" in Joyce's writing from "The Dead" onward in "Dead Ends: Joyce's finest moments," *Semicolonial Joyce*,

esp. 34–36. However, I would suggest instead that Joyce's writing continues to *alternate* between aestheticization and critique.

24. Joyce, "Fenianism: The Last Fenian," *Occasional, Critical, and Political Writings,* 138.

25. As observed by Terence Brown, introduction to *Dubliners,* xxx; Joyce added "The Dead" to the volume in 1907.

26. Brown notes that in fact MacHale was not even present at the Vatican Council when the declaration of papal infallibility was made (*Dubliners,* 303).

27. Joyce, "Ireland: Island of Saints and Sages," *Occasional, Critical, and Political Writing,* 125. In this lecture, Joyce questions what Ireland had ever gained by its unswerving "fidelity to the Papal crown," 122–23.

28. Brooker has usefully analyzed the views of Thomas MacGreevy, Flann O'Brien, and Patrick Kavanagh, among others, on the question of Joyce's Catholicism. Brooker, *Joyce's Critics,* 195–202. For a robust recent assertion of Joyce's loyalties to Catholic culture and an account of his hostility to Irish Protestantism, see Platt, *Joyce and the Anglo-Irish.*

29. In this regard, Dedalus has much in common with such fin de siècle writers as Oscar Wilde, Charles Baudelaire, and J.-K. Huysmans, who found in the Church an alternative to the bland dreariness of bourgeois civilization. See Ellis Hansen, *Decadence and Catholicism* (Cambridge, Mass.: Harvard Univ. Press, 1998).

30. Brown suggests that Kernan alludes here to the Marian apparitions at Knock in Co. Mayo in 1879; skeptics had suggested that the images of the Virgin Mary, St. Joseph, and St. John had been contrived by magic lantern images (*Dubliners,* 304). If this was the case, it demonstrates how traditional beliefs could be manipulated by the use of modern technology.

31. Foucault traces the generalization of the confession in modern culture, arguing that for the first time "a society has taken upon itself to solicit and hear the imparting of individual pleasures." Foucault, *The History of Sexuality,* vol. 1, trans. Robert Hurley (1976; reprint, New York: Vintage, 1980), 63.

32. Among numerous recent discussions of Joyce and masochism, see in particular Frances Restuccia, *James Joyce and the Law of the Father* (New Haven: Yale Univ. Press, 1989).

33. Lawrence Birken, *Consuming Desire: Sexual Science and the Emergence of a Culture of Abundance, 1871–1914* (Ithaca: Cornell Univ. Press, 1988), 42.

34. Benedict Anderson, *Imagined Communities: Reflections on the Origins and Spread of Nationalism* (London: Verso, 1991). See also Susan Buck-Morss, *Dreamworld and Catastrophe: The Passing of Mass Utopia in East and West* (Cambridge, Mass.: MIT Press, 2000), for a detailed description of how early-twentieth-century commodity culture, in both the United States and the Soviet Union, was deeply bound up with fantasies of a mass utopia. It is only in the late twentieth century, she asserts, that such utopian yearnings were entirely eliminated from "advanced" capitalist societies.

35. An argument advanced as late as the early 1990s by Derry Desmond and Paul Keating, *Culture and Capitalism in Ireland* (Aldershot: Avebury, 1993), 175.

36. J. J. Lee summarizes the prevailing view: "The clergy, strong farmers in cassocks, largely voiced the concerns of their most influential constituents, whose values they instinctively shared and universalised as 'Christian.'" Lee, *Ireland, 1912–1985: Politics and Society* (Cambridge: Cambridge Univ. Press, 1989), 159; see also Tom Garvin, *Preventing the Future: Why was Ireland So Poor for So Long?* (Dublin: Gill and Macmillan, 2004), esp. 40–43.

37. Ben Singer analyzes the melodramatic mode as an aesthetic response to the instability of modern life that is particularly attuned to the experiences and tastes of the urban working class. Singer, *Melodrama and Modernity* (New York: Columbia Univ. Press, 2001).

38. See Franco Moretti's account of the contrasting images of Paris and London in a number of key nineteenth-century *bildungsromane*. Moretti, *Atlas*, 100–101.

39. Enda Duffy, "Disappearing Dublin: Ulysses, Postcoloniality, and the Politics of Space," *Semicolonial Joyce*, esp. 48.

40. This is despite Dedalus's famous salute to the peasant with his "redrimmed horny eyes" at the end of *Portrait*; there he acknowledges his alienation from the old man, although declaring that he means him "no harm" (*Portrait*, 274). I would suggest that this passage has more to do with Joyce's rejection of the revivalist appropriation of the peasant than with any attempt to define his own artistic project.

41. Joyce, "The city of the tribes: Italian memories in an Irish port," *Occasional, Critical, and Political Writing*, 198.

42. Ibid., 197. See Howes's discussion of the "ambiguous and uneven modernity" of Galway in Joyce, *Colonial Crossings*, 74.

43. Benjamin, *Arcades Project*, 17.

44. The interpolation is in part a parody of a medieval poem, "Aelfrid's Itinerary," which celebrates the delights of the four provinces of Ireland. Joyce was familiar with this text through a translation by James Clarence Mangan. See Don Gifford and Robert J. Seidman, *Ulysses Annotated*, rev. ed. (Berkeley: Univ. of California Press, 1988), 318.

45. See my *Joyce and Nationalism*, chap. 3.

46. See Gifford and Seidman, *Ulysses Annotated*, 59.

47. Stanley Cavell, *Cities of Words* (Cambridge, Mass.: Harvard Univ. Press, 2004), 83.

48. In 1882, a splinter group of Fenians known as the Invincibles assassinated Lord Frederick Cavendish, the new chief secretary of Ireland, and Thomas Henry Burke, an undersecretary in Dublin Castle, in the Phoenix Park, stabbing them with surgical knives.

49. Benjamin, *Arcades Project*, 416. Luke Gibbons further argues that there are several points in *Ulysses* at which "the pressure of the past forces its way into the present"

in a series of "flash-cuts," demonstrating how the colonial past resists relegation to the realm of private memory. Luke Gibbons, "Spaces of Time through Times of Space: Joyce, Ireland and Colonial Modernity," *Field Day Review* 1 (2005): 85.

50. For an analysis of Joyce's many allusions to the Phoenix Park murders in *Ulysses*, see James Fairhall, *James Joyce and the Question of History* (Cambridge: Cambridge Univ. Press, 1993), chap. 1.

51. Connerton, *How Societies Remember*, 20. Connerton reports how in the 1930s, Southern Italian peasants in a remote village had apparently forgotten about the Great War, but vividly remembered the brigands of the previous century.

52. See my *Joyce and Nationalism*, 36–47.

53. Fredric Jameson, "*Ulysses* in History," in *James Joyce and Modern Literature*, ed. W. J. McCormack and Alistair Stead (London: Routledge, 1982), 129. Jameson observes that in previous societies it was nature, rather than the world created by human labor, that was usually perceived as meaningless or antihuman.

54. On the Irish Censorship of Publications Act of 1929, see Terence Brown, *Ireland: A Social and Cultural History, 1922–2002* (London: Harper Perennial, 2004), 57–67.

55. Andrew Gibson, *James Joyce* (London: Reaktion, 2006), 159.

56. Seamus Deane, "Joyce the Irishman," in *The Cambridge Companion to James Joyce*, ed. Derek Attridge (Cambridge: Cambridge Univ. Press, 1990), 50.

57. On Joyce's interest in Irish radio, see Gibson, *James Joyce*, 147.

58. Quoted by John V. Kelleher, *Selected Writings of John V. Kelleher on Ireland and Irish America*, ed. Charles Fanning (Carbondale: Southern Illinois Univ. Press, 2002), 101.

59. Joyce alludes to the lyric by Moore that begins "At the mid hour of night, when the stars are weeping, I fly." Moore, *Poetical Works*, 259. The song tells of a grieving lover who imagines he can hear the voice of his beloved answering his song from the Kingdom of Souls. Blight is the common name for the disease that destroyed the potato crop during the Great Famine.

60. Quoted by Michele Dowling, "'The Ireland that I would have': De Valera and the Creation of an Irish National Image," *History Ireland* 5, no. 2 (Summer 1997): 39.

61. On the peculiarity of the Irish relationship with the land or soil, especially as this is reflected in the writings of Thomas Davis and James Fintan Lalor, see Deane, *Strange Country*, 72–78.

62. On the later Yeats and on the counter-revivalist reaction against modernism in Ireland, see my "Modernism and the Irish Revival," *The Cambridge Companion to Modern Irish Culture*, ed. Joe Cleary and Claire Connolly (Cambridge: Cambridge Univ. Press, 2005), 157–72.

Bibliography

Note: Names of publishers given only for works published after 1900.

Primary works

Banim, John. *The Anglo-Irish of the Nineteenth Century.* 1828. 3 vols. With an introduction by Robert Lee Wolff. New York: Garland, 1978.

———. *The Boyne Water.* 1826. New York, 1885.

———. *The Denounced; or, the Last Baron of Crana.* 1830. By the O'Hara family, with introduction and notes by Michael Banim. Dublin, 1866.

———. *The Nowlans.* 1826. With an introduction by Kevin Casey. Belfast: Appletree Press, 1992.

Banim, John, and Michael Banim. *The Peep O'Day; or John Doe; Crohoore of the Bill-hook.* 1825. By the O'Hara family, with introduction and notes by Michael Banim. Dublin, 1865.

Banim, Michael. *The Croppy.* 1828. With an introduction by Robert Lee Wolff. 3 vols. New York: Garland, 1978.

Blundell, Francis [M. E. Francis, pseud.]. *Miss Erin.* New York, 1898.

Carleton, William. *The Autobiography of William Carleton.* 1896. Revised edition with a preface by Patrick Kavanagh. London: McGibbon and Kee, 1968.

———. *The Emigrants of Ahadarra.* London, 1848.

———. "The Late John Banim." *The Nation* 1, no. 50 (23 Sept. 1843): 794–95.

———. *Traits and Stories of the Irish Peasantry.* 1830–33. 2 vols. With a foreword by Barbara Haley. Gerrards Cross: Colin Smythe, 1990.

Griffin, Gerald. *The Collegians.* 1829. With an introduction by John Cronin. Belfast: Appletree Press, 1992.

———. *The Rivals; Tracy's Ambition.* 1829. With an introduction by Robert Lee Wolff. 3 vols. New York: Garland, 1979.

Joyce, James. *Dubliners.* 1914. With an introduction and notes by Terence Brown. London: Penguin, 1992.

————. *Finnegans Wake.* 1939. London: Faber and Faber, 1975.

————. *Occasional, Critical, and Political Writings.* Edited by Kevin Barry. Oxford: Oxford Univ. Press, 2000.

————. *A Portrait of the Artist as a Young Man.* 1916. Edited by Seamus Deane. London: Penguin, 1992.

————. *Selected Letters.* Edited by Richard Ellmann. London: Faber, 1975.

————. *Ulysses.* 1922. Edited by Hans Walter Gabler. London: The Bodley Head, 1986.

Keegan, John. *Legends and Poems.* Edited by J. Canon O'Hanlon, with a memoir by D. J. O'Donoghue. Dublin: Sealy, Bryers and Walker, 1907.

Kickham, Charles J. *Knocknagow or, The Homes of Tipperary.* 2d ed., 1879. With an introduction by John Kelly. Washington, D.C.: Woodstock Books, 2002.

————. *Sally Cavanagh or, the Untenanted Graves: A Tale of Tipperary.* Dublin, 1869.

Lawless, Emily. *Grania: The Story of an Island.* London, 1892.

————. *Hurrish: A Study.* 1886. With an introduction by Val Mulkerns. Belfast: Appletree Press, 1992.

Moore, George. *A Drama in Muslin.* 1886. Gerrards Cross: Colin Smythe, 1981.

————. *The Lake.* 1905. New York: Carroll and Graff, 1986.

————. *The Untilled Field.* 1903. With a foreword by T. R. Henn. Gerrards Cross: Colin Smythe, 1976.

[Moore, Thomas]. "Irish Novels." *Edinburgh Review* 43 (Feb. 1826): 356–72.

————. *The Life and Death of Lord Edward Fitzgerald.* 2 vols. London, 1831.

————. *Memoirs of Captain Rock, the Celebrated Irish Chieftain, with Some Account of His Ancestors. Written By Himself.* London, 1824.

————. *Memoirs of Captain Rock, the Celebrated Irish Chieftain, with Some Account of His Ancestors, Written By Himself.* Edited by Emer Nolan. Dublin: Field Day Publications, forthcoming.

Moore, Thomas. *The Journal of Thomas Moore.* Edited by Wilfrid S. Dowden. 6 vols. Newark: Univ. of Delaware Press, 1983–91.

————. *The Letters of Thomas Moore.* Edited by Wilfrid S. Dowden. 2 vols. Oxford: Clarendon Press, 1964.

————. *The Poetical Works of Thomas Moore.* New York, 1887.

Morgan, Sydney (Lady). *The Wild Irish Girl.* 1806. Edited by Claire Connolly and Stephen Copley. London: Pickering and Chatto, 2000.

Mulholland, Rosa. *Marcella Grace.* London, 1886.

O'Brien, William. Introduction to *The Heart of Tipperary: A Romance of the Land League,* by W. P. Ryan, ix–xv. London, 1893.

————. *When We Were Boys.* 1890. With an introduction by Robert Lee Wolff. New York and London: Garland Press, 1979.

O'Donovan, Gerald. *Father Ralph.* 1913. With an introduction by John F. Ryan. Dingle: Brandon Press, 1993.

————. *The Holy Tree.* London: Heinemann, 1922.

Sheehan, Patrick (Canon). *The Graves at Kilmorna.* New York, 1915.

[Tonna,] Charlotte Elizabeth. *The Rockite.* London, 1829.

Trollope, Anthony. *The Landleaguers.* 1883. With an introduction by Mary Hamer. Oxford: Oxford Univ. Press, 1993.

Secondary Sources

Anderson, Benedict. *Imagined Communities: Reflections on the Origin and Spread of Nationalism.* Revised edition. London: Verso, 1991.

Armstrong, Nancy. *Desire and Domestic Fiction.* Oxford: Oxford Univ. Press, 1987.

————. "Gender and the Victorian Novel." In David, *The Cambridge Companion to the Victorian Novel,* 97–124. Cambridge: Cambridge Univ. Press, 2001.

————. *How Novels Think: The Limits of Individualism from 1719–1900.* New York: Columbia Univ. Press, 2006.

Atherton, James S. *The Books at the Wake: A Study of Literary Allusions in Joyce's Finnegans Wake.* New York: Viking Press, 1959.

Attridge, Derek, and Marjorie Howes, eds. *Semicolonial Joyce.* Cambridge: Cambridge Univ. Press, 2000.

Bakhtin, Mikhail. *Rabelais and His World.* Translated by H. Iswolsky. Cambridge, Mass.: MIT Press, 1968.

Barrell, John. *The Dark Side of the Landscape: The Rural Poor in English Painting, 1730–1840.* Cambridge: Cambridge Univ. Press, 1980.

Barrington, Jonah (Sir). *Personal Sketches of his Own Times. With a memoir of the author; an essay on Irish wit and humour; and notes and corrections by Townsend Young.* 2 vols. London, 1869.

Bartlett, Thomas. *The Fall and Rise of the Irish Nation: The Catholic Question, 1690–1830.* Dublin: Gill and Macmillan, 1992.

Beames, Michael. *Peasants and Power: The Whiteboy Movements and Their Control in Pre-Famine Ireland.* Brighton: Harvester Press, 1983.

Belanger, Jacqueline. Introduction to *The Irish Novel in the Nineteenth Century: Facts and Fictions.* In Belanger, *Irish Novel,* 11–33.

————, ed. *The Irish Novel in the Nineteenth Century: Facts and Fictions*. Dublin: Four Courts Press, 2005.

Benjamin, Walter. *The Arcades Project*. Translated by Howard Eiland and Kevin McLaughlin. Cambridge, Mass.: Harvard Univ. Press, 1999.

Bhabha, Homi K. *The Location of Culture*. London: Routledge, 1994.

Birken, Lawrence. *Consuming Desire: Sexual Science and the Emergence of a Culture of Abundance, 1871–1914*. Ithaca: Cornell Univ. Press, 1988.

Bourke, Angela. *The Burning of Bridget Cleary: A True Story*. London: Pimlico, 1999.

————, et al., eds. *The Field Day Anthology of Irish Writing: Irish Women's Writing and Traditions*, vols. 4–5. Cork: Cork Univ. Press, 2002.

Boyd, Ernest. *Ireland's Literary Renaissance*. London: Grant Richards, 1923.

Brooker, Joseph. *Joyce's Critics: Transitions in Reading and Culture*. Madison: Univ. of Wisconsin Press, 2004.

Brown, Terence. *Ireland: A Social and Cultural History, 1922–2002*. London: Harper Perennial, 2004.

————. *Ireland's Literature: Selected Essays*. Mullingar: Lilliput Press, 1980.

Buck-Morss, Susan. *Dreamworld and Catastrophe: The Passing of Mass Utopia in East and West*. Cambridge, Mass.: MIT Press, 2000.

Burdy, Samuel. *The History of Ireland*. Edinburgh, 1817.

Cahalan, James M. "Forging A Tradition: Emily Lawless and the Irish Literary Canon." In Kirkpatrick, *Border Crossings*, 38– 57.

————. *Great Hatred, Little Room: The Irish Historical Novel*. Dublin: Gill and Macmillan, 1983.

————. *The Irish Novel: A Critical History*. Dublin: Gill and Macmillan, 1988.

Cavell, Stanley. *Cities of Words*. Cambridge, Mass.: Harvard Univ. Press, 2004.

Chatterjee, Partha. *The Nation and Its Fragments: Colonial and Postcolonial Histories*. Princeton: Princeton Univ. Press, 1993.

Chaturvedi, Vinayak, ed. *Mapping Subaltern Studies and the Postcolonial*. London: Verso, 2000.

Cleary, Joe. *Outrageous Fortune: Capital and Culture in Modern Ireland*. Dublin: Field Day, 2007.

Comerford, R. V. *Charles J. Kickham: A Study in Irish Nationalism and Literature*. Dublin: Wolfhound Press, 1979.

————. *Ireland*. London: Hodder Arnold, 2003.

Connerton, Paul. *How Societies Remember*. Cambridge: Cambridge Univ. Press, 1989.

Connery, James. *The Reformer, or, an infallible remedy to prevent pauperism and the periodical returns of famine*. London, 1836.

Coulter, Colin and Steve Coleman, eds. *The End of Irish History? Critical Reflections on the Celtic Tiger*. Manchester: Manchester Univ. Press, 2003.

Corkery, Daniel. *Synge and Anglo-Irish Literature*. 1931. Cork: Mercier Press, 1966.

Croker, Thomas Crofton. *Researches in the South of Ireland. Illustrative of the Scenery, Architectural Remains and the Manners and Superstitions of the Peasantry with an Appendix containing a Private Narrative of the Rebellion of 1798*. London, 1824.

Cronin, John. *The Anglo-Irish Novel*. Vol. 1, *The Nineteenth Century*. Belfast: Appletree Press, 1980.

David, Deirdre, ed. *The Cambridge Companion to the Victorian Novel*. Cambridge: Cambridge Univ. Press, 2001.

Davitt, Michael. *The Fall of Feudalism in Ireland*. London: Harpers, 1904.

Deane, Seamus. *Celtic Revivals*. London: Faber and Faber, 1985.

———. "Dead Ends: Joyce's Finest Moments." In *Semicolonial Joyce*, edited by Attridge and Howes, 21–36.

———. *Foreign Affections: Essays on Edmund Burke*. Cork: Cork Univ. Press, 2005.

———. "Joyce the Irishman." In *The Cambridge Companion to James Joyce*, edited by Derek Attridge, 31–53. Cambridge: Cambridge Univ. Press, 1990.

———. *Strange Country: Modernity and Nationhood in Irish Writing since 1790*. Oxford: Clarendon Press, 1997.

———, ed. *The Field Day Anthology of Irish Writing*, vols. 1–3. Derry: Field Day, 1991.

de Paor, Liam. *Tom Moore and Contemporary Ireland*. Ó Riada Memorial Lecture. Cork: Univ. College, Cork, 1989.

Desmond, Derry, and Paul Keating. *Culture and Capitalism in Ireland*. Aldershot: Avebury, 1993.

de Valera, Eamon. "The Undeserted Village Ireland." In Deane, *The Field Day Anthology of Irish Writing* 3:747–50.

Donnelly, James S., Jr. "Pastorini and Captain Rock: Millenarianism and Sectarianism in the Rockite Movements of 1821–4." In *Irish Peasants: Violence and Political Unrest 1780–1914*, edited by Samuel Clark and James S. Donnelly, Jr., 102–39. Dublin: Gill and Macmillan, 1983.

Dowling, Michele. "'The Ireland that I would have': De Valera and the Creation of an Irish National Image." *History Ireland* 5, no. 2 (Summer 1997): 37–41.

Doyle, James Warren [J. K. L., pseud.]. *A Vindication of the Religious and Civil Principles of the Irish Catholics*. Dublin, 1823.

Duffy, Charles Gavan. *Four Years of Irish History*. New York, 1882.

Duffy, Enda. "Disappearing Dublin: *Ulysses*, Postcoloniality, and the Politics of Space." In *Semicolonial Joyce*, edited by Attridge and Howes, 37– 57.

Dunne, Tom. "Haunted by History: Irish Romantic Writing, 1800– 1850." In *Romanticism in National Context*, edited by R. Porter and M. Teich, 68–91. Cambridge: Cambridge Univ. Press, 1988.

———. "The Insecure Voice: A Catholic Novelist in Support of Emancipation." In *Culture et pratiques politiques en France et en Irlande, XVIe–XVIIIe siècle*, edited by P. Bergson and L. Cullen, 213–33. Paris: Centre De Recherches Historiques, 1988.

———. "Murder as Metaphor: Griffin's Portrayal of Ireland in the year of Catholic Emancipation." In *Ireland and Irish Australia: Studies in Cultural and Political History*, edited by Oliver MacDonagh and W. F. Mandle, 64–80. London: Croom Helm, 1986.

———. "Representations of Rebellion: 1798 in Literature." In *Ireland, England and Australia: Essays in honour of Oliver MacDonagh*, edited by F. B. Smith, 14–40. Canberra: Australian National University, 1990.

Eagleton, Terry. *Crazy John and the Bishop and Other Essays on Irish Culture*. Cork: Cork Univ. Press, 1998.

———. *Heathcliff and the Great Hunger: Studies in Irish Culture*. London: Verso, 1995.

Erikson, Kai. "Notes on Trauma and Community." In *Trauma: Explorations in Memory*, edited by Cathy Caruth, 183–99. Baltimore: Johns Hopkins Univ. Press, 1995.

Fairhall, James. *James Joyce and the Question of History*. Cambridge: Cambridge Univ. Press, 1993.

Ferris, Ina. *The Romantic National Tale and the Question of Ireland*. Cambridge: Cambridge Univ. Press, 2002.

Fielding, Penny. *Writing and Orality: Nationality, Culture and Nineteenth-century Scottish Fiction*. Oxford: Clarendon Press, 1996.

Flanagan, Thomas. *The Irish Novelists, 1800–1850*. New York: Columbia Univ. Press, 1959.

Foley, Tadhg, and Sean Ryder, eds. *Ideology and Ireland in the Nineteenth Century*. Dublin: Four Courts, 1998.

Foster, R. F. "Yeats, Carleton and the Irish Nineteenth Century." In *The Irish Story: Telling Tales and Making It Up in Ireland*, 113–26. London: Allen Lane, 2001.

Foucault, Michel. *The History of Sexuality.* Vol. 1. 1976. Translated by Robert Hurley. New York: Vintage, 1980.

Frazier, Adrian. *George Moore, 1852–1933.* New Haven: Yale Univ. Press, 2000.

Garvin, Tom. *Preventing the Future: Why was Ireland So Poor for So Long?* Dublin: Gill and Macmillan, 2004.

Gibbons, Luke. "Between Captain Rock and a Hard Place: Art and Agrarian Insurgency." In Foley and Ryder, *Ideology and Ireland*, 23–44.

———. *Cinema and Ireland.* With Kevin Rockett and John Hill. London: Routledge, 1988.

———. "'Have you no homes to go to?' James Joyce and the Politics of Paralysis." In Attridge and Howes, *Semicolonial Joyce*, 150–71.

———. "Republicanism and Radical Memory: The O'Conors, O'Carolan and the United Irishmen." In *Revolution, Counter-Revolution and Union*, edited by Jim Smyth, 211–37. Cambridge: Cambridge Univ. Press, 2000.

———. "Spaces of Time Through Times of Space: Joyce, Ireland and Colonial Modernity." *Field Day Review* 1 (2005): 70–85.

———. *Transformations in Irish Culture.* Cork: Cork Univ. Press, 1996.

———. "'Where Wolfe Tone's statue was not': Joyce, Monuments and Memory." In *History and Memory in Modern Ireland*, edited by Ian McBride, 139–59. Cambridge: Cambridge Univ. Press, 2001.

Gibbons, Stephen. *Captain Rock, Night Errant: The Threatening Letters of Pre-Famine Ireland, 1801–1845.* Dublin: Four Courts Press, 2004.

Gibson, Andrew. *James Joyce.* London: Reaktion Books, 2006.

———. *Joyce's Revenge: History, Politics and Aesthetics in* Ulysses. Oxford: Oxford Univ. Press, 2002.

Gifford, Don, and Robert J. Seidman. Ulysses *Annotated.* Revised edition. Berkeley: Univ. of California Press, 1988.

Ginzburg, Carlo. "Checking the Evidence: The Judge and the Historian." *Critical Inquiry* 18 (1991): 79–92.

———. *The Cheese and the Worms: The Cosmos of a Sixteenth-Century Miller.* Translated by J. and A. Tedeschi. London: Penguin, 1992.

Gledhill, Christine, ed. *Home is Where the Heart is: Studies in Melodrama and the Woman's Film.* London: British Film Institute, 2002.

Guha, Ranajit. "The Prose of Counter-Insurgency." In *Selected Subaltern Studies*, edited by Ranajit Guha and Gayatri Spivak. Oxford: Oxford Univ. Press, 1988, 45–86.

Hansen, Ellis. *Decadence and Catholicism*. Cambridge, Mass.: Harvard Univ. Press, 1998.

Hawthorne, Mark D. *John and Michael Banim (The "O'Hara Brothers"): A Study in the Early Development of the Anglo-Irish Novel*. Salzburg: Universität Salzburg, 1975.

Hazlitt, William. *The Spirit of the Age: or, Contemporary Portraits*. London, 1825.

Hobsbawm, E. J. *Bandits*. Harmondsworth: Pelican, 1972.

Hodgart, Mathew, and Mabel P. Worthington. *Song in the Work of James Joyce*. New York: Columbia Univ. Press, 1959.

Howes, Marjorie. *Colonial Crossings: Figures in Irish Literary History*. Dublin: Field Day, 2006.

"Ireland." *Edinburgh Review* 41 (Jan. 1825): 356–410.

Jameson, Fredric. "Third World Literature in the Era of Multinational Capital." *Social Text* 15 (fall 1986): 65–88.

———. "*Ulysses* in History." In *James Joyce and Modern Literature*, edited by W. J. McCormack and Alistair Stead, 126–41. London: Routledge, 1982.

Joannon, Pierre. "O'Connell, Montalembert and the Birth of Christian Democracy in France." In O'Connell, *Daniel O'Connell*, 98–109.

Jordan, Hoover H. *Bolt Upright: The Life of Thomas Moore*, vols. 1–2. Salzburg: Universität Salzburg, 1975.

Kelleher, John V. *Selected Writings of John V. Kelleher on Ireland and Irish America*. Edited by Charles Fanning. Carbondale: Southern Illinois Univ. Press, 2002.

Kelleher, Margaret. "'Factual Fictions': Representations of the Land Agitation in Nineteenth-Century Women's Fiction" (forthcoming).

———. "Prose Writing and Drama in English, 1830–1890: From Catholic Emancipation to the Fall of Parnell." In Kelleher and O'Leary, *Cambridge History of Irish Literature* 2:449–99.

———. "Women's Fiction, 1845–1900." In Bourke et al., *The Field Day Anthology of Irish Writing* 5:924–75.

Kelleher, Margaret, and James H. Murphy, eds. *Gender Perspectives in Nineteenth-Century Ireland*. Dublin: Irish Academic Press, 1997.

Kelleher, Margaret, and Philip O'Leary, eds. *The Cambridge History of Irish Literature*. 2 vols. Cambridge: Cambridge Univ. Press, 2006.

Kelly, John. Introduction to *Knocknagow*, by Charles J. Kickham, 5-41.

Kiberd, Declan. *Irish Classics*. London: Granta, 2000.

———. *The Irish Writer and the World*. Cambridge: Cambridge Univ. Press, 2005.

Kilfeather, Siobhán. "Sex and Sensation in the Nineteenth-Century Novel." In Kelleher and Murphy, *Gender Perspectives*, 83–92.

King, Jason. "Emigration and the Anglo-Irish Novel: William Carleton, 'Home Sickness', and the Coherence of Gothic Conventions." *Canadian Journal of Irish Studies* 26, no. 2 (fall 2000)/27, no. 1 (Spring 2001): 105–18. This double issue of the journal is in fact one volume numbered continuously throughout.

Kirkpatrick, Kathryn, ed. *Border Crossings: Irish Women Writers and National Identities*. Dublin: Wolfhound Press, 2000.

Laird, Heather. *Subversive Law in Ireland, 1879–1920: From "Unwritten Law" to the Dáil Courts*. Dublin: Four Courts Press, 2005.

Larkin, Emmet. *The Historical Dimensions of Irish Catholicism*. 1976. Washington, DC, and Dublin: Catholic Univ. of America Press and Four Courts Press, 1984.

Lee, J. J. *Ireland, 1912–1985: Politics and Society*. Cambridge: Cambridge Univ. Press, 1989.

Leerssen, Joep. *Remembrance and Imagination: Patterns in the Historical and Literary Representation of Ireland in the Nineteenth Century*. Cork: Cork Univ. Press, 1996.

Lennon, Joseph. *Irish Orientalism: A Literary and Intellectual History*. Syracuse: Syracuse Univ. Press, 2004.

Lewis, George Cornewall. *On the Local Disturbances in Ireland*. London, 1836.

Lewis, Wyndham. *Time and Western Man*. 1927. Edited by Paul Edwards. Santa Rosa: Black Sparrow Press, 1993.

Lloyd, David. "Afterword: Hardress Cregan's Dream For Another History of the Irish Novel." In Belanger, *Irish Novel*, 229–37.

———. *Anomalous States: Irish Writing and the Post-Colonial Moment*. Dublin: Lilliput Press, 1993.

———. "Counterparts: *Dubliners*, Masculinity and Temperance Nationalism." In Attridge and Howes, *Semicolonial Joyce*, 128–49.

———. *Ireland After History*. Cork: Cork Univ. Press, 2000.

———. *Nationalism and Minor Literature: James Clarence Mangan and the Emergence of Irish Cultural Nationalism*. Berkeley: Univ. of California Press, 1988.

Loeber, Rolf, and Magda Loeber, with Anne Mullin Burnham. *A Guide to Irish Fiction, 1650–1900*. Dublin: Four Courts Press, 2006.

Lukács, Georg. *The Historical Novel.* 1937. Translated by H. and S. Mitchell. London: Merlin Press, 1962.

MacDonagh, Oliver. *O'Connell: The Life of Daniel O'Connell.* London: Weidenfeld and Nicolson, 1991.

MacDonagh, Oliver, and W. F. Mandle, eds. *Ireland and Irish Australia: Studies in Cultural and Political History.* London: Croom Helm, 1986.

MacSharry, Ray, and Padraic White. *The Making of the Celtic Tiger: The Inside Story of Ireland's Boom Economy.* Dublin: Mercier Press, 2000.

Marx, Karl. *Selected Writings.* Edited by David McLellan. Oxford: Oxford Univ. Press, 1977.

Mathews, P. J. *Revival: The Abbey Theatre, Sinn Fein, the Gaelic League and the Co-operative Movement.* Cork: Cork Univ. Press, 2003.

McCormack, W. J. *Ascendancy and Tradition in Anglo-Irish Literary History from 1789–1939.* Oxford: Clarendon Press, 1985.

Meaney, Gerardine. "Decadence, Degeneration and Revolting Aesthetics: The Fiction of Emily Lawless and Katherine Cecil Thurston." *Colby Quarterly* 36, no. 2 (June 2000): 157–75.

Mokyr, Joel. *Why Ireland Starved: A Quantative and Analytical History of the Irish Economy, 1800–1845.* Revised edition. London: George Allen and Unwin, 1985.

Morash, Christopher. *Writing the Irish Famine.* Oxford: Clarendon Press, 1995.

Moretti, Franco. *Atlas of the European Novel, 1800–1900.* London: Verso, 1998.

———. "Conjectures on World Literature." *New Left Review* 1 (Jan.–Feb. 2000): 54–68.

———. *Modern Epic.* Translated by Quintin Hoare. London: Verso, 1996.

———. *The Way of the World: The Bildungsroman in European Culture.* London: Verso, 1987.

Murphy, James H. *Catholic Fiction and Social Reality in Ireland, 1873–1922.* Westport, Conn.: Greenwood Press, 1997.

———. "'Insouciant Rivals of Mrs Barton': Gender and Victorian Aspiration in George Moore and the Women Novelists of the *Irish Monthly.*" In Kelleher and Murphy, *Gender Perspectives,* 221–28.

———. *Ireland: A Social, Cultural and Literary History, 1791–1891.* Dublin: Four Courts Press, 2003.

———. "'Things Which Seem to You Unfeminine': Gender and Nationalism in the Fiction of some Upper Middle Class Catholic Women Novelists, 1880–1910." In *Border Crossings,* edited by Kirkpatrick, 58–78.

Murphy, Willa. "Secrecy and Solidarity in the Fiction of John and Michael Banim." In *Was Ireland a Colony? Economics, Politics and Culture in Nineteenth-Century Ireland*, edited by Terrence McDonough, 280–98. Dublin: Irish Academic Press, 2005.

Nolan, Emer. *Joyce and Nationalism*. London: Routledge, 1995.

———. "Modernism and the Irish Revival." In *The Cambridge Companion to Modern Irish Culture*, edited by Joe Cleary and Claire Connolly, 157–72. Cambridge: Cambridge Univ. Press, 2005.

O'Callaghan, Margaret. "New Ways of Looking at the State Apparatus and the State Archive in Nineteenth-Century Ireland: 'Curiosities from That Phonetic Museum'—Royal Irish Constabulary Reports and Their Political Uses, 1879–91." *Proceedings of the Royal Irish Academy*. Vol. 104C, no. 2 (2004): 37–56.

O'Connell, Daniel. *A Memoir on Ireland Native and Saxon*, vol. 1. Dublin, 1843.

O'Connell, Helen. "The Fiction of Improvement." In Belanger, *Irish Novel*, 110–38.

[O'Connor, Roger]. *Letters to his majesty, King George the fourth, by Captain Rock*. Dublin, 1828.

Ó Ciardha, Eamon. *Ireland and the Jacobite Cause, 1685–1766: A Fatal Attachment*. Dublin: Four Courts Press, 2002.

Ó Cios áin, Niall. "The Irish Rogues." In *Irish Popular Culture, 1650–1850*, edited by J. S. Donnelly, Jr., and Kerby A. Miller, 78–96. Dublin: Irish Academic Press, 1998.

———. *Print and Popular Culture in Ireland, 1750–1850*. London: Macmillan, 1997.

O'Connell, Maurice, ed. *Daniel O'Connell: Political Pioneer*. Dublin: Institute of Public Administration, 1991.

O'Ferrall, Fergus. "Liberty and Catholic Politics, 1790–1990." In O'Connell, *Daniel O'Connell: Political Pioneer*, 35–56.

O'Halloran, Clare. "Irish Re-creations of the Gaelic Past: The Challenge of Macpherson's Ossian." *Past and Present*, no. 124 (1989): 69–95.

O'Riordan, Michael (Rev). *Catholicity and Progress in Ireland*. London: Kegan Paul, Trench, Trübner and Co., 1906.

[O'Sullivan, Mortimer]. *Captain Rock detected: or, the Origin and Character of the Recent Disturbances, and the Causes, both Moral and Political, of the Present Alarming Condition of the South and West of Ireland, fully and fairly considered and exposed: by a Munster Farmer*. London, 1824.

O'Sullivan, Patrick. "A Literary Difficulty in Explaining Ireland: Tom Moore and Captain Rock." In *The Irish in Britain: 1815–1939*, edited by Sheridan Gilley and Roger Swift, 239–74. Dublin: Gill and Macmillan, 1989.

O'Sullivan, Tadhg. "Captain Rock in Print: Literary Representation and Irish Agrarian Unrest, 1824–1833." M.Phil thesis, Univ. College Cork, 1998.

———. "'The violence of a servile war': Three Narratives of Irish Rural Insurgency Post-1798." In *Rebellion and Remembrance in Modern Ireland*, edited by Laurence M. Geary, 73–92. Dublin: Four Courts Press, 2001.

[Otway, Cesar]. *Sketches in Ireland: Description of Interesting and Hitherto Unnoticed Districts, in the North and South*. London, 1827.

Pateman, Carole. *The Sexual Contract*. Cambridge: Polity Press, 1988.

Pick, Daniel. *Faces of Degeneration: A European Disorder, c. 1848–1918*. Cambridge: Cambridge Univ. Press, 1989.

Platt, Len. *Joyce and the Anglo-Irish: A Study of Joyce and the Literary Revival*. Amsterdam: Rodopi, 1998.

Plunkett, Horace. *Ireland in the New Century*. 1904. Foreword by Trevor West. Dublin: Irish Academic Press, 1983.

Pope-Hennessy, John. "What Do the Irish Read?" *The Nineteenth Century* 15 (June 1884): 920–32.

Pykett, Lynn. "Sensation and the Fantastic in the Victorian Novel." In *Cambridge Companion to the Victorian Novel*, edited by David, 192–221.

Radek, Karl. "James Joyce or Socialist Realism?" 1934. In *James Joyce: The Critical Heritage*, edited by Robert H. Deming, 2:624–26. London: Routledge and Kegan Paul, 1970.

Rainey, Lawrence. *Institutions of Modernism: Literary Elites and Public Culture*. New Haven: Yale Univ. Press, 1998.

Restuccia, Frances. *James Joyce and the Law of the Father*. New Haven: Yale Univ. Press, 1989.

Review of Moore, *Memoirs of Captain Rock*. *Westminster Review*, 1 April 1824, 492–504.

Richetti, John. "The legacy of Ian Watt's *The Rise of the Novel*." In *The Profession of Eighteenth-Century Literature: Reflections on an Institution*, edited by Leo Damrosch, 95–112. Madison: Univ. of Wisconsin Press, 1992.

Roberts, Paul E. "Caravats and Shanavests: Whiteboyism and Faction Fighting in East Munster, 1802–11." In *Irish Peasants*, edited by Clark and Donnelly, 64–101.

Scott, Malcolm. *The Struggle for the Soul of the French Novel: French Catholic and Realist Novelists, 1850–1970.* Houndmills: Macmillan, 1989.

Simms, J. G. *Jacobite Ireland, 1685–91.* London: Routledge and Kegan Paul, 1969.

Singer, Ben. *Melodrama and Modernity.* New York: Columbia Univ. Press, 2001.

Sloan, Barry. *The Pioneers of Anglo-Irish Fiction, 1800–50.* Gerrards Cross: Colin Smythe, 1986.

Sommer, Doris. *Foundational Fictions: The National Romances of Latin America.* Berkeley: Univ. of California Press, 1991.

Spivak, Gayatri. "Three Women's Texts and the Critique of Imperialism." In *The Feminist Reader,* edited by Catherine Belsey and Jane Moore, 175–95. London: Macmillan, 1989.

Stallybrass, Peter, and Allon White. *The Politics and Poetics of Transgression.* London: Methuen, 1986.

Thompson, E. P. "The Crime of Anonymity." In *Albion's Fatal Tree: Crime and Society in Eighteenth-Century England,* edited by Douglas Hay et al., 255–308. London: Allen Lane, 1975.

———. *Customs in Common.* London: The Merlin Press, 1991.

Thuente, Mary Helen. *The Harp Re-strung: The United Irishmen and the Rise of Irish Literary Nationalism.* Syracuse: Syracuse Univ. Press, 1994.

Tompkins, Jane. *Sensational Designs: The Cultural Work of American Fiction, 1790–1860.* Oxford: Oxford Univ. Press, 1985.

Townshend, Charles. *Political Violence in Ireland: Government and Resistance Since 1848.* Oxford: Clarendon Press, 1983.

Tracy, Dominick. "Squatting the Deserted Village: Idyllic Resistance in Griffin's *The Collegians.*" In Belanger, *Irish Novel,* 94–109.

Tracy, Robert. *The Unappeasable Host: Studies in Irish Identity.* Dublin: Univ. College Dublin Press, 1998.

Trumpener, Katie. *Bardic Nationalism: The Romantic Novel and the British Empire.* Princeton: Univ. of Princeton Press, 1997.

Valente, Joseph. "Joyce's Politics: Race, Nation, and Transnationalism." In *Palgrave Advances in James Joyce Studies,* edited by Jean-Michel Rabaté, 73–96. Basingstoke: Palgrave Macmillan, 2004.

van Boheemen-Saaf, Christine. *Joyce, Derrida, Lacan, and the Trauma of History: Reading, Narrative, and Postcolonialism.* Cambridge: Cambridge Univ. Press, 1999.

Vance, Norman. *Irish Literature since 1800.* London: Longman, 2002.

———. "Protestant Form and Catholic Fiction?" in Belanger, *Irish Novel*, 139–49.

Watt, Ian. *The Rise of the Novel: Studies in Defoe, Richardson and Fielding.* Berkeley: Univ. of California Press, 1957.

Weber, Max. *The Protestant Ethic and the Spirit of Capitalism.* 1904–5. Translated by Talcott Parsons, with an introduction by Anthony Giddens. London: Routledge, 1992.

Whelan, Irene. *The Bible War in Ireland: The "Second Reformation" and the Polarization of Protestant-Catholic Relations, 1800–1840.* Dublin: Lilliput, 2005.

Whelan, Kevin. *The Tree of Liberty: Radicalism, Catholicism and the Construction of Irish Identity 1760–1830.* Cork: Cork Univ. Press, 1996.

White, Harry. *The Keeper's Recital: Music and Cultural History in Ireland, 1770–1970.* Cork: Cork Univ. Press, 1998.

[Whitty, Michael J.], ed. *Captain Rock in London; or, the Chieftain's Gazette.* London, 1825–26.

Wicke, Jennifer. *Advertising Fictions: Literature, Advertisement, and Social Reading.* New York: Columbia Univ. Press, 1988.

Wilde, Jane (Lady). *Notes on Men, Women, and Books.* London, 1891.

Wilde, William (Sir). *Irish Popular Superstitions.* Dublin, 1852.

Wolff, Robert Lee. Introduction to *The Boyne Water,* by John Banim, v–xlvii. 1826. 3 vols. New York: Garland, 1978.

"Works on Ireland." *Blackwood's Edinburgh Magazine* 15 (May 1824): 544–58.

Yeats, W. B. *Representative Irish Tales.* 1891. Compiled with an introduction and notes by W. B. Yeats and a foreword by Helen Mary Theunte. Gerrards Cross: Colin Smythe, 1979.

———. *Uncollected Prose,* vol. 1. Edited by John P. Frayne. London: Macmillan, 1970.

Index

The names of fictional characters are not inverted and are denoted by (fict.) following the name. Pseudonyms are denoted by (pseud.).